GLOUCESTER
CRESCENT

GLOUCESTER CRESCENT

Me, My Dad and Other Grown-Ups

WILLIAM MILLER

P

PROFILE BOOKS

First published in Great Britain in 2018 by
PROFILE BOOKS LTD
3 Holford Yard
Bevin Way
London WC1X 9HD
www.profilebooks.com

1 3 5 7 9 10 8 6 4 2

Typeset in Garamond by MacGuru Ltd
Printed and bound in Great Britain by Clays Ltd, Elcograf S.p.A.

A CIP catalogue record for this book is available from the British Library.

ISBN 978 1 78816 036 0
eISBN 978 1 78283 440 3

FSC
www.fsc.org
MIX
Paper from
responsible sources
FSC® C018072

For Trine, Daisy, Stella and my parents, Rachel and Jonathan

CONTENTS

PROLOGUE

Autumn 2017
(Age 53)

When we were children, my father would take me and my brother up Primrose Hill. At the top he'd look out across London, and tell us how he'd spent his life moving very slowly around Regent's Park, and had never lived anywhere else. With his arm outstretched he'd take aim, squinting, his cheek resting on his arm, and draw a line across the city with his great big index finger. Pointing at a crescent of tall white houses at the bottom of Regent's Park, he'd tell us that this was where he was born. His finger would move over the park to St John's Wood, where he lived before and after the war. Dropping to the bottom of Primrose Hill, he'd point at the big bird cage in London Zoo, whose designer, Cedric Price, was best man at his wedding. Then he'd swing back to the other side of the hill and to the mouldy basement flat on Regent's Park Road where he and my mother moved after they got married. Finally, his finger would arc up over the rooftops of Chalcot Square and across the red-brick walls of my primary school on Princess Road. When he stopped, he would be pointing to where a mass of green trees explodes between the roofs of a circle of tall houses. Holding his finger steady, he'd smack his lips and say, 'And this is where we are now – Gloucester Crescent. You see, we haven't gone very far in all that time.'

The events in this story are a lifetime ago. More than forty years have passed, and I am married with my own family to take climbing up Primrose Hill. But the memories of my childhood and the community I grew up in are as vivid as ever. My parents moved to Gloucester Crescent in the 1960s, and over the next three decades great friendships were forged, hearts were broken, professional rivalries were fuelled and needless fallings-out took place as the celebrated occupants of Gloucester Crescent came together and allowed their lives to become entwined.

As children, we were free to roam across the back gardens and wander in and out of our neighbours' houses. We explored, climbed trees and leaped over walls, spent hours in each other's homes and crossed the invisible boundaries that our parents unconsciously created with their rivalries. My closest friends had parents much like mine: most had been educated at the same small collection of public schools and knew each other well from either Oxford or Cambridge and then through their work. Together they'd found a common and worthy cause to believe in, born out of the post-war euphoria of the 1945 Labour landslide, which created a radical new way of thinking: full employment, a cradle-to-grave welfare state and a national health service that would be free to all. The promise of a fairer society led our parents to become left-leaning, idealistic as well as anti-establishment, with a strong distaste for the old-school approach to authority and power. They made the conscious decision to give their children a radically different childhood from their own. We were sent to the local state schools, where we could mix with children from every walk of life, and were encouraged to be free spirits. They frequently left us to our own devices while they went off and expanded their utopian vision and pursued glittering careers. We all looked up to our gifted parents and hoped that one day we might be like them, but as we got older many of us found ourselves left behind and struggling to keep up. It began to seem that we'd been part of an experiment driven by their principles, rather than their care. Despite the huge privilege of our birth, we were left feeling bewildered, and a few of us, like me, longed to escape to a way of life that was more structured and conventional.

Within this community and at the centre of the story are my parents, Jonathan and Rachel Miller. An ever-present figure in our home was their close friend (and one of my father's three partners from *Beyond the Fringe*) Alan Bennett, who started off living in my parents' basement and then bought the house across the road. Other friends in the street were the jazz singer and writer George Melly and his wife, Diana. In the mid-1970s the Mellys sold their house to another friend, Mary-Kay Wilmers, the ex-wife of the film director Stephen Frears. She later took over the editorship of the *London Review of Books* from my maternal uncle Karl Miller. Across from the Mellys were the artist David Gentleman and the Labour MP Giles Radice and, two doors away, the writer Claire Tomalin and her journalist husband, Nick. He was killed in Israel in 1973 by a Syrian missile while reporting on the Yom Kippur War, and she later married the playwright Michael Frayn, who in turn moved into the Crescent.

Immediately behind us, in Regent's Park Terrace, were the eminent philosopher Sir A. J. Ayer (known to his friends as Freddie) and his American wife, the author and broadcaster Dee Wells, along with their son, Nick, and her daughter from a previous marriage, Gully Wells. Next to them were Shirley Conran and her sons, Jasper and Sebastian. Further along the Terrace were the writers Angus Wilson, V. S. Pritchett and A. N. Wilson. Across the road from us and next door to Alan Bennett were the novelist Alice Thomas Ellis (aka Anna Haycraft), her publisher husband Colin Haycraft and their six children. Colin's publishing house, Duckworth, was based in an old piano factory rotunda at the top of the Crescent. They published many of my parents' friends, including Oliver Sacks, Beryl Bainbridge, the American poet Robert Lowell (who was also my godfather) and his wife, Caroline

Blackwood. Three doors from our house was Sir Ralph Vaughan Williams's widow, Ursula, and across the road from her the artistic director of the Royal Court, Max Stafford-Clark, who lived with his wife, Ann, and the son she had with Sam Spiegel, the producer of films like *On the Waterfront*, *The African Queen* and *Lawrence of Arabia*. There was also Miss Shepherd, the eccentric homeless woman who in the late 1960s arrived in the Crescent in her van and stayed for twenty years. After several years of moving her van up and down the Crescent, she eventually parked it in Alan Bennett's driveway, where she remained until she died in 1989. In nearby streets were others in my parents' circle, such as the documentary film-maker Roger Graef, Kingsley Amis and his son Martin, Beryl Bainbridge, Sylvia Plath and Joan Bakewell.

Most of the time our parents were happy to share their homes and meals with their friends in the street, but relationships occasionally became strained when they either wanted to sleep together or to kill each other. To the outside world it was a community that seemed to operate as if it were a closed society. It was often misunderstood or maligned by its critics and became the focus of much mockery in the press and on television. But it was my home.

As a child who was overshadowed by these extraordinary people, I longed to have a voice and be heard. Whenever I could, I went in search of the grown-ups who would tell me their stories and listen to my thoughts about the world as I knew it.

This is that boy's story of Gloucester Crescent. Sandwiched between the bustling chaos of Camden Town and the leafy tranquillity of Primrose Hill, I did everything I could to get away from it, and when I did finally leave, I thought I'd gone for good. But things don't always go the way you think they

Kate, me, Tom and Mum, Antibes, 1971

will, and to my surprise I've ended up right back where I started. Having returned, I find myself doing exactly what my father did all those years ago: sitting at his desk staring out the window thinking about life when he should have been writing.

When I was a child, I'd listen to the rhythmic clatter of manual typewriters coming from the open windows of houses along the street. Staring out of my study window, I can see why some, like my father, lost their train of thought as they sat at their desks and got distracted by life in the gardens: the sounds of children at play, grown-ups chatting and laughing and then the views across the dense foliage that bursts into life each spring. The branches of the vast London plane trees heavy with leaves that sway in the breeze, sending hypnotic ripples of reflection over the windows of the tall houses in the terrace opposite.

Now, over four decades later, I have the ghosts of my past to distract me as well. Occasionally, I am sure I see something moving out of the corner of my eye – a child in the garden racing down the back steps of a house opposite. He crosses the garden and then vaults effortlessly over the wall, but then I look up and there's no one there, just a single cat slipping quietly through a bush that overhangs the wall.

PART ONE

August 1975
(Age 11)

Mum, me and Tom, back garden at Gloucester Crescent, 1975

1

COMPETITIVE TYPING

The best thing my parents ever did was to buy our big old rambling house in the Crescent. I'm not sure we'd be known as 'the Millers' if we lived somewhere else. Maybe we'd just be that family up the road with the blue front door. Pretty soon after they bought the house Mum and Dad turned it into the perfect family home, even though at the time they didn't have any children. Now they have three, and the house is always filled with people, who come and go all day long, and in some cases, come and then stay for ever.

In the middle of all this coming and going is one thing that never changes and I hope never will: my Mum – she's lovely, pretty and warm and the person who holds it together for all of us. She's the rock everything in our lives is built on. She makes it possible for us to go to school in the morning, and then, when we come back home, we find everything we need is there. I know if it was left to Dad we'd stay up past midnight, never get to school on time and we'd probably all starve. He couldn't be more different from Mum, who, for starters, doesn't think the whole world is against her. Dad's a bit like our television – everything is in black and white: he either loves you or hates you, and people are either good or bad. It's a bit like his politics, where everyone is either a nice kind Labour person or an evil and cruel Tory. Much of the time he's far too busy with work and his big ideas to think about family life and leaves Mum to deal with all that. His head is filled with getting on with writing for a book or magazines (which he doesn't seem to like), travelling and directing plays and operas and having to go on the telly. Before I was born, he was a comedian, and before that a doctor, but he gave that up and never stops telling us how much he wishes he hadn't.

Mum gives him the freedom to do all these different jobs and makes it possible for him to try new things with his work. This sometimes means he goes away for weeks or months. And he does it knowing that, when he comes home, life in the Crescent will be exactly as he left it. I think lots of the dads in the street are like this and seem to live on another planet from their families. An American friend of Mum and Dad's, who I'll tell you about later, always says, 'The dads live on Planet-Do-I-Give-A-Shit', but I think the lucky dads are the ones who were sensible enough to marry mums like mine.

Mum and Dad met at school, when she was 16 and he was 18. Mum was really pretty, whereas Dad was tall and gangly with curly red hair and I don't think knew much about girls. It's no surprise that he fell madly in love with her the minute he saw her, but she wasn't interested in him at all. In fact, she thought he was a show-off, and it took a lot of work for him to convince her he wasn't. I think he was also a bit hopeless at courting and would turn up to take her out with his two best friends from school, Oliver Sacks and Eric Korn. She eventually changed her mind after Dad went to Cambridge and she went to see him in a comedy show where he was on stage dressed as Elizabeth I in sunglasses. When she realised he was talented and quite funny, and even rather handsome, she thought it might be worth giving him another chance. I don't

Mum, 1954, age 18   Dad, 1954, age 20

think he's stopped loving her ever since, and I know he would be completely lost without her. Dad isn't the easiest person to be married to, and I've often seen her lose her temper with him or cry when things aren't going well. What's amazing is that, with all she has to take care of and in spite of all the comings and goings and the number of people who turn up unannounced at the kitchen table, she also manages to be a hard-working doctor. She has all these patients who phone up in the middle of the night and make her go out and see them when all they probably have is a cold or a headache.

When Mum and Dad first got married, they moved into a damp basement flat on Regent's Park Road in Primrose Hill. They were happy there until Dad's books started to go mouldy with the damp and they decided they had to move. They couldn't really afford to, but Mum's Great Aunt Brenda gave them some money to help them buy a house of their own. At the time Dad was doing a comedy show in the West End called *Beyond the Fringe* with Alan Bennett and two other friends called Peter Cook and Dudley Moore. According to Dad, everybody really liked the show, so he went to the bank

Dad's one-man show, *Poppy Day*, Cambridge, 1953

with all the reviews from the newspapers, thinking that they might convince them to give him a loan. It worked, and the man at the bank lent him some money. With Great Aunt Brenda's money and the money from the bank they were able to buy our house in Gloucester Crescent. Dad's not very good with money, so borrowing it gave him sleepless nights. I told my best friend, Conrad Roeber, who lives two doors from us, that our house cost a million pounds. I thought that seemed like a fair price because I imagined that's what most big things grown-ups bought probably cost. Conrad believed me, but his older brothers just laughed, so I felt a bit stupid when Dad told me it only cost £7,000. Mum and Dad didn't have children yet, so the house must have seemed enormous and bigger than anything they ever thought they would own.

I've always thought Gloucester Crescent is one of nicest streets in London. It's filled with tall houses that sit on either side of a road that slopes down a hill. Joining one end of

Dad shortly after buying the house in Gloucester Crescent, 1961

the Crescent is another street with a row of identical houses called Regent's Park Terrace. These look over the backs of the houses on our side of the Crescent, which means we can see the people who live in them and they can see us. Between these two streets is a big jungle of gardens, which are divided by brick walls with a long one that runs all the way down the middle. Although it's quite high, for kids it's a bit like a path that connects all the gardens.

Gloucester Crescent, 1975

Half-way down the Crescent at the bottom of the hill is Inverness Street, which comes off it like the branch of a tree. It takes you through a fruit and veg market, and at the end is another world – Camden Town. You see all sorts of people there: rich and poor, black and white, Indian, Greek and a lot of Irish. Wandering around in the middle of it are the families who have come out of the Underground station and are looking for London Zoo. They always seem a bit shocked as they step over the scruffy old men (and sometimes women) lying in doorways, asleep or drunk on cider.

If you walk in the other direction from Gloucester Crescent, you won't believe how different it is: a few streets away is Regent's Park, with enormous and very grand white houses around the edge. And then there's Primrose Hill.

I can't tell you how many times Dad has taken us up Primrose Hill and done exactly the same thing. We get to the top of the hill and he starts telling us about how he's lived his whole life near Regent's Park. I don't mind him repeating himself as I like hearing about it. I love where we live and, most important, I like the fact that we have never moved from here, and I hope we never will.

Plus, Primrose Hill is my favourite park and has been for as long as I can remember. I've pushed my bike up the steep path to the top with Mum, Dad or my friends, and when it snows I've tobogganed with Tom and the Roebers from the top all the way to the very bottom at terrifying speeds. Primrose Hill is a proper green and grassy hill in the middle of a big city. If you climb to the top and don't look back till you get there, it's amazing and worth it when you finally do. Everything in London can be seen from the top of Primrose Hill. You can see all the way to Greenwich in one direction, and to the south there's a really tall metal tower that comes out of the mist on the top of another hill. Dad once told us it was the Eiffel Tower, though I know it's a lie – it's the television mast at Crystal Palace, and it's miles away. From here London looks much smaller than it is. It feels like you can almost touch the buildings that take so long to get to by car or on the bus or Tube, like St Paul's Cathedral, Big Ben, King's Cross Station, the Post Office Tower, Battersea Power Station and loads more.

We once had a nanny whose husband built an enormous balsa-wood glider, which he took with me and Tom to fly from the top of the hill. On its first flight I lay in the long grass and watched it soar higher and higher in the warm air. I've always wanted to fly, and I lay there imagining what it would be like to be the pilot of this glider as it flew across the rooftops. I would glide silently over the houses and hear the different sounds of each street: children playing, babies crying and grown-ups arguing. Finally, as I cross over Gloucester Crescent, I would hear the familiar comforting sounds of pianos and violins and recorders being played, along with the clickety-clacking of all the typewriters. Then I'd drop between the trees at the back of our house, where I'd see Dad sitting in his study in front of an open window and he would wave at me. As I land gently on our lawn, I climb out of the cockpit to be met by Mum, who gives me a big hug before taking me indoors for lunch. All the usual people would be there – Alan, my grandparents and various other friends. They would all be chatting away, and I would be dying to tell them about my flight but struggle to get a word in edgeways.

There's one sound I've only ever heard in the gardens of Gloucester Crescent. And it goes on all day, every day of the week: the sound of grown-ups working. Lots of them work at home on typewriters which they sit at with the windows wide open. Dad and Alan talk about the other people in the street who do lots of typing, and how, when they eventually finish, their friends come over and they have a party to celebrate that they've stopped.

Every typewriter in the street sounds different. Some are fast and go on and on for ages, whereas others aren't fast at all. Some begin really fast, then suddenly stop and it all goes very quiet. After a while it starts up again and the typing goes so fast you think the typewriter's going to fall to pieces. There are also one or two where the typing is so slow you wonder why they bother doing it at all. Mum says these are the 'tortured ones', which I was a bit worried about because I think Dad might be one of those. When you hear all the typewriters going at the same time, from all the different windows, you could easily think they're having a big typing competition to see who can type the fastest. There are times when the sound of all the typewriters going together is like one of those films where hundreds of people are tap dancing on a stage.

When I was about four, I was curious to see some of this typing in action. I crawled on my front like a crocodile, working my way across the landing outside Dad's study. Without him knowing, I half-entered the room and lay on the floor watching him work. I decided he was definitely one of those who hit the typewriter keys slowly and then stop for ages. When he's not typing, he's staring out of the window, thinking and smoking. He starts by taking a slow, deep drag on his cigarette and then holding the smoke in his lungs for as long as he can as he stares down at the typewriter. Then, when he's ready to start typing, he lets the smoke out of his mouth. Sometimes he holds the smoke in his lungs for so long that when he opens his mouth nothing comes out and I wonder where all the smoke's gone – maybe it's seeped into his flesh, which might be why he sometimes smells like an ashtray.

He is definitely one of the tortured ones. I know this because I've heard him tell Mum that, whenever he can't think of anything to write and hates the work he's doing, he says the best way out of it would be to kill himself. That scares the life out of me. I sometimes think him not being able to type and holding the smoke in his lungs for as long as he can is all part of the trying-to-kill-himself thing. But then suddenly it's like a light comes on in his head and he stubs out his half-smoked cigarette and everything changes. He starts typing like a madman, poking away at the keys with his index fingers. This is very different from Alan's way of working, which I know because I've seen him typing as well. He sits at a desk in a window on the ground floor of his house, which looks out onto the Crescent. I've noticed that he uses all his fingers, like someone playing the piano.

I think a big part of Dad's problem is that, when he stops typing, instead of silence and time to think, he has to sit and

Dad at Sue's desk, with the window cleaner, 1968

listen to the sound of all the other typewriters going really fast in the houses next door or across the gardens in Regent's Park Terrace. Knowing that everyone else is getting on with their writing and having no trouble at all must drive him nuts, and I don't think he's alone in feeling this.

Whether he likes typing or not, for Dad his study is also a place to get away from all the things he can't stand about family life. Although it's on the first floor of the house, I think his study is what a shed at the end of the garden is to other dads. Unless his friends come over for lunch or supper, family meals are his idea of hell. He can't bear the way Tom, Kate or me sometimes refuse to eat what's put in front of us. And nothing makes him crosser at mealtimes than all of us shouting over each other or talking about what we've been watching on telly as if it's the most important thing in the world. What he really wants is a family who, if they can't talk about something intelligent, sit in silence and let him do the talking so he can lecture us about Charles Darwin or what the Germans did to everyone in the war. I really don't want to hear about Darwin, and Dad's stories about the war frighten me.

When he was our age, there was no TV, but he says they had a radio and that he listened to something called *The Goon Show*. He made me listen to it once, and I didn't think it was funny at all. He said one of the men on *The Goon Show* (who I saw in the *Pink Panther* film) had also been in Dad's *Alice in Wonderland* film. He once called Dad up and asked him to fly all the way to Hollywood to talk to him about making a film. He even sent him an aeroplane ticket. Dad got on the plane, flew all the way there, waited in his hotel but the man never showed up. So he got on the plane and came home and told Mum the man was a 'little shit'. I thought he was pretty funny in the *Pink Panther* and I was really excited that Dad might work on something like that instead of all his serious stuff he does, but it wasn't to be.

When Mum and Dad bought our house, the whole area, including our street, was shabby and run down. Only a few years before, there were steam trains in the freight yard a few streets away. These trains filled the air with black smoke that covered the houses in soot and left a stink in the air. Some of the houses, like ours, had always been family homes, but most of the others were boarding houses for Irish labourers or divided up into bedsits. Everything changed around the time Mum and Dad moved in: the steam trains went, as did the soot and the smell of the smoke that came from them, and the Crescent became somewhere people wanted to live. Along with Regent's Park Terrace, the houses in our two streets started to fill with either Mum and Dad's friends

'The Stringalongs', by Mark Boxer, *The Listener*,
1968. Bernard Goldblatt is on the right.

or people just like them. Before Alan even moved into the
street he wrote a comedy series for the BBC called *On the
Margin*, which had a bit in it called *Streets Ahead: Life and
Times in NW1*. This was all about a family like ours and all
their friends, who lived in a street that was just like Gloucester Crescent. Then a friend of Dad's made a cartoon called
'The Stringalongs' for a magazine that my uncle Karl was the
editor of, and in the cartoon there was a man called Bernard
Goldblatt, who looked just like Dad.

Gloucester Crescent is the only place we've ever lived as
a family, apart from New York. A year after Mum and Dad
bought the house, and not long after Tom was born, they went
to live in America for a few years. I was born there, just before
they came back to London, which makes me an American and
a little bit different from the rest of my family. Mum says I was
born in the same hospital that the lady in the film *Love Story*
dies in. We saw it on TV a few years ago and Mum shouted
out, 'Look, there's the hospital William was born in!' I thought
that was pretty amazing, but Tom just rolled his eyes and said
maybe I could die there too. He says that sort of thing a lot.

Alan Bennett

The reason they went to New York was because Dad went to do *Beyond the Fringe* on Broadway with Alan, Peter and Dudley. Alan lived in our basement before they all went to New York and now lives in his own house across the street from us. He still has a key to our house, and Mum invites him to meals almost every day, so it feels very much like he's part of the family.

All the mums and dads are friends, as they either know each other through work or they went to university together. One way or the other, everyone seems to be connected. I know they all grew up in a time when things were very different from the way they are now. They were all born before the war, and they talk a lot about what it was like back then. Dad told me that when he was my age everyone was expected to look

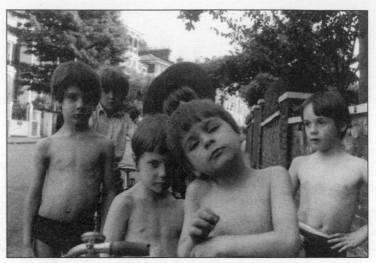

Gloucester Crescent children, 1969: left, Tom; front, me

up to important people like politicians, army generals and the royal family. Then, when he became a grown-up, lots of people like him thought these people were out of touch with what was going on in the world. When Alan and Dad did *Beyond the Fringe*, they made jokes about them that made everyone think they might all be a bit backward-looking, which Dad says was really easy to do.

Apart from Alan, all of Mum and Dad's friends went to private schools, which they now think is wrong. So they decided to try something completely different with their own children. They said that's why we all go to the local schools, which they don't pay for, and we get to mix with all sorts of children and it's fairer. They also want us to be free and independent, because their childhoods were too strict and organised, which is why we're left to do what we want for most of the time. When we're not at school, we're running wild and climbing over the garden walls and crashing in and out of each other's houses to play – and that feels like freedom.

2

THEY ARRIVE AND NEVER LEAVE

I used to think all the coming and going, the crashing in and out of each other's houses, the competitive typing and all the other stuff went on everywhere else too. Then you go and stay at a friend's house in another street and you can't believe how quiet and calm everything is. Gloucester Crescent houses are filled with people all the time. They come and go, night and day, and in some cases arrive and then never leave. Colin and Anna Haycraft live opposite us and have six children – Will, Joshua, Tom, Oli, Arthur and Sarah. Their house is full of all sorts of people who don't live there but drop in and stay all day. They even had a real-life burglar who lives with them now. Colin's office is in an old piano factory at the top of the Crescent that publishes loads of books and is called Duckworth. His writers come over to the house and hang about in the basement chatting, smoking and drinking.

Anna Haycraft is a writer, but on all the books she's written she calls herself Alice Thomas Ellis. I don't know why, as I've never heard anyone call her Alice. Her best friend is a writer called Beryl, and she comes round to hang out at the Haycrafts' house too. Whenever I go over there, Anna is sitting with Beryl at the kitchen table with a cigarette in one hand and a glass of wine in the other. I've never seen Anna get up from that chair. When she wants one of her children to come

Beryl Bainbridge and Anna Haycraft

down to the kitchen she just screams their name at the top of her voice. You can hear her doing this from our house across the road. Anna seems to spend a lot of time at the table talking to other people about their books. I don't know when she gets time to write her own, but I know she does as I've seen them on the shelves in our downstairs loo, and they're always having parties at their house for them. We're sometimes allowed to go to the parties with Mum and Dad, even when they're for someone else who's written a book for Colin.

At one point Anna and Colin decided not to send any of their children to school, and instead teachers would come to their house. I'm not sure that idea worked very well as it wasn't long before they were all sent back to proper schools.

I really like going to the Haycrafts' house because there's always something going on. Oli Haycraft is a year older than me and also friends with Nick Ayer, my friend in Regent's Park Terrace. Oli knows everything about the war and tanks and uniforms. There's a shop in Euston called Laurence Corner that sells army surplus clothing. Some of Oli's older brothers went there and bought all these Japanese uniforms from the Second World War. Oli and Nick then decided that they would go to Laurence Corner and get themselves German uniforms. When they got home, they put them on and went up and down the street, goose-stepping like the Nazis in a war film. They stopped old Mr Pablovich in the street – he lives at number 66 and came here from Yugoslavia after the war – and when Nick and Oli asked him for his identity papers he was furious. Mr Pablovich marched them back to the Haycrafts' and gave Colin a telling-off too.

Oli was so keen on the whole German thing that his parents got him a tutor, Mr Knox, who came on Sunday afternoons to teach him German. Mr Knox would then come across the road to teach me, but that didn't last very long. He gave me a book called *Sprich Mal Deutsch*, but in the end he told Mum and Dad I was unteachable as I just wanted to chat in English about my train set or something I'd seen on the television. I don't think I was really that interested in learning German but liked having Mr Knox come and chat.

The only problem with visiting the Haycrafts is that they have a bulldog, who, like Anna's best friend, is called Beryl. Beryl (the dog), a lot like Beryl (the friend), likes to sit next to Anna in the kitchen all day. Beryl (the dog) doesn't like visitors much and tries everything to get them to leave before they've even got through the basement door and into the laundry room to get to the kitchen. If you get any further than that, she goes completely berserk and tries to bite your ankles. Beryl (the dog) once trapped me in the corner of the laundry room and was bouncing up and down barking at me so much I thought she was trying to bite my neck. It's amazing how high so much blubber and fur can jump when it really wants to. For a second or two I was screaming like a girl. I didn't think I could scream like that, but I did and had to be rescued by their nanny, who dragged Beryl off me so I could escape up the stairs to look for Oli. After that I discovered the trick was to creep through the basement door and then make a run for it up the staircase to Oli's bedroom before Beryl wakes up. For some reason, she never goes upstairs. Oli says it's because she's frightened of Colin, who has a study on the first floor and hates Beryl (the dog).

Anyway, back to the burglar! One day Colin, or maybe it was Anna, caught a boy breaking into their house. This was before they got Beryl (the dog), so the burglar could go anywhere he wanted in the house. I say 'breaking in', but it wasn't really. To make it easier for their friends, and Colin's writers, to come and go, the Haycrafts never lock their basement door, so the burglar just walked in like everyone else. Instead of calling the police, Colin and Anna felt sorry for him and invited him to stay, and he's been like their seventh child ever since. He's called Alfie and fits in pretty well, even if he is, or was, a burglar. Alfie now works for Colin up the road at Duckworth, and you see him all the time bringing packages to Anna from the office.

As well as all the other people who hang around the Crescent, there are the drunks and old men who live in a big red-brick building around the corner in Arlington Road. Everyone in the street calls it the Doss House, but it's actually called Arlington House. The men who live there get chucked out in the mornings, so they spend the day getting drunk on cider before being allowed back in the evening. They drink their cider sitting on milk crates by the back doors of the cinema on Arlington Road. The dads in the Crescent are always saying that if they can't get any work or if their books don't get published or their plays are a failure, they will end up in Arlington House and will be found drinking cider round the back of the Odeon cinema. Maybe seeing all those men standing around drinking and peeing against the doors or down their trousers is what makes the dads do all that typing.

Some of the men from Arlington House like to wander up to the Crescent and ring on the doorbells asking for money. I think they choose our house because Dad always gives them something and likes talking to them, or at them. They know he's a soft touch, but Mum or anyone else in our house never gives them a thing. If one of us comes to the door they say, in a drunk voice, "'ello, young man, is Dr Jon in by any chance?" like he was their best friend. Dad comes down from his study and often knows them by their first name and stands on the porch talking to them about something or other and then gives them some money. I think most of them get pretty fed up with Dad's talking and his long lectures and just want him to hand over the dosh. He comes back in and says to Mum things like, 'That was Michael and he was really interested in what I had to say about the government', or 'John is really quite a fan of Tolstoy, so I gave him your copy of *Anna Karenina*.' Mum just rolls her eyes and tells Dad that the last thing they want is one of his lectures, but it never stops him giving them.

Another person who turned up one day and never left is Miss Shepherd, who lives in a van parked in the street. According to Alan, she was on the run from the police and her van broke down when she was trying to escape. She saw Gloucester Crescent and thought it would be a good place to hide. She'd managed to get some men to help push her van into the street and she never left. That was years ago, and she still thinks the police are looking for her. Miss Shepherd believes that if she keeps changing the colour of her van the police won't recognise it. This is why she's always painting it, which she does with little pots of paint and a stiff old paint brush. The van was brown when she first arrived in the Crescent, but it's now custard yellow and looks like one of those bad paintings Dad showed me when we went to see Jackson Pollock at the Tate Gallery.

Every now and then, to confuse the police, she gets the dustmen to push the van to a new spot in the street. She thinks that if the van is moved a few houses down from where it was the police won't think it's the same one. When this happens, Miss Shepherd sits at the steering wheel with the door open and her arm sticking out the side to let the dustmen know when she wants to stop. These moves always worry everyone in the street because no one knows if the van, with Miss Shepherd in it, will end up parked outside their house. We've had it outside ours quite a few times and the smell is terrible, but it's now been outside the Roebers' for some time and it looks like it might be there to stay.

Like the Haycrafts, we also have someone who came and never left. She's called Jeanie, but she isn't a burglar and doesn't live in a van. Mum and Dad always call Jeanie their daughter and introduce her to everyone as that. Me, Tom and Kate call her our sister, which has always felt totally normal. She isn't really our sister, as we know her mum, who's Jamaican and used to be our nanny and housekeeper. I really love Jeanie, she's like the big sister all my friends wish they had. Although she's fifteen years older, she never minds playing with me, is really kind if I'm ever sick and is always around in the same way that Tom and Kate are. She comes on holidays with us and takes me to classical music concerts at the Festival Hall with her friends.

Miss Shepherd's van outside number 61

Jeanie's real mum is called Beatrice, and now lives in a tower block near Euston Station. Beatrice came over from Jamaica on her own and got a job as a cleaner in a hospital called the Royal Free, where Mum was working. This was all before I was born, but she came to clean our house and then had to stop when Mum, Dad and Tom went to live in New York. Then I was born and we moved back to Gloucester Crescent, and Mum and Dad asked Beatrice to come and work for us as a nanny and housekeeper. By then her two daughters, Jeanie and Esther, had come over from Jamaica too, so they all moved into the flat on the top floor of our house. Jeanie was 15 and Esther was 13, and it wasn't long before they started coming downstairs and hanging out and playing with me and Tom. Beatrice was our first nanny, but we've had quite a few since her: there was Christine, who had a baby called Janey-Waney with the man who ran the junk stall down on Inverness Street. Then there was Cathy, followed by Jean, whose husband, Dave, made me and Tom balsa-wood gliders, and then finally Marina González, who's our nanny now.

Anyway, Beatrice was useless as a nanny because no one ever knew if she was going to appear in the morning or stay in bed claiming to be sick. This was hard on Mum, as she works as a doctor every day. If Dad was at home, he wasn't going to get up and make us all breakfast or cook us tea when we got back from school. I was only a baby at the time, and Tom was two, so when Beatrice had one of her staying-in-bed days Mum would have to run around trying to find someone else to look after us so she could go to work. Quite often it would be my grandparents, Ruth and Bob. They live in Northwood in Middlesex, so they'd have to get on a train and come all the way into London.

All in all, Beatrice's staying-in-bed thing messed up everyone's day. Eventually, Mum and Dad decided they needed someone they could rely on, and Beatrice was asked to leave. Jeanie liked living with us in Gloucester Crescent, and when Beatrice packed her bags and left, Jeanie refused to go. Mum and Dad did a lot of talking and even went to see Jeanie's headmaster at her school to get his advice. He told them that, because she'd just turned 16, she could do what she wanted. What she wanted was to stay with us. I don't think it was an easy decision for Mum and Dad, but in the end they said Jeanie could stay for as long as she liked. Beatrice was furious with everyone, especially Jeanie. When the new nanny

Jeanie with Kate, 1967

moved into the flat on the top floor, Jeanie was given her own bedroom next to me and Tom, and from that moment on she became one of the family.

Just like Alfie over at the Haycrafts, it all seemed pretty normal. Jeanie lived with us as our sister. She ate with us and came on holidays with us – in fact, she did everything with us. Mum and Dad always knew how clever Jeanie was and insisted she stay on to finish school and then go to college, which they helped her do. Dad is always buying her books that he thinks she'd be interested in, and also paid for her to have piano lessons, which she is now really good at.

Another person who turned up at our house and is around a lot is someone called Keith McNally. Jeanie actually lives with us and feels like a real sister, and even though he doesn't live with us, Keith feels a bit like an older brother. He was an actor in a play Alan wrote called *Forty Years On* and first turned up in the Crescent when he came to help Alan decorate his house, and sometimes, when Alan goes away, Keith stays and looks after it. I was trying to remember the first time he ever came to our house, but like lots of people he just started coming and was then around a lot. I know he likes Mum's cooking, but I think he likes having a laugh with Dad as, unlike me and Tom, he listens to every word Dad says and really likes being taught things by him. Keith was at lunch once when Mum and Dad were having a big argument about something. It can't have been that serious as they are still together, but Dad said to Keith, 'Whatever you do, don't ever get married.' That made me really worry that they might get divorced one day, as there does seem to be a lot of it happening in the Crescent. In fact, one morning, when we were going to school, one of the dads in the street brought his children to our car for the drive to school and said to Mum, 'They might seem a bit odd this morning as Sandra and I have decided to get a divorce.' The children looked like their world had come to an end, and I couldn't stop thinking about the way he told Mum about the divorce as if he was telling her they were all going to France for a holiday. If divorce was so easy to do, it could happen to my family just like that. This was another thing to add to all the other things that worried me, like Dad saying he wanted to kill himself and nuclear war.

3

A SECOND HOME, EASTER 1967

The first car we ever had was a Morris Traveller, which was dark green with a funny wooden frame on the outside with doors on the back like a delivery van. Inside it had springy grey leather seats, which had a nice comfy smell in hot weather. Mum and Dad bought the car when I was four and just after my sister Kate was born. Before that Dad went around on a Lambretta, but one day he fell off it. He cut his leg and ruined one of his favourite suits, so he got rid of the scooter. Dad didn't learn to drive a car for a long time, so after the scooter accident Mum had to do all the driving.

It wasn't long after Kate was born that they bought the car, and we all went on holiday in it to Scotland to visit Dad, who was making a film. It was a strange film about how they make whisky, which Dad said no one would ever see as it was made to help the company sell their whisky abroad. He hadn't wanted to make the film in the first place, but the film company told him he would get lots of money and his family could have a holiday in Scotland.

We put the car on the overnight sleeper train, which arrived in Scotland early the next morning. We hadn't slept much on the train, and then we had to drive for hours up and down big mountains and along small, winding roads. It was going up one of these mountains that the nice smell of leather in the car changed to a smell of burning. Jeanie, who was sitting in the front and had Kate on her lap, was the first to notice the smell and told Mum it was something called the clutch. Mum looked a bit worried, so we stopped at the top of the mountain and got out and waited for the smell to go and then it was fine.

As we started to come down the mountain the fields became greener, and after driving along the edge of a river we came to a sign on the road that said, 'Rothes Glen Hotel, Shooting and Fishing Parties Welcome'. Across a big field was a huge castle with turrets that looked like witches' hats. Mum turned into the drive and stopped, and we all stared at the castle in silence. In the field in front of the castle was a herd of shaggy Highland cows, who were standing in muddy puddles looking miserable. Mum turned round and looked at the two of us sitting in the back. Tom was sulking and refused to look at the castle, but I couldn't take my eyes off it. It was like one of the castles in my Ladybird book on knights and dragons. I loved that book and would look at it for hours, imagining living in that time with castles and dragons.

'Right, who's had enough and wants to ride up the drive on the roof rack?' Mum asked, trying to break the angry silence in the back seat. With so little sleep we were all pretty tired, fed up and bad-tempered with each other, and Mum knew she needed to cheer us up before we arrived at the hotel. Tom was suddenly interested. Mum knew if she didn't come up with something a bit crazy, like a ride on the roof rack, someone would get well and truly punched. Annoyingly, that usually ends up being me. We've always loved riding on the roof of the car, even if our next-door neighbour, Mr Jefferson, thinks it's dangerous and stupid. He once gave Mum a telling-off when she let us do it along Gloucester Crescent with all the

Jeanie, Tom and me at Rothes Glen Hotel, Scotland, 1967

Roebers. This time we were so excited we were bouncing up and down on the back seat. Jeanie got out and then helped me and Tom onto the roof. We climbed over the suitcases and found a place where we could hang on to the roof rack. Mum headed slowly up the drive with the two of us screaming and cheering at the top of our voices.

As we got closer to the hotel, we could see people starting to gather at the windows on the ground floor. We thought they were coming to greet us. It wasn't until we pulled up at the front of the hotel that we could see their faces – and they didn't look happy. A big man in a tweed suit came running out of the front door waving his arms. He came right up to the car and put his hands on the bonnet like he was trying to stop Mum driving through the front door. Obviously she wasn't going to do that, but he just stood there staring. I realised he wasn't looking at Mum but instead had his eyes fixed on Jeanie, who was still sitting in the car. Mum got out, went straight up to him and shook his hand. He was trying to get a better look at Jeanie over Mum's shoulder, and she was now waving at him, which he didn't seem to like at all. I think all the people standing in the windows were staring at Jeanie too, because they were starting to point. It then crossed my mind that they might never have seen a black person before. We'd driven through a town soon after getting off the train, and Jeanie had asked Mum why there were no black people. I'd been to the countryside loads of times, but I'd never really noticed until then that you never saw a black person outside London. The guests were now standing in the front hall, trying to get a better look at us, or rather Jeanie, who was starting to get a bit annoyed. This sort of thing never happened at home, where everyone seemed fine when they were told Jeanie was our sister, even if she is a different colour. No one ever thinks it's strange that she lives with us as part of our family, and nobody points or whispers. But in Scotland they looked like we'd just arrived from Mars and Jeanie was an alien, which made me feel bad for her as it wasn't fair to make her feel different from her family.

The man in the tweed suit told us that Dad was out with his film crew at a local distillery and would be back for tea. When some of the hotel guests realised we were Dad's family, everything changed and they decided to be nice to us. Now they were chatting to Mum about how much they liked Dad, and some of them were telling her that they'd seen him on television, and that they loved having someone famous in the hotel.

For Tom, Jeanie and me this massive castle was the best adventure playground we'd ever been to. You could sit at the top of the shiny banisters and slide really fast, all the way down to the reception desk. And running in your socks, you could skate down the corridors so fast without stopping that when you hit the door to the bedroom at the end it made a crashing thump. And the sofas in the sitting room were big enough to skydive off the back of.

The distillery where Dad was making his film was on the edge of a village called Knockando. To get there from our hotel you had to drive along a winding road and up a steep hill. As the car climbed higher, we could see heather-covered hills, and behind them big mountains. When we couldn't go any higher, we drove past fields and a forest until we came to a village called Archiestown. It had two shops and a hotel on the edge of a big square. We were driving up the high street when Tom suddenly shouted, 'Fire! Look at those flames!' He was right – there was one, and it was the Archiestown village hotel that was on fire.

As we drove into the village square, the road was blocked by fire engines parked outside the hotel. It was brilliant – huge flames were shooting out of two of the windows, and there were firemen throwing suitcases and bits of furniture out of another. For me and Tom, watching the firemen at work and seeing a building in flames had to be more exciting than watching Dad making a film about whisky. Mum pulled over so we could get a better look. Climbing out of the car with Jeanie, who was carrying Kate, we found a place to watch all the action on the steps of a war memorial in the middle of the square. As we sat there, Mum, who wasn't at all interested in fires, went for a walk around the village.

Every now and then I would look to see where she'd got to. I was worried in case she'd forgotten us and got back in the car and driven off without us. She and Dad have done that a few times. The worst was actually a few years later, when we'd been to the beach for the day. There was all of us and another family and we'd gone in two cars. It wasn't until we were half-way home that someone in our car said, 'Where's Kate?' She definitely wasn't in our car and, as it turned out, she wasn't in the other one either. I don't think I've ever seen Mum drive so fast. When we got back to the beach, there was Kate, perfectly happy, playing in the sand. I thought Mum was going to have a heart attack. Dad pretended to be calm, but I could tell he was freaked out. When we found Kate, Mum burst into tears and told Dad it was all his fault, which seemed a little unfair.

Fortunately, this time Mum didn't leave us behind. I saw her walking through the front gate of a big house at the top of the square. I thought this was a bit strange, as I didn't think we knew anyone in this village. She went around the garden and then stood on the door steps looking out across the square with this big smile on her face. Then she walked all the way to the bottom of the square and into a shop. She was in there for ages, and when she finally came back, the fire had gone out. Me and Tom were talking to the firemen, who had taken us to look at one of their fire engines. They were really nice, but some of the people in the village came out of their houses and, instead of looking at the fire, they stood there staring at Jeanie, who was now feeling cross again.

When Mum finally walked back to where we were sitting, she pointed to the big house at the top of the square and asked us what we thought of it. That seemed like an odd question, but the next one was even odder. 'Do you think we should get Dad to buy it for us as a holiday home?' This was exciting, although I knew Dad was hardly going to agree to Mum's plan. I hoped she hadn't gone and bought it already, as Dad would be furious. He loves London and can't stand the countryside. Lots of my friends have houses in the country, and Mum sometimes says it would be nice to have a place we can all go away to. Whenever she mentions it to Dad, he either changes the subject or launches into one of his speeches about how ghastly everyone is in the countryside. This plan of Mum's was obviously one she hadn't discussed with Dad, and it was going to be very interesting when she did. We didn't have to wait long as the place where Dad was making his film was only a few miles from Archiestown.

Mum had gone into the distillery to collect Dad, and when they came back he had his angry face on. 'Are you out of your bloody mind?' he said to Mum as he climbed into the front seat of the car. Jeanie and Kate were now squeezed into the back seat with me and Tom, and we were all watching Mum and Dad. 'What would we want with a house all the way up here? Do you know how many miles we are from London – hundreds, if not thousands?' This was pretty much how I thought it was going to go.

I never knew why they bought the Morris Traveller, as Dad always had to bend his head and twist his body to get into it. And I don't think the car was meant to have two children, a teenager and a baby in the back. Dad had his knees pressed against the dashboard with his head bent sideways so he could look Mum in the eyes. He started on a long list of reasons why buying a house anywhere outside London was such a terrible idea.

He was still going on about how far it was from London, but he was having trouble putting a figure on the distance. I knew exactly how many miles it was, as me and Jeanie had worked it out on a map in the hotel – 570, to be precise. Dad has never been very good with distances. He either totally exaggerates them or thinks they're very small. Maybe it was because he didn't drive until recently. In London he measures everything by how many stops it is on the Underground. If you asked him how far it is to the Science Museum, he would say, 'It's eleven stops, but then it depends where you change trains.'

After a while Dad came up with another reason for not buying a house in the countryside, which we'd all heard before. 'You do know everyone's either a Tory or an anti-Semite?' Mum just laughed, but Dad reminded her of the awful little man wearing breeches who sat next to us at supper in the hotel. Dad had said something to him about borrowing money, and the man said something about someone he knew who worked in a bank and he called him a 'hook-nose'. Dad managed to stay calm, but he was now telling Mum that he'd wanted to 'rip his oesophagus out through his nose and make him eat it'. He turned round and explained to us that this was a typical anti-Semitic way of saying someone is a Jew. The man had then started talking about 'those people from Darkest Africa', then raised his eyebrows and looked over at Jeanie, who he called our 'negro au pair'. I think this was the point when the man's oesophagus was about to be removed, which would have been great fun to watch.

Dad had that pleased look on his face that said 'I am winning this argument', but Mum wasn't going to be put off by Dad's dislike of everyone in the countryside, or his fear of distances. She pointed out that, with three children and Jeanie, we were going to take a lot of entertaining over the school holidays. There would be Easters, Christmases and summers as well as half-terms, and she was going to have her work cut out while he 'buggered off' around the world or stayed put in London leaving her to look after us. According to Mum, we now needed a lot of space to run around, and she couldn't wait for friends to invite us to their houses in the country. The next thing she said seemed a bit unfair: she claimed it wouldn't be long before our family was banned from every hotel in the country. As far as I could tell, it was only the horrid owner of the Rothes Glen Hotel who got cross with our rowdiness and the sliding down the banisters, and I knew Dad was worried he was going to get a bill for repainting the dining room ceiling after we flooded the bathroom above it. He reminded Mum how the owner had liked him before we all turned up. Now he was just the 'father of that unruly mob'. After a while the whole car fell silent. I knew Mum wasn't going to let this one go and that this conversation was going to carry on when they were back in their hotel room. Poor Dad, he didn't look happy about it at all – he knew he was about to lose this argument and that it was going to cost him a lot of money.

The next morning at breakfast Mum was looking a lot happier, and Dad, for now, had stopped talking about all the people he hated. It was his morning off from filming, and Mum decided we were all going to a town called Elgin. It turned out Dad had run out of excuses and Mum had won her argument about the house, and now they were going to see a man about buying it. Mum looked excited, but Dad looked like a man on his way to prison. He kept saying things like, 'I'll be bankrupt' and 'It's going to clean us out.' Mum wasn't having any of it and said that they didn't know how much the house was going to cost yet.

It didn't take us long to get to Elgin, and we soon pulled up outside an office in a side-street. Mum and Dad got out of the car and went inside. They were in there for what seemed like hours, but when they came out I could tell Mum was trying her best not to smile, and an old man in a grey suit was shaking Dad's hand. For some reason Dad was smiling too. When they got back in the car he started to laugh. 'Bloody hell,' he said, 'that was less than it cost us to buy this dreadful car.' That sounded barmy: how could a house cost less than a car? Something had happened in that office, and Mum was about to give Dad an earful.

'Jonathan, negotiating is not offering someone £750 when they clearly said "£650 would be more than sufficient, sir."' I was a bit confused by all of this, but Mum carried on having a go at Dad. 'Negotiating is when someone says £650 and you come back with £550.' Mum was teasing him now, and he was looking embarrassed. 'You don't put the price up in a negotiation, you go down – pushing the price up is his job, but you seem to have done it for him.'

I was even more confused when Mum said the house wasn't exactly ours yet. It turned out that they still had to write the number of pounds they wanted to pay on a piece of paper and put it in an envelope. Later, the man in Elgin would open the envelope and if their number was the biggest of all the envelopes, then the house was ours. It would be amazing to come here for our holidays, and I was sure the locals would get to know and like Jeanie, and eventually they might stop staring at her like she was from outer space. Jeanie was also really excited about us all coming to Scotland for holidays, even if, she said, some of the people might be 'racists'. So we were all crossing our fingers. If the envelope thing worked, we were going to have our own house in the country! It didn't matter that it was 570 miles from London and you couldn't get to it on the Northern Line.

4

THE OLD MANSE

It was December 1967 when Mum got the call from the man in Elgin. It turned out that the number Dad had put in the envelope was more than enough, and the Old Manse was ours. Mum was thrilled and, because her birthday is in December, Dad said it could be her present from him. He still went on about being broke and kept telling everyone that it would be quicker to get to New York than Scotland, which turned out to be true. Now Mum can do what so many of her friends like doing – shopping for knives and forks and furniture and curtains and spending hours in antique shops while their children are left sitting in their cars, bored senseless.

The Old Manse has lots of bedrooms, and Mum didn't want to be spending holidays making beds or running around with a Hoover. To help look after the house she found a really nice housekeeper called Mrs Thain, who lives in a house on the village high street, just past the sweet shop. It turns out she lived in the Old Manse when she was a little girl. Dad thinks Mrs Thain looks like the wife of a duke as she's tall and grand-looking, with a kind face. I think she's more like a saint as she's so nice to us and makes the house warm and cosy when we arrive at the beginning of every holiday. Some mornings she comes up to my bedroom at the top of the house, leans on her broom in the doorway, wags a finger and tells me off for still being in bed at ten o'clock. I always write to her when I get back to London and tell her about my friends and school. She writes back with the village gossip, news about her family and how the house is getting on without us.

The Old Manse has a big garden, and since Dad was never going to mow the lawn, plant trees or grow vegetables, Mum had to find someone who would. The gardener she found used to work in a distillery and is called Willie Moggach. He and his wife live in a white cottage along a little back lane from the Old Manse. He has a wonderful garden where he keeps bees, which means we also have all the honey we can eat. Mrs Moggach is very small, with snow-white hair, and speaks as if her voice-box has been crushed and she is choking on water. Mum takes us to visit her at the beginning and end of every holiday. She is usually sitting in an armchair beside the fireplace, where she likes to burn chunks of peat. We sit there listening to her wheeze and gurgle, and we nod politely, pretending to understand what she is saying when we clearly don't, but we try our best not to show it.

Willie seems to find Tom, Kate and me amusing and spends hours helping us fix our bikes or find the things we need to build camps in the garden. One of our favourite games is to pinch his cloth cap (exposing his shiny bald head) and then take it in turns to run around the garden wearing it. I think it's really interesting that he has a full set of false teeth, which

Kate, Willie Moggach, Tom and me at the Old Manse, 1969

he takes enormous pleasure in removing for us. He throws them in the air and then pops them back in his mouth with a big smile.

Mum bought Willie a big green lawn mower with blades that spin on a barrel on the front. To start the engine you have to pull a rope on the side really hard. If you lose your balance, you could fall straight into the spinning blades and die, which was why it is a good thing Dad didn't want to mow the lawn. Alan nearly chopped his foot off with his Flymo when he was mowing his lawn in London. He came straight over to show us what he'd done and he looked very pale. He was still wearing the Wellington boot that the mower had sliced through. There was a large hole right over his toes. You could see them wiggling around in a grey sock – any closer and there wouldn't have been any toes for him to wiggle. Alan was quite shaken and had to sit down while Mum made him a cup of tea. When he recovered, he went back across the road and carried on mowing. Alan was lucky – if it had been Dad

The view from Mum and Dad's bedroom across the garden
to the hills beyond the Old Manse, by Nicholas Garland

with Willie's new mower, he would have lost an entire arm or
a leg or even his head. Alan eventually decided having a lawn
was too dangerous for him, bricked over his garden and threw
the mower away.

5

YOU'LL BE DEAD BY THEN! - 1968

I pushed the full weight of my body against our heavy front door. It swung open, crashing against the wall as I fell forward onto my hands and knees. Picking myself up, I went back to slam the door shut. All the doors in Gloucester Crescent have their very own sound when they're being slammed shut. Ours closes with a big thud, and you can hear bits of the house shaking. Next door, at the Thackers', I think the door must be thin as it rattles like it's going to fall to pieces. The Roebers' door is heavy, like ours, but has more of a shush and then a thud. From our house, if you close your eyes and listen, you can tell who's coming and going just from the sound of the front doors opening and closing.

I stood very still in the hallway, trying not to breathe so I could listen to the sounds of our house. I could tell someone was in the house on their own as I couldn't hear the usual voices and laughing when Mum and Dad have visitors. Our nanny, Cathy, had collected me from school and was heading down to the kitchen and I could hear her shoes on the wooden stairs, but I was much more interested in following the sound of a typewriter coming through the half-open door of the sitting room.

As quietly as I could, I crossed the loose tiles in the hall and then stretched a foot across the old floorboards in the doorway of the sitting room. I stood there, holding my breath. I was right, there was a new person, a woman, who carried on typing as she sat very straight at the little desk in the window looking out onto the street. She had long blonde hair swept over one shoulder and she was looking down to one side at something on the desk and she was typing without looking at the keys. Not the sort of typing I was familiar with, having, at the time, only ever watched Dad and Alan doing it. This was real typing like I'd seen on TV. I moved forward slowly until I was only a few feet away. I could now smell her scent, which was really nice and new and different from Mum's or Cathy's. Without stopping typing she coughed and said, with a laughy sort of voice, 'I think there is someone very small and quiet behind me.'

I froze on the spot as she turned round and reached out to shake my hand. 'Hello, I'm Sue Coltman-Rogers. Who are you and what, may I ask, is under the plaster on your forehead?' 'My eyebrow,' I informed her, which seemed fairly obvious to me. Mum had put the plaster on after I'd had a fight with a sharp toy before breakfast. Although there wasn't any blood, Mum decided having a plaster might stop me whining and it would impress my friends at school. I could see that the plaster was going to come in pretty handy if I could use it to get some sympathy from this lovely-smelling and beautiful new person in our house.

I asked what she was typing, and she said it was letters for my dad, and that there were an awful lot of them. 'That's what my dad usually does.'

'What does your dad do?' she asked.

'Typing – that's what my dad's work is – smoking, typing and getting paid for it.' I thought that was a pretty good

Sue Coltman-Rogers

response and would show her that nothing went unnoticed by me in our house.

I knew Dad had started writing a book. Not a story book but one about a real man called Marshall Something-or-other, who was a philosopher, just like Nick's dad, Freddie Ayer. I don't think anyone other than Dad and Freddie had ever heard of this man, which might be why Dad was having so much trouble writing about him. He would come down to the kitchen and read what he'd written to Mum, then walk off screwing the bits of paper up and throwing them on the floor, saying, 'It's all hopeless.' He'd go back to his study and sit for hours, smoking and staring at his typewriter. Then he'd come back down again and say to Mum, 'I have got to get myself out of writing this dreadful book or I'm going to have to kill myself.'

There it was again, the killing himself thing. Every now and then there would be lots of activity from his study, followed by long periods of getting nowhere, and the idea of him killing

Dad reading his work to Mum, Gloucester Crescent, 1965

himself would be very much on my mind and everyone else's. Mum told him he should speak to his agent, Elaine Green, and explain why it was taking him so long to write the book. When Elaine came to see Dad, she always seemed clever, so I was sure she would know what to do – and she did. But there was another problem: along with his book, there were piles of unanswered letters lying around the house. One of the many things Dad hated was writing letters. He loved writing them to Mum and some of his friends when he was away, but he hated doing them for work. There is one other kind of letter he really likes writing and that's the angry ones to people he doesn't like. Tom showed me one Dad had written that was printed in a magazine (*Private Eye*), which he kept with lots of others in a drawer. Tom and I really liked reading this letter because it was full of swear words that we knew made Mum cross. This is what his letter to the magazine said:

> You stupid bloody irresponsible cunts!! You had no per-
> mission and therefore no right to use my medical title as a
> heading to the article. Are you all so completely frivolous
> and insensitive as not to be able to understand that such a
> fucking stupid blunder could well mean me being struck
> off the register? God rot the lot of you!
>
> Jonathan Miller

The piles of letters around the house were getting bigger, and someone had to sort them out. Elaine was always quite calm about these things, but I could tell she was worried that Dad would never finish his book and that staring at his unanswered letters might be stopping him from getting on with writing it. She spoke to a friend of hers called Deborah Coltman-Rogers, who is an agent too (as Deborah Rogers), and she said her younger sister had just finished at a school for secretaries. Mum and Dad liked Sue the minute they met her and gave her the job on the spot.

I liked Sue too, and the day after I met her I was certain I had fallen in love with her. She was so different from the other women in my life. At the time there was one other grown-up woman I really liked, and her name was Miss Laing. She was the teacher in the next-door classroom at Primrose Hill Primary. She was beautiful too, and I thought she looked like a princess in a painting. Since the beginning of the year I'd wished Miss Laing could have been my teacher. On the first day of the school year everyone has to stand in the playground as the teachers call out the names of the children going into each class. Miss Laing was standing waiting with a clipboard and was looking so beautiful, then she stepped forward and started calling out names. I was holding my breath, with my fingers and toes crossed, hoping she would call mine. The names stopped, and off she marched to her classroom with all her new pupils following her. It felt like the world had suddenly come to an end and none of this school stuff would be worth doing any more. Conrad came over and shoved me. 'Come on, William, wake up, we're off to Mr Connor's class', which just made the situation worse. Mr Connor was small and chubby and nothing like Miss Laing. I carried on thinking about her every day, wondering what my life would be like if we were married. I decided that we'd probably live on a farm in Scotland and go on holidays to France or America and have beautiful children – maybe a girl who would look like a miniature version of Miss Laing.

With the arrival of Sue at Gloucester Crescent my thoughts about Miss Laing seemed to have gone away. Now I was thinking about what life would be like when I married Sue. They both had lovely blonde hair and blue eyes, and Sue wore that nice perfume. More importantly, Sue was in my house and not in the classroom next door with twenty-five other children.

Tom didn't get how lovely Sue was, but as far as I was concerned this was a good thing – I didn't need any more competition. She would have already met Alan, who would have been around for elevenses. This happens every weekday at eleven o'clock, when everyone stops working for an hour and they meet in the kitchen for coffee. If Dad is home, he comes down from his study and Alan comes from across the road. I knew Sue would like Alan. Most people do, and what's more, he doesn't have a girlfriend.

When I got back from school, I decided I had to let Sue know how I felt. But before I did that I thought it would be a good idea to get Tom to be a witness, though I didn't tell him what it was all about. At some point I would need to bring Conrad in on it too. That was going to be trickier as the two of us had a made a plan of our own, and if Sue said yes I would need to get out of that. I found Tom and took him into the sitting room, where Sue was busy working on a pile of Dad's letters. Marching straight up to her desk, we stood waiting for her to stop typing. It did cross my mind that this could go horribly wrong, but before she started on the next letter I came straight out with it.

'Sue, I've been thinking and I thought you should know that when I'm older there are three people I would like to marry.'

'Three?' she asked with surprise.

'There were two who I've actually asked. First there's Louise.' This was a girl who lived three doors away. 'And then me and Conrad have been talking about getting married too, but now I'm not sure. And since you turned up in our house I've decided I would really like to marry you, so that makes three.' I didn't mention Miss Laing, as I hadn't had the chance to tell her how I felt, so she wasn't on my list. Conrad and Louise were, and I knew I'd have to get out of the marriage thing with them if I was going to marry Sue.

Sue tilted her head and smiled at me, but I could see she was trying not to laugh. Tom didn't know where to look. He tried staring at the pattern in the carpet then over at me to see if I was serious, then back to Sue to see if she thought I was as mad as he did. Then Tom burst out laughing and said, 'Don't be stupid, Sue will be dead by then!'

There was another silence as I glared at him with my I'll-kill-you stare. Then Sue burst out laughing too. When she recovered, she took my hand and said, 'I wouldn't be too sure of that, Tom, I think it's a lovely offer.' Well, she hadn't said no, which had to be a good thing. She thanked me and said she would bear it in mind. She also felt I should talk to Louise and Conrad, as they might have something to say about all of this.

6

ANOTHER WORLD – 1969

I liked the old coins we had before decimalisation. They felt worn and soft, like they could tell a story. When Decimal Day happened a few years later, it was as if an old world had ended and everything was now going to be modern. The threepenny bit was my favourite, with all its corners around the edge. It had the Queen on one side and a portcullis from a medieval castle on the other. I think I only ever used it for dinner money at school. We got the big brown pennies with Britannia on one side for buying sweets and, if we were lucky, half a crown or a two-shilling coin for toys. When I was little, the old one penny coin was almost the same size as the palm of my hand.

Guy Coltman-Rogers handed me one he'd taken out of his pocket. It was still warm as he pressed it into my hand, and I squeezed up next to him on the sofa. He was so tall, with long legs like a giraffe that twisted around themselves when he sat down. We were sitting together in his library, opposite a roaring fire and the biggest television I'd ever seen. He gave me the penny and told me to choose a horse that was running in one of the races we were about to watch.

One of the things I loved about Guy when I first met him was his grand, raspy old voice. Usually he speaks very softly, with a gurgly croak that sounds like there's a lump of jelly stuck

Guy Coltman-Rogers

in his throat. Sometimes it suddenly changes when he gets excited and starts shouting. When a rider falls at a fence, he'll shout at the television, 'Ya bloody fool!', and then goes quiet again. If a big pheasant walks across the lawn outside the library window, he'll point and shout, 'Bloody hell, Stella, get mi gun, the buggers missed one.' He sometimes ends a shout with a little croaky laugh, so you know he's only joking. Then he gets his pipe out and sticks it in his mouth and mumbles to himself. He shouts at Stella a lot – she's his wife, but I don't think he's ever really angry with her. If my horse wins, he reaches into his pocket and while searching for the right coin he mutters, 'Bloody good choice, old boy, should have listened to ya in the first place.' Then he hands over my winnings, a shilling or two, and we settle down and start betting on the next race.

I don't know anyone else like Guy. He's so not like Grandad or my other grandfather, Bob. I think he's probably the grandfather I wished I could have had. I know that's a bit unkind, but Guy is always funny, badly behaved and likes talking to me and showing me new things, like how to bet on the horses. In the mornings he lets me sit in a big armchair in his dressing room while he's shaving, and I can ask questions about all sorts of things, like growing old or how to shave. Once, when he told me how old he was, I said I was worried he might die soon. He smiled and told me we were all going to die one day, and that I wasn't to worry about him as he was old on the outside but, pointing to his head, young in here. I was very happy with this answer and ran off to find Stella to let her know what Guy had said.

Quite soon after I told Sue that I wanted to marry her, she told me about her Mum and Dad, Guy and Stella Coltman-Rogers. They live in a big castle in Wales called Stanage Park, which was where Sue grew up. I couldn't believe they lived in a real castle, so she promised she would take me there and show me. Then one day she said that she had managed to get through all of Dad's letters and didn't have any work to do. As Mum and Dad were going away and it was half-term, they asked Sue if she wanted to take me to stay with her parents. I was only five years old and it was the first time I'd ever been away on my own.

The journey to Stanage goes on for ever, and just as you feel like it must be nearly over you turn off the road at a lodge and head up a long drive. You don't see the castle straight away, but as you go further up the drive you see the turrets and chimneys, and then slowly the rest of it starts to appear and you can see how really big it is. Getting to Stanage and coming up the drive is one of my favourite moments. As you pull up outside the house, the gravel makes a crunching noise. When Stella hears it, she comes out to meet you with her dogs, a black Labrador called Juno and Tao-Chi, a blonde and angry Pekinese who likes chasing sheep and cows.

Stella Coltman-Rogers in her twenties as an actress

I think Stella is one of the most amazing women I've ever met. She was once a Hollywood actress, but that was a long time ago. It was when she came back from Hollywood that she met Guy at a party. She was only 21 and he was 48. He fell in love with her straight away and they got married soon after that.

When you walk into the front hall at Stanage, the first thing you notice is the smell. It's a delicious mixture of the big log fire and the flowers on the table. I even know the name of the flowers – azaleas. Wherever I am, the smell of azaleas always makes me think of Stanage. It's now a smell that makes me feel calm and happy. Mum once told me about a French-man who lived a long time ago, and every time he dipped a cake into his tea he was reminded of things that made him happy. And that's what the flowers and the log fire smell at Stanage do to me.

In the really old days there were lots of staff who worked and lived at the castle. There's a long corridor that goes down the back of the first floor and has lots of bedrooms off it. This is where all the servants once slept. The only person who sleeps there now is Maggie, the housekeeper. She had a budgie she kept in a cage in her bedroom, but Stella's dog Juno got into the room and ate it. I don't know how Juno opened the cage, but she did and that was that. There is also a cook called Mrs Preece, but everyone calls her Preecie. She's married to the gardener, Willy, and they live in a cottage at the end of the kitchen garden. She calls me Mr William, which I like, and knows that my favourite thing to eat is treacle sponge pudding. As a special treat she makes it for me whenever I come to stay.

On my first visit to Stanage they had a pheasant shoot at the weekend. Guy doesn't shoot any more, but the men who were shooting came back to have their lunch in the house. They sat at a round table in front of the big windows at one end of the dining room. The rest of us sat at the long dining table at the other end of the room. The men were having a conversation about their morning out shooting when Guy suddenly shouted 'BIRD!' All the men stood up in their breeches and stared out of the window looking for the bird. As he pointed at the window he said, 'Bloody hell, didn't you see it? You're supposed to shoot the buggers.' Then he snorted and laughed into his soup. There wasn't a bird, but with their backs turned he stuck his tongue out at them. I thought this was hilarious, although Stella didn't and tried to hit him with her napkin. Stella knew that if Guy made me laugh I was likely to fall off my chair. To stop this happening she put me in a big chair with arms that touched the table to keep me in.

When the men sat back down, Guy moved on to his other favourite trick. This was sticking his finger right up his nose so it got stuck, pretending it had come off and that he would need a corkscrew to get it out again. Stella has to play along

Stanage Park, Radnorshire

with him for this trick as he does a lot of shouting at her with things like 'Stella, quick, my bloody finger's stuck up my nose' and 'For God's sake, old girl, get the corkscrew from the pantry.' When he finally reattaches his finger, he brings his hand up from under the table and licks the finger clean. When he did it over lunch, the men on the other table sat there looking at him in horror. Guy just smiled and mumbled to himself, 'That's better, nearly lost the old chap.' When he thought no one was looking he leaned over and said, 'That got 'em, the silly buggers!'

Gloucester Crescent is amazing in all sorts of ways, but when I went to Stanage it made me realise that my home wasn't as perfect as I thought. Stanage has always felt like a safe place that I can escape to, where the grown-ups want to talk to me and spend time with me in a way that no one does at home. Sometimes I feel torn, as I know Stanage is the sort of place that Dad really doesn't like, and for that reason I can't really tell him about it. He doesn't understand why I like it so much and why I feel so happy when I'm there. I once tried to tell him about some of the things I'd done and how much fun it was being with Guy and Stella. He just said that their fortune was probably built off the slave trade: most of the grand houses in Britain were. Then he gave me a history book, which he said was about slavery and that I should read it, but I didn't. He said it was important to remember that lots of upper-class people hate Jews, and that they will always let you down. I certainly don't think Guy or Stella hate Jews, or anyone else for that matter, and of all the people I know I can trust them not to let me down.

In Dad's world there are two kinds of people – the ones he likes, who are good, and the ones he hates, who are bad. The good ones are people like his close friends and the drunks who come to the door and anyone who votes Labour. Since Dad finds it easier to hate people than to like them, there are quite a few on his bad list, which includes people like Idi Amin, because he's mad and eats human flesh, Hitler and his generals, the upper classes, because they hate Jews *and* vote Conservative, and then all theatre critics. You often hear the mums and dads in the Crescent complaining about someone or other being upper-class or a Tory. If you ask me, I think they're all a bit confused and don't realise that anyone who doesn't know the people in the Crescent probably thinks they're all upper-class when they first meet them. I once heard a recording of Dad talking on the radio from a long time ago, and he sounded even posher than Prince Charles.

One of the things I like about going to Stanage and what makes it so different from Gloucester Crescent is that no one there ever talks about other people's class or goes on about who they hate. They're kind and generous to everyone, and I know they didn't make their money from the slave trade.

7

APOLLO 11 TO THE MOON
(WEDNESDAY, 16 JULY 1969)

We don't normally have a Saturday kind of family lunch on a Wednesday, but we did with this one, and it was a lunch I knew I would remember for ever. Big family lunches usually take place on the weekend, and there's always an odd mix of people, including a few who drop in uninvited. Mum does it without any kind of fuss and always cooks enough food to go around. Saturdays are usually when my grandparents come to lunch. They are Mum's mother and father, but we've always just called them Ruth and Bob. There are other people who come too, like Dad's sister, Sarah, who he's never really got on with. Apart from Christmas, when Mum feels she has to ask her to come, I don't think Sarah ever actually gets invited to lunch but then she just turns up. She lives on her own with a cat in Richmond and has a very bad stutter, which is sad as I think she has a lot to say and doesn't get to say much of it. I'm sure one of the reasons she comes over is to annoy Dad and make him feel guilty about being what he calls a 'bad Jew'. The thing is, he doesn't care about being a bad Jew, but Sarah does, so she usually leaves feeling even angrier than Dad.

Alan is always invited and is really good at talking to Ruth and Bob. They like that, because everyone around the table talks so fast and over each other that they find it hard to keep up. There are always a lot of jokes, which Ruth complains about as she says she doesn't understand them. Then Bob misunderstands quite a lot because he's a bit deaf. The other day Alan said something like, 'I like to be on my own,' and Bob said, 'Oh yes, the Mayan civilisation, I like them too.' I didn't get what was wrong, but I could see Mum and Dad and Alan were trying not to laugh. Then Mum said, 'No, Dad, Alan said he likes to be on his own – "I-like-to-be-on-my-own", not that he liked the Mayan civilisation.' It didn't make any difference – he still carried on talking about the Mayans.

Quite often Dad's friends Eric Korn and Oliver Sacks come to lunch too. Eric sells old books, and Oliver is a doctor and does something with brains that I don't really understand. He wrote a book which Colin Haycraft published. Dad says Colin had to lock Oliver in a room to get him to finish it. Eric and Oliver know Sarah from when they were at school with Dad, so they often talk about when they grew up together. Like Sarah, Oliver has a stutter, which might actually be worse than hers. Sometimes they try saying something at the same time and they both get stuck on a word and it ends up sounding like two people with machine guns. When this happens, everyone looks down at their plates because they're too embarrassed to interrupt them. It's also a bit unfair on Oliver because Dad and him are quite competitive about the things they know about science and the brain. If Oliver is trying to make a point and gets stuck on a word, Dad goes straight in there and talks over him with his own theory. I once saw Oliver get so frustrated with this sort of situation that he twisted one of Mum's silver spoons under the table as he stuttered until it looked like a corkscrew.

Apart from the fact that it was the first day of our summer holiday, there was one big reason why Mum had decided to do a Saturday lunch on a Wednesday: the Americans were going to the Moon. This wasn't a fly-round-the-Moon trip, like the one before. This time they were actually going to go there and land on it, or, as we kept being told, they were going to *try* to land on it. Everyone I knew was going to watch the launch on telly, and for all of us in Britain it was going to happen right in the middle of lunch. People were talking about it everywhere – on television and in every newspaper, in the street, at all the fruit and veg stalls in the market on Inverness Street, in the library off Regent's Park Road and, of course, at school. Dad said that the last time everyone in the world was this obsessed by a single event was the Cuban Missile Crisis, which he had to explain to me and then I wished he hadn't, as it frightened me that we could have been so close to a nuclear war and the end of the world. Alan disagreed and said it was the Coronation, and Mum said it was when JFK was shot. I didn't care – the Moon landing was more important than anything for me. I'd been thinking and talking about it non-stop on the walk to school, during class, playing with friends and alone in my bedroom. I'd been reading a brilliant book that Dad bought me in America about everything you needed to know about the Apollo space programme. I was now quite an expert on the subject, and ready to answer any questions anyone might have.

I don't think I can remember a time before, or after for that matter, when we all sat down as a family and watched television together. Like most of the houses in the Crescent, our basement had been knocked through to make one big kitchen-dining room. Mum was cooking at one end while everyone else sat around the dining table waiting for the food to arrive. The grown-ups were only half-watching the TV, which sat on a high shelf above one end of the dining table.

This was the end of the room where me, Tom and Jeanie had sat ourselves, and we were glued to the snow and fuzz on the screen as we waited for Dad to sort out the picture.

He had his back to us, as he tried to reach up to the TV and adjust the dial. I could hear him swearing as he turned it back-wards and forwards looking for the right channel and a clearer picture. Dad's never been able to make the TV work. Alan, who thinks he can, shouted at Dad from the table, 'Come on, Jonathan, it's a good thing you're not a rocket engineer at NASA!'

'Oh ha bloody ha,' Dad shot back. 'Let's hope they aren't having this much trouble at Cape Canaveral.'

I've never understood why Dad insisted on putting the TV high up on that shelf where no one could reach it. Most of my friends from school have big TVs in proper cabinets that stand on one side of the room. Everyone can reach it and watch whatever they want whenever they like. But my Dad hates the television. He hates it more than he hates the people who are on his long list of those he hates most. It drives him crazy when we watch it during supper. He thinks everything on it is rubbish and that if we watch it for long enough our brains will start to rot. But he seems to know lots of people on it, and he talks about them in the way you do when you know someone really well. He shakes his head and says, 'Look, it's poor old Larry, he loathes doing TV,' or 'poor Tony' or poor someone else. Somehow I don't think any of these poor people hates being on TV as much as Dad thinks they do. The other week my uncle Karl was on it, talking about football, of all things. I didn't even know he liked football, but apparently he does and there he was, on the television, discussing a football match with some other men. The thing is, when I see Dad on TV he always looks happier than he does when he's at home. But you will never see my Dad on the telly talking about football, so Uncle Karl has one over him there, and they both know it.

Alan was now standing next to Dad, having pretty much taken over the dial setting and, with a few slow careful turns, found the right channel. Alan's not technical: he's just patient in a way that Dad isn't. At last, there it was, with steam swirling around its base, the huge Saturn V rocket of Apollo 11, which I've drawn loads of times at home and for our big 'Going to the Moon' project at school. I'd followed all the Apollo missions, and this one was finally going to the Moon, and with any luck the astronauts would get out and walk on it. It wasn't going to be like the last ones, where they went all the way there, flew around the Moon and came home. On Apollo 10 they got the lunar module less than ten miles from the surface of the Moon, looked out of the window and said, 'Yep, we can do that,' and then came back. Last Christmas, the crew of Apollo 8 went all the way to the Moon and one of the astronauts called Frank Borman said something from the Bible about God making the Heaven and the Earth. Then they came home. Dad was furious and said how could an intelligent man believe in God when he'd gone to the Moon, having flown through space for days on end to get there and never saw God or passed him on the way? 'Where, for God's sake, is God if not up there?'

According to Dad, when the Russian cosmonaut Yuri Gagarin came back from his mission he said, 'I flew into space but did not see God.' Dad said, 'Now, that's the sort of intelligent man I like.' I heard him talking to Freddie Ayer about this on Boxing Day when we went round to their house for drinks. Freddie is a philosopher and talks a lot about there being no God, but this time his wife, Dee, said he 'shouldn't take it all so fucking literally' (she swears a lot). Then she said something about how if the American astronaut hadn't said something about how God had made the Heaven and the Earth, especially on Christmas Day, NASA wouldn't get any more money to keep sending people to the Moon. Either way, I actually thought what the astronaut Frank Borman said was pretty amazing and I totally got it. But I was never going to tell Dad I thought that, as I'd just get one of his long speeches about science and how anyone who believes in God is an idiot.

Everyone was now sitting down at the table and tucking into chicken and baked potatoes. The action on the television kept going back to a man called Cliff behind a desk in a studio. He was trying to explain what was going on at Cape Canaveral, and for some reason he also thought he knew what the three astronauts were feeling up there in the rocket. Ridiculous, I thought, how could he possibly know what they were feeling? But Cliff turned to his friend in the studio and said, 'Patrick, what do you think is going through Neil's mind right now?' How would Patrick know?

The picture on the TV was now back on the rocket and, judging by the big countdown clock on the bottom of the screen, mission control at NASA were about to say those all-important words I'd used so many times when acting out this exact moment: '10-9-8, Ignition sequence start, 4-3-2-1, we have lift off!'

At last, everyone in the room shut up and we were all staring at the TV in silence as the Apollo 11 rocket rose from the launch pad and climbed into the sky. Just at that moment, Mum said loudly that she'd heard James Burke on the radio talking about how the three astronauts were going to have a breakfast of steak and eggs before heading out to the launch pad. Now all the grown-ups started talking over each other again and making jokes about it.

'Steak and eggs?' Alan said. 'You must be joking? Only an American would eat steak and eggs before pulling off a stunt like that.'

Why do grown-ups always have to make stupid jokes right when the biggest thing ever is happening, and at the very moment we've been waiting for all year? There wouldn't have been any stupid jokes over at the Roebers. They would have been sitting quietly in a row enjoying every minute. Their mum wouldn't dream of interrupting. Me, Tom and Jeanie were now standing up so we could get closer to the television and have a better chance of hearing what they were saying at the BBC. What I really wanted to know was what the astronauts and the men in the white short-sleeved shirts at mission control were saying to each other as the rocket got smaller and smaller on the screen. It was the same for all the Apollo launches: the soft, calm American voices that always have a little beep at the end of each thing they say.

'We are systems go, Neil – Beep.'

'God speed, Apollo 11 – Beep.'

'Looking good here, Gene – Beep.'

'Clear for main engine shut down – Beep.'

How could the astronauts remain so calm when right behind their seats all that rocket fuel is exploding and the safety of the Earth is slipping away?

I had repeated these phrases with my own little beeps so many times when playing Apollo missions in my bedroom or on the climbing frame in the back garden. I even had an Airfix model of the Saturn V rocket with sections that came apart just like the real thing. Now it was happening in front of me on the telly, but I had to fight to hear what was going on.

Alan and Dad were now pretending to be two gay astronauts deciding whether they wanted their eggs 'over easy' or 'sunny side up'. Why couldn't they take this one big event seriously? I love it when Dad and Alan are silly, but not right at that very moment.

Before long, the astronauts and their rocket were so high that the cameras couldn't see them any more. All I could think about was how, at that very moment, while we were sitting around the table eating our lunch back on Earth in Gloucester Crescent, Neil, Buzz and Mike had left the Earth and were up there looking down at all of us from space.

Dad got up and announced that there was only so much of this he could take and switched the TV off without asking any of us if we were still watching it – which we were. This was the big moment, the one we had been waiting for all this time and which was an important thing to us, even if it wasn't to the grown-ups. Now it was back to being like any old Saturday lunch with everyone talking over each other. Alan had made the pudding – tapioca again, which only the grown-ups like and Tom and I think looks like sick.

I knew the Roebers would have stopped watching the TV by now and might be out in the garden talking about the launch. I got down from the table and headed into the garden and climbed onto the wall. The Roebers are the ones I play with the most. There are four of them – Bruno, Nicky and James, who are identical triplets and almost the same age as my brother, Tom, and then Conrad, who's my age and is my best friend. They live two doors away from us. When the triplets were born, they lived above a launderette around the corner on Parkway, and my mum went to visit them because she was interested in identical triplets. She was so surprised to see their mum and dad, nanny and three babies living in such a small flat that she said they should come and live in our house when her and Dad went to live in New York for two years. They moved in to our house in 1962 and then later bought the house two doors from us. I think it was quite hard for their mum because their dad left, came back and then left again and went to live with someone else in Maida Vale who he eventually married. Now though, their mum has married a nice man called Will Camp, who lives with them and does something important for the Labour Party.

By standing on our wall I could see across to the Roebers' garden, and sure enough they were all sitting on the garden steps talking. I could hear James explaining to his brothers what was going on right now on Apollo 11. Keen not to miss out on any of this conversation, I did what I'd done a thousand times and jumped over our wall into the Jeffersons' garden. I ran across their lawn into a big flowerbed with lots of broken plants in it, then down with a bump into the Roebers' garden. Tom and I had done this so many times that there was now a worn path with no grass right across the Jeffersons' lawn. Surprisingly, bearing in mind the damage we caused, they never complained. The Jeffersons are quite old-fashioned and not really like the other families in the Crescent. They are the only family who go to church on Sunday, which of course Dad doesn't approve of.

By the time James finished explaining how rocket thrusters worked, I headed back home over the walls. Life across the Crescent had settled back into its usual middle-of-the-week routine, with all the sounds I found so comforting. Alan had gone across the road to his house and would no doubt be back for tea, and maybe again for supper. I could see Sue wasn't in the kitchen any more, so she must have gone back to her desk in the sitting room, which meant Dad was most likely in his study on the floor above, staring at his typewriter and smoking.

I stood in our garden for a moment and listened to all the typewriters starting up again and felt happy the summer holidays had started and life was carrying on in the way it always does in the Crescent. In spite of the chaotic lunch, it had been a great day, and the crew of Apollo 11 were finally on their way to the Moon. There was going to be a lot more about it on the television, and I knew we would be allowed to stay up late and watch the Moon landing on Sunday.

8

THE SCHOOL RUN

Tom's first school was called The Hall. He hated it so much that after one term Mum and Dad took him out and sent him to Gospel Oak School with Nick Ayer, the Mellys and the Haycrafts. I'm not sure why he went to The Hall in the first place, especially since Mum and Dad had to pay for it, which they always say they think is wrong. He had to wear a smart uniform with grey shorts and a pink and grey blazer. Tom never liked the uniform, but then he didn't like anything pink. I think I would have liked it. I said this to Tom once, and his response was that I would have liked it because I'm a 'ponce'. I don't think I'm a ponce, it's just that The Hall is a serious school and Primrose Hill isn't. Maybe the uniform at The Hall made it feel like that. At Primrose Hill we could wear whatever we wanted. If we spilled breakfast all over our clothes or had a hole in our trousers, no one cared. We've always worn scruffy clothes. Mum and Dad don't think they should be spending money on new clothes and that it's better if we hand them down. I get all of Tom's old clothes and Kate gets mine, and then there is some swapping with the Roebers too. Most of the time we look like ragamuffins.

None of my friends or anyone else in the street goes to a private school. Dad always says it's because everyone in Gloucester Crescent votes Labour and that only Tories go to

Me and Kate, Gloucester Crescent, 1969

private schools. I don't understand that because Mum, Dad and all their friends went to private school and they never stop talking about how great it was and how important it is to get a good education. But I don't think anyone in the Crescent is properly rich, and most of them only seem to have money when they've just written a best-selling book or a play in the West End or do something on the television.

The Roeber triplets were at Primrose Hill School with me but have now left to go to secondary school. Conrad's in the same year as me, and we've been in the same class together ever since we were five years old. I like most of my teachers, but there are a few who think it's funny to make jokes about me and Conrad being posh. It's a bit confusing as we've never thought of ourselves as posh or upper-class, and neither do the other kids. There's one really annoying teacher who thinks it's hilarious to imitate how me and Conrad speak, which she does in front of the whole class and enjoys making us look stupid. She's called Miss Crosby, and for some reason she's had it in for the two of us from the start. When she tries to imitate us it sounds nothing like the way we speak; in fact, it's more like Derek Nimmo from the telly. It gets a laugh from everyone in our class, but I don't think they know why they're laughing.

Miss Crosby is angry most of the time. She's very big and wears T-shirts and bad trousers that are too small for her, so she often looks like Humpty Dumpty. She's the only teacher who looks messier than the children. One Christmas she found another way of making me and Conrad look stupid in front of the rest of the school. We did a play about the Queen and Princess Anne switching on the Christmas lights, and instead of choosing Janet and Melissa or Emily and Zoe to play the Queen and Princess Anne, she made me and Conrad do it. We had to wear make-up, dresses and jewellery and carry handbags. Annoyingly, Mum and Dad came to see the play and thought it was brilliant and talked about it with their friends all the time over Christmas, and they thought it was hilarious too. Me and Conrad felt completely humiliated, and we knew that for Miss Crosby it was just a cruel joke that she would get to laugh about in the staff room.

Getting everyone in the Crescent to school in the morning was like an army exercise. It involved several cars and nearly all the mums and dads. Although you could walk to Primrose Hill, for a long time we were all packed into cars and taken there. The kids in the street who didn't go to Primrose Hill went to Gospel Oak, which you couldn't walk to as it's up near Parliament Hill. On weekdays there might be a couple of cars going to Primrose Hill and a couple going to Gospel Oak, and all that has to be worked out so the mums and dads can take it in turns. Dad didn't drive us to Primrose Hill to begin with, as he didn't have a driving licence. It took him ages to get one because every time he went for the test he failed it. I think the driving examiner must have made a mistake when he did finally get his licence. Soon after he got it he nearly crashed into a van on Regent's Park Road. The man driving the van looked very tough and scary and shook his fist out of the window. Dad pulled up next to him at the traffic lights and rolled down his window, but the man got in there first.

'Learn to drive, you idiot!' the man shouted.

'Bugger off or the next time I will rip your fucking thyroid out,' Dad shouted back.

'Fuck off, big nose,' the man said as the lights changed.

When we drove off, Dad had a look on his face that said, 'That told him.' I don't think it told him anything, and I think it was a really stupid thing to do.

A couple of times a week there's a minicab that takes a few of the children to the Tavistock Clinic in Swiss Cottage and then, after an hour with their therapists, they go on to school. Dad says it's all to do with a man called Freud, and they make them sit in a room with a grown-up (called a psychotherapist) who waits for them to say something interesting. Then they write it down in a notebook. I know this because the boys who went made a pact to sit there and say nothing to the therapists, which only made the parents worry even more. The more they worried, the longer their children had to keep going. It crossed my mind that it was probably the parents who needed the therapy. I was quite curious about the Tavistock as I think I would have liked to go somewhere like that. It sounded like a place where you could have a proper talk with a grown-up and they would give you all their attention and be really interested in listening to you. Sometimes I wish Dad would listen to me like that.

9

SHOOTING AND FISHING

Since Mum and Dad bought the house in Scotland we've been going there almost every holiday. Mum has the whole journey worked out pretty well now, and Dad either goes along with it or doesn't come at all. We usually leave on the night that school finishes and take the car on the Motorail sleeper train. In the summer it goes from a station called Kensington Olympia, which opens specially for all the people going to Scotland for the shooting and fishing. I really like this station as the shooting and fishing people remind me of Guy and Stella at Stanage and they're all very friendly and jolly. The men wear tweed jackets and funny-looking trousers called plus-fours and the women wear tweed skirts and headscarves. I think for the tweedy people the train to Scotland is like a big party. When we get to the station, Dad scowls at them and says they're the kind of people he loathes most of all.

One summer Jeanie's sister Esther came with us to Scotland. Apart from Dad getting cross with everyone on the way to the station, it all seemed to be going well, until we got to Kensington Olympia and someone shouted at the top of their voice the one word that Mum and Dad told us no one should ever use – the 'N' word. Dad says only really racist people use that word. We heard it yelled again, and we all stopped. I'm not even going to use the whole word here, but I think you'll know the word I mean. In the middle of the station there was this man standing in his plus-fours shouting the word over and over again, and everyone around him had just frozen and stared at us. He kept shouting it, and getting louder. No one knew which way to look except at Esther and then at this man. She looked shocked and hurt. Dad looked like he was going to explode. Then, the man yelled 'Heel!' and 'Sit!' and we realised he was shouting at his dog. Through the crowd we saw a black Labrador run up to the man and sit down in front of him. Mum hurried us along, pushed us all onto the train and locked us in the sleeper compartment. If Mum hadn't pulled Dad onto the train at that moment, I think he would have gone up and strangled the man.

I love going on the sleeper to Scotland. Once the train has left the station I like to sit on the lid of the basin in our compartment and watch as we pass all the houses and gardens and factories as we get further out of London. When I can't stay awake any longer, I get into my bunk and the rocking of the train sends me to sleep. When it's still dark, the train stops at Edinburgh and I get woken up by people shouting with Scottish accents and train doors being slammed and then a whistle blowing as the train pulls out of the station. I open the blind at the end of my bed and wait for the train to go over the Forth Rail Bridge. When it does, I can see the sun coming up over the sea. As it gets lighter, mountains start to appear and I know I'm really in Scotland and it's the beginning of a wonderful long holiday.

When we arrive at Perth, Mum and Dad take us to the station hotel for breakfast while we wait for the car to be taken off the train. When we finally get to the car and climb in, it smells delicious from the coffee beans Mum buys for the holiday. I don't think Mum and Dad and their friends can live without their coffee beans: their elevenses happens whether they're in London or France or Scotland.

The road from Perth to Archiestown is the longest and twistiest I've ever been on. One time, somewhere near Balmoral, we had to pull over to let a line of cars go by. There were lots of them, as well as police cars, and then a really big car with the Queen and Prince Philip in it. Dad always gets irritated when anyone says anything about the royal family. He says they don't serve any purpose and that they 'enforce our terrible class structure'. So he was pretty annoyed when we had to wait for them to pass on the road. I quite like the royal family and saw a television programme about them that said how much they like coming to Scotland and that they do lots of shooting and fishing.

One of Alan's favourite stories is about a lady who was fishing on the River Spey. He said there was another lady fishing there too. They were standing in the middle of the river in those rubber waders that go right up over your tummy. The first lady started shouting at the other one, 'Private waters, get oorf!' It always makes me laugh when Alan tells this story and shouts 'Get oorf' like that. Anyway, the lady was getting crosser and shouting up the river at the other lady. Eventually, the other lady turned round and it was the Queen Mother! The shouting lady was so embarrassed when she realised who it was that she curtsied in the river. She curtsied so low that her waders filled with water and she couldn't stand up again. In the end the gamekeeper had to jump in the river and save her before she drowned.

I don't know how much Dad likes going to Scotland when it's just us, as he never really seems to enjoy family holidays. I think it's the idea of being stuck in a house with children where there is no chance of intellectual conversation. He also

Left to right: Keith McNally, Stephen Frears, Mary-Kay Wilmers, Tom, Alan Bennett, me, Kate, Mum, Auchindoun, Moray, 1972

doesn't like leaving London, unless it's to go to somewhere like America for work. One summer he came with us on the train to Scotland, and as soon as we got to the Old Manse the phone rang. Dad answered it and put on his concerned face. He turned to Mum and said he had to go back to London straight away. An hour later a taxi arrived to take him to Aberdeen airport. I remember thinking he was definitely trying not to smile as he got into the taxi. It's very different if the Old Manse is filled with his friends, and Mum often makes sure it is, so that he's happy. This means all sorts of people come to stay with us. When the house is full of their friends, it's really just like being in Gloucester Crescent.

Dad did eventually find a way of enjoying himself when there are no friends staying, and it involved his love of medicine and science. He went to a shop in Euston and bought a microscope and a set of tools for dissecting animals. He then set himself up at the Old Manse kitchen table so he could give us biology lessons. It was the first time I'd seen Dad really happy to be on holiday with his children. As soon as he gets his classroom ready, he tells us we need to find a dead but fresh animal. So every time we drive back from the shops, a walk or the beach he makes us look out for anything dead on the road. As soon as we see something Mum jams on the brakes and Dad jumps out and peels it off the road. When we get home, he nails its arms and legs stretched out on a bread board and we gather around the table and he starts to dissect it. Mum once told us that when she first married Dad he brought a brain home from the hospital and dissected it for her on the kitchen table in their flat. She was learning to be a doctor, and he thought it might be useful, but it sounded a bit Dr Frankenstein to me.

Dad is really brilliant at dissecting, and you can see how much he likes doing it. He talks us through every part of the animal as he peels the skin back, opens up the chest and takes out the organs. Then he shows us where the nerves and veins are. One year he bought each of us a biology kit and sent us to the woods to look for the stinkiest ponds we could find. When we brought the dirty water back in our test tubes, he showed us how to get it ready to look at under the microscope. I was amazed at how much tiny life there was in one dirty brown pond. There, under our microscope, were microorganisms that Dad described in the same way that he does when he's being rude about people he doesn't like – 'a useless amoeba' or 'a dirty little invertebrate'. He also shows us how to cut thin slices of plants with a sharp blade so we can look at their cells under the microscope. I know Dad's never going to teach us things like football or swimming, but I love learning about biology and I can really see he likes teaching, and, best of all, it makes him happy to be with us on holiday.

Soon after we first arrived in Archiestown the people in the village seemed to take a lot of interest in what we were up to.

Dad opening the Archiestown village fête

They're fascinated by Dad, who they refer to as 'Television personality Jonathan Miller', which really annoys him. I'm not sure they know he's a theatre and film director or that he was once a doctor. A local newspaper started announcing our arrival in Scotland for our holidays. They always use a photo of Dad when he opened the Archiestown village fête the year they bought the house. Dad called it a 'fête worse than death'.

They write the same thing underneath the photo every time: 'Television personality Jonathan Miller and his family have arrived in Archiestown for their summer holiday.' Dad once showed it to Mum and said, 'Is that all they can say? What about: "Leading theatre director Jonathan Miller is taking a break from doing Chekhov to come and waste his time in Scotland"?' One time, coming back from a visit to an old castle, we had to stop for petrol. We sat in the car as the man filled the tank, then his whole family came out and stood there looking at us. When the man finished, he tapped on the window to get Dad to wind it down, then stuck his head right into our car and said, 'You were super on Parky. That'll be a fiver.' As we drove off, Dad said to Mum, 'Why does it always have to be the Parkinson show? That man really should see my *Alice in Wonderland*.'

Once they've announced it in the local newspaper, people start knocking on our door to say hello. One of the people who knocked first was Margery Swinton. She's English and lives in the next village and is a teacher at the local primary school. This was the same summer that Mum and Dad decided to bring Jeanie's sister Esther to Scotland. What Esther liked doing most in the evenings was sitting on the railing of the war memorial in the village square, watching the cars go by and listening to pop music on her transistor radio. It wasn't long before she made friends with some of the older boys in the village, who sat with her listening to her radio. Before Esther, Jeanie was probably the only black person they'd ever seen in this part of Scotland, so news of another black person spread quickly. It soon reached Margery, who happened to be captain of the local women's tug-of-war team. This team was made up of housewives from the villages of Knockando, Cardhu and Archiestown. I think it must have been when Margery saw Esther sitting on the war memorial that she came up with the idea. Esther looks nothing like her sister, who is normal height and thin, whereas Esther is a normal height but big and probably quite heavy too. What Margery wanted more than anything was to get the Highland Games Women's Tug-of-War trophy back for Archiestown, and what the tug-of-war team needed was something called an anchor. This is the person who holds onto the end of the rope and tries not to move. When Margery saw Esther, she knew she would be perfect for the job.

It was in the middle of supper that Margery first turned up at the Old Manse. She knocked on the front door and the

Esther in Scotland, 1970

next thing we knew, she was standing in front of us holding out a pair of heavy black 'tackety' boots (which is Scottish for hobnail). Esther was going to need these if she was to help the team win the trophy back. After that we didn't see much of Esther for the rest of the summer as she was off most days, travelling around the Highlands in a minibus with Margery and her housewives. The good news was they were now winning wherever they went, and every night when Margery came back with Esther she looked like she'd won the pools. Esther even got to be in our local newspaper.

Like most people who knocked on our door in the middle of a meal, Margery was soon invited to sit down and have supper with us. And, like many of the people who do that in London, Margery never stopped coming to supper. Some of Mum and Dad's friends think it's a bit odd that no one ever actually invites her, but there she is, every night. And what's more, everyone has to wait for her to arrive before supper can start. Most people seem to like Margery, but Dad told Mum they needed a plan to deal with the waiting-for-supper problem. In the end, it was quite simple – Margery turned out to be allergic to fish! So whenever someone is staying who doesn't like having to wait for Margery, Mum lets her know there will be fish on the menu for quite a few nights. Sure enough, without saying a thing, she doesn't turn up.

I wish the grown-ups didn't feel like that about Margery as I think she's amazing and I would be happy to see her every night. She's another one of my grown-up friends who properly listens, and she takes me to places Mum and Dad would never go to, like skiing in the Cairngorms or helping out on farms. At one point she was added to my list of people I would like to marry when I grow up. Tom and Kate aren't that bothered about Margery, so often she takes me on trips on my own and I get to meet her friends. She also writes to us when we get back to London and lets us know all the news. She always mixes the good news with the bad, all in one sentence. Her letters say things like 'Cathy McPherson's son was killed on his motorbike, Alastair's dog Suki has had puppies' or 'Eddie McDonald's house burned down with his son inside, we're going to pick tatties this weekend.'

One of the farms Margery takes me to is right on the edge of the village. The farmer's eldest son, Alastair, runs it, and I think he quite likes Margery because he always blushes and stutters when she's around, and he lets her drive his tractor.

With the farm being so close to our house I often go there on my own to help out, and Alastair lets me come with him on the tractor to take food to his cows. One summer I was holding a gate open for the tractor when Alastair accidentally ran right over my foot and I had to go to hospital and have it put in a cast.

The summer Esther came to stay and joined the tug-of-war team was also the summer Grandad died. He was in hospital in London, and Dad was with us in Scotland. One afternoon, after we all got back from a long walk, Dad's sister, Sarah, called to say that he had to get back to London straight away.

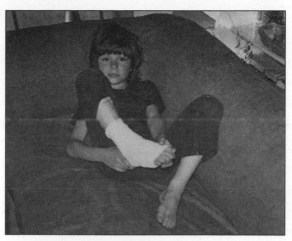

Me with my broken foot, Archiestown, 1973

The next night Mum was reading us a story and Dad called in the middle of it to tell us Grandad had died. It was the first time anyone I knew had died, and I wasn't sure what to do or say. We all sat there in silence, and then Esther burst into tears, which I thought was odd as she'd never met Grandad. I asked her why she was crying and she said it was because it was sad for us that someone in our family had died. Mum went over and put her arm around her, and then everyone started crying.

The funeral happened when we were still in Scotland, so no one other than Dad went to it. I don't even know where Grandad is buried as Dad has never taken us to look at the grave or put flowers on it. Whenever I think about this, it all feels so sad, even though I knew Dad never got on with Grandad. He was a lot older than Dad's mum, Betty, who died when she was only 55. Dad told me he was much closer to his mother because his father wasn't very interested in his children and never gave them hugs or kisses. Dad likes a hug but if you try to kiss him he squirms and dodges like he's

Dad's mother, Betty Miller

going to fall over and you end up kissing the back of his head. Now that both of Dad's parents are dead, I suppose it makes him an orphan, which also makes me feel sad.

10

GODDAMMIT

Nick, Freddie and Dee Ayer

Lots of Dad's friends are philosophers, which means he likes to talk about philosophy quite a bit. I didn't really know what a philosopher does, so one day I asked Nick Ayer's dad, Freddie, as he's supposed to be a really famous one, whose real name is Sir A. J. Ayer. Freddie's answer was: 'When a tree falls in a forest and no one is there to hear it, does it still make a sound?' I said I wasn't sure, and he said, 'Well, that's philosophy.' Even now I'm not sure what it means, and I can't believe Freddie makes any money from it.

Nick Ayer's house is the easiest of my friends' to get to as they live right behind us in Regent's Park Terrace and their garden backs onto ours. All you have to do is climb a tall brick wall, get over a broken trellis and jump down into their garden. Unlike ours, which Mum tries to keep nice and tidy and which we use all the time, the Ayers only use theirs as a loo for their two dogs, Jane and Gucci. Trying not to step in the dog poo, you go up some slippery wooden steps and through an unlocked door into a bathroom. Not just any bathroom – this is Freddie's bathroom.

Dad says I shouldn't go barging through Freddie's bathroom like that, as it's where one of Britain's greatest minds goes to soak in a hot bath and read *The Times*. When Freddie isn't in Oxford or sitting at his desk thinking about what happens to trees when they fall down, he's in his bath, the only place he says he can get any peace and quiet from Nick, his wife, Dee, or stepdaughter, Gully. Having crashed into his bathroom, I run right across it, leaving Freddie splashing about trying to get bits of his newspaper out of the water. He shouts the same thing every time as I race up the stairs to the second floor: 'It's that bloody William Miller!' For some reason Nick and Dee think this is hilarious as it's part of what they call 'Freddie-baiting'.

If I go really fast I can get from our back door to the Ayers' kitchen on the second floor in less than two minutes. As I run up each flight of stairs, I sometimes have to slow down and stand completely still as two familiar words come screaming down the stairs. Those words are usually 'Goddammit, Nicholas', but sometimes it's 'Goddammit, Freddie' or 'Goddammit, Gully'. I know that whenever 'Goddammit' is the first thing I hear from upstairs it's a good idea to stop, count to three and then walk into the kitchen pretending nothing's happened.

Unlike Freddie, who is very English, Dee is very American. I think being an American is glamorous and exciting, like something out of a film. Nick is Dee and Freddie's son, and he's a year older than me. Dee has a grown-up daughter called Gully from someone she was married to before Freddie. Most of the time the reason I come to the Ayers' is to see Nick, who's friends with me and Tom. But when I was about nine, I started to realise how funny and interesting Dee can be and how much I like spending time talking to her. Strange really, as my first memory of her is definitely not a good one.

When I was over at the Ayers' one day playing with Nick, she called me into her study and asked if I would do her a favour. The favour was to dial a number written on a piece of paper. I did this, held the phone to my ear and waited for someone to answer. I could tell Dee was pretending to read something on her typewriter while watching me out of the corner of her eye. When someone finally answered it was a man who said in a posh voice, 'Buckingham Palace. May I help you?' I slammed the phone down and stood there in shock. Dee and Nick couldn't stop laughing, especially when she shook her head and said, 'Jesus H Christ, William, you're in deep shit now.' She told me the police or, worse, the Household Cavalry would be round in minutes to take me away. Nick kept running to the window and shouting, 'I can hear them coming down the Terrace, run William run!' There was something odd about the way Nick was so in on this and didn't want to help me out. Either way, I wasn't going to hang around to find out what was going to happen. I ran down the stairs, through Freddie's bathroom and straight home.

Trying to catch my breath, I told Dad what had happened. He sat me down and explained that it was just one of Dee's ridiculous jokes, and that no one was coming from the Palace to get me. He even showed me the number for Buckingham Palace printed right there in the London phone book and told me they get these calls all the time. I was now feeling like an idiot for getting so scared and upset. Although I could see it was a trick Dee and Nick liked doing together, I didn't like the way Nick had enjoyed frightening me so much. After a while I found myself sneaking past his room and going straight to see Dee instead. Freddie saw me doing this, and wasn't happy about it. Nick and Dee fought and argued a lot, and I don't think he liked the fact that I might have got on with Dee more than Nick did. He also noticed that Tom still preferred to hang out with Nick and wasn't interested in Dee in the way that I was. This might have been why Freddie was always nice to Tom and he ended up being the one who got invited to go on holidays with them.

The Ayers are now quite used to me turning up uninvited. And I've got used to Dee's bad language and have been known to try some of it out at home and at school, but it hasn't gone down that well. Of course, there's a bit of swearing at home, but only from Dad, and it's nothing like the amount I hear at the Ayers'. Mum never swears, and I've heard her tell Dad off for saying things he shouldn't. I don't think I know any house where people swear as much as the Ayers do. As well as Dee's 'Goddammit' and 'Jesus H Christ', there's also 'Goddamn son-of-a-bitch' and a few others. She might use these if she's cross with an object like an oven, a tin opener or her type-writer when the keys jam. But most of the time it's aimed at a person, and that's either Nick, Gully or Freddie, who all just ignore it as though someone has left the radio on.

I saw something Anna Haycraft wrote in a magazine Mum was reading. It said: 'Men love women, women love children and children love hamsters.' I thought about that, and then thought about Dee and how she likes children but doesn't seem to love them, and what she really loves is dogs and other animals. I think it's probably because they're loyal, don't argue with her and are helpless. I don't know what it is about people like Dee and Anna, but for some reason what they truly love is an angry dog. Dee's dog Jane is a terrier that looks like Nipper, the dog on all the record covers made by His Master's Voice. Jane likes to spend most of her day standing guard on the first-floor landing, trying to stop anyone from coming past. This is one of the reasons I have to run so fast up their stairs. If you keep going and try really hard not to look her in the eyes she lets you past, but if you stop for even a second you're going to get bitten by her. I once made the mistake of stopping to pat her, thinking she must surely know me by now and that we could be friends. Next thing I knew she was hanging off my arm and Dee was screaming down the stairs, 'For Christ's sake, William, how many goddamn times have I told you? Never stop and talk to that fuckin' dog.'

Gucci is a different kind of dog altogether – she's a sausage dog with short, silky brown fur and got her name because Dee says she looks like a Gucci loafer. Whereas Jane likes hanging out on the stairs, Gucci prefers to lie on a soft mohair blanket on Dee's bed. When you come into Dee's room, she's usually lying across the bed blowing raspberries into Gucci's warm hairless tummy. If you blew raspberries into Jane's tummy, she'd rip your nose off. Sad really, as Jane just sits on the stairs being angry and misses out on the chance to get a lot of the love and attention Gucci gets.

When she's not blowing raspberries into Gucci's belly, Dee sits at a large desk in one corner of her bedroom. Like Dad, when she's working she needs to smoke to do any typing, but her style is very different from his. For a start, she lights up a cigarette and then leaves it in an ashtray by the side of her typewriter. Then, without stopping, she types really fast for a few seconds. When she stops, she picks up the cigarette and takes a long, deep drag on it and leans forward to read what she's typed. Without taking her eyes off the paper, she half opens her mouth and lets the smoke escape between her lips, sucking it up through her nostrils like an upside-down waterfall. She can make this waterfall of smoke last long enough to read what she's written. Finally, she puts the cigarette back in the ashtray and starts the whole thing again. I guess this is how she wrote her book *Jane*. I was a bit confused by the title, as the book isn't about Jane the dog: it's about an American lady who lives in London and has lots of affairs and is called Jane. Mum and Dad said it was probably total rubbish and the sort of book you'd buy in an airport or station. So they refused to read it, but it sold millions of copies. She hasn't written another one since, but she still does a lot of typing.

Whatever Dee is up to she always seems to have time to sit and talk to me, even if she's working at her desk or cooking in the kitchen. She has all these drawers and boxes where she stores things she's found or collected, such as a dead beetle with a shiny green body like a mirror, the dried skin of a snake, an old fountain pen or a penknife with lots of blades and tools. She really likes showing me things from her collection, and then we talk about them for ages. Dee is someone I can really talk to about the world and the things I'm interested in. Even if I'm worried about something, I feel I can talk to her about it and she'll put my mind at ease. She does this in a way that's so different from how Dad does it, where he wants to give me all the facts, however terrifying they are. My conversations with Dee go something like: 'Look-it, William, isn't nature so goddamn beautiful? This little guy has these tiny fuckin' hairs coming out of his legs to help him grip.' Then she'll surprise me by saying, 'Sometimes that idiot man upstairs does amazing things. The rest of the time he's an arsehole.'

'Who's upstairs?' I ask.

'God,' she says. Now I'm confused and I tell her Dad is always saying God doesn't exist, and that when my sister went to church with the next-door neighbours she came back saying, 'God is Love,' and Dad was furious. He's the same about Father Christmas. I totally believed in him until I woke up in the middle of the night one Christmas Eve. I pretended to be asleep, waiting to see him in his big red coat and white beard, but when I opened my eyes I just saw Dad standing there, stark naked, at the end of my bed holding a shopping bag. Out of it he was stuffing presents into my stocking and swearing and complaining to Mum about how it was all non-sense and a waste of money. Dad wasn't at all guilty when I confessed on Christmas Day that I'd seen him in my room and now knew Father Christmas was made up: a myth I'd busted, like Dad had busted God.

I might go on to say, 'Dad says Darwin gave the beetle the hairs on his legs, and probably the green colour too. It's called Evolution.' Dee wouldn't want me thinking she'd gone religious and would come straight back with, 'For God's sake, kiddo, I wasn't speaking literally. I know there's no fuckin' man upstairs.' Then she would point out that Darwin didn't put the hairs on the beetle's legs either and how he just had a theory about how things evolved. Alarmed by my confusion over God, she'd add: 'For God's sake don't go telling silly old Freddie about it or you'll be stuck with him all afternoon.'

I once asked Dee what Freddie really did at his desk all day.

I noticed that he writes with a big pen in one hand and plays with a thin silver chain in the other. And, like everyone else, he smokes when he works. 'Listen,' she said, 'whatever silly old Freddie does, it takes him to Oxford for the week and gets him out the house and out of my hair, and that's good enough for me.'

Having got bored of the conversation about God and Darwin, we eventually go into the kitchen. 'Now, milk shake or French toast or both? And let's see if we can get Prince Nicholas away from that fuckin' TV?' Dee always calls Nick 'Prince Nicholas' and Gully 'Princess Gully-Gully'. I don't think it helps, as it just makes them think they're some kind of royalty and can get away with their bad behaviour.

When I first started coming over the garden wall, the Ayers' kitchen was in the basement. Then Gully came back from Oxford and they turned it into a flat for her. The kitchen was moved all the way up to the second floor, next to Dee's bedroom and study. Apart from when Dee leaves the house to go somewhere, she spends most of her time on the second floor. In our house the kitchen has always been in the same place and nothing changes, whoever's coming over to eat with us. Dee likes to completely change her kitchen, depending on who's eating in it. At lunchtime Freddie stops writing and fiddling with his silver chain and comes up for his lunch. According to Dee, he likes to think he's in his gentlemen's club. So she puts out the silver knives and forks, a big ham, a glass jug of celery, a pot of Gentleman's Relish, which smells like cat sick, and Stilton cheese with the blue mould. In the middle of the table is a round silver box filled with Bath Olivers and water biscuits, which no one is allowed to eat other than Freddie. As soon as he's finished his lunch he goes back downstairs to work and everything gets put away. Then it goes back to being a family kitchen, which now serves American diner food for Nick and Gully, their friends and anyone else dropping by. Dee starts making pancakes, French toast and milk shakes, followed by ice-cream with lots of toppings.

Once the food is on the table, Nick comes up from watching TV and is usually in a bad mood with everyone. He's often cross with me for ignoring him and spending so much time with his mum. The trouble is, I feel like I have to try to explain myself to get back on his good side, but the more I do, the deeper I seem to dig myself into a hole. Somehow, I hope that saying something friendly like 'Your mum's been showing me that green beetle with the hairy legs and now we're having French toast' will break the ice. It doesn't, and now both me and his mum are in trouble.

'No shit, William, the fucking beetle again?'

'French toast, Nick, or would you prefer arsenic?' Dee asks. Nick's usual response to his mum is 'Fuck off,' followed by a dig at her. His favourite one is to tell whoever's in the room how, when Dee is really old, he's going to have all the counters, the oven and the sink raised up so she can't reach anything from her wheelchair. This is a game Nick and Dee play to see who can be the nastiest to the other. Dee's response will be something like, 'That's a Brain-of-fuckin'-Britain idea. Then you can get your hopeless father to do the cooking and washing up,' or 'Then Princess Gully-Gully can take you to restaurants with one of her rotten boyfriends who you hate so much.'

Sooner or later Gully comes up to the kitchen so she can have a gossip with her mum. She's thirteen years older than me, very beautiful and can be just as mean as Nick and Dee. When you get the three of them in the same room, you start to wish you'd stayed at home. Gully acts like she doesn't have time for boys like me and Nick and only wants to tease us or talk about herself. When she comes into a room, she has this way of walking where she slinks and sways her hips from side to side so her whole body moves like a snake. She has thick blonde hair which is all perfect and she wears perfume that smells lovely. She wears glamorous dresses with high-heeled shoes or boots that make her look taller. The trouble with Gully is she knows that men think she's beautiful – all she has to do is that slinky hip and bum thing and they'll do anything for her. She also knows how to annoy Nick and embarrass me. Every time it's the same and I never know what to do.

As she slinks into the kitchen, she walks over and gives me a big hug with a sloppy kiss. It would be nice if she did this because she liked me rather than to show me up in front of everyone else. 'Ohhh look, it's Freddie's favourite person, that "bloody William Miller",' which she says in a deep, Freddie-like voice. I can feel my cheeks going red and for a minute I can't speak. She then goes over to Nick and starts sniffing his hair.

'Mmmm, what do you think, Mummy? Something tells me our little Prince Nicholas has been smoking his daddy's cigarettes.' At this point the sparks start to fly and Nick responds with, 'Get off, you bloody bitch,' and then he has a go at Gully about one of her boyfriends and calls her a stupid tart. Gully's had a lot of boyfriends, and Nick hates all of them apart from her first one ever, Martin Amis. Everyone likes him, and he still comes over to Regent's Park Terrace to visit and chats with us.

Gully is right about the cigarettes, which is one of his worst-kept secrets, but Nick hates it when Gully is being a snitch. He was only ten when he started stealing Freddie's cigarettes. When he does, he sneaks back to his bedroom, where he lies on the bed smoking and reading comics.

Nick's mood changes the minute Gully turns her attention

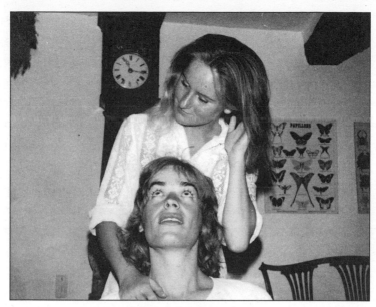

Gully with Martin Amis

back to me, which she does with one of her favourite jokes, which is that Miss Shepherd is my grandmother. Gully never misses a chance to bring this up whenever I'm in the house. I don't know why it makes me so cross, but I always feel helpless when everyone laughs along with her. I also don't like it when she tries to make Mum seem bad by saying something like 'The smell from the poo your granny leaves in those shopping bags under the van is terrible,' followed by, 'Why doesn't your nice mummy invite her in to use your loo? I think the Millers are all very mean to their poor old granny.'

This is when I hope Dee might tell Gully to back off and leave me alone. But she doesn't – she thinks Gully's jokes about Miss Shepherd being my granny are the funniest thing ever. I wish I knew not to argue with Gully, but I can't help it. The more I try to explain that Miss Shepherd isn't related to me, the deeper she sticks the knife in. In the end, whoever's getting it in the neck from Gully, Nick gets bored with it. He also knows that, as soon as she's stopped making me look stupid, she's going to turn on him again. After feeding half his French toast to Jane and Gucci under the table, Nick orders me to come downstairs to play.

'Right, now that you've finished stuffing your face and sucking up to my mother, let's go downstairs and play Commandos, then Gul' can bore mum about all the men she's been shagging.'

Gully is the only person I know who talks about all the sex stuff in front of other people. Dad might sometimes say something silly about sex as a joke, but Gully does it because she knows it will annoy Nick, embarrass Freddie and impress Dee. Whatever it is that she's doing, she certainly likes to make out she's doing it all the time. Me and Nick sometimes stand just outside the kitchen and listen to Gully banging on about it with her mum, hoping to get clues as to what all this sex stuff actually is. I've heard Dee making jokes about sex too, but I don't really understand them.

Commandos is a game Nick and I play a lot. We crawl around his house on our stomachs, trying not to be seen. The aim is to take things from rooms with grown-ups in, or play a joke on them without them knowing. It's usually Dee or Freddie we do it to. We did it to Gully once, but that was a completely different mission. We managed to crawl all the way down to Gully's basement flat in search of evidence that she was having all this sex she talked so much about. There was one major problem with the mission – neither me nor Nick knew what to look for that would count as proof. But it felt exciting, and so much more interesting than stealing candlesticks, books or paintings off his mum and dad.

Sir A. J. Ayer at work

Playing Commandos on Freddie was a pretty stupid thing to do as it only made him dislike me more. He works at a large round table at the back of a drawing room on the first floor, where he sits for hours with his back to the window. Me and Nick pull ourselves across the floor until we get under his desk. Then Nick starts tying Freddie's shoelaces together, and I have to try not to laugh. We make our way back across the floor, disappear behind a sofa and wait. Freddie is either a brilliant actor or thinking too hard about philosophy to have noticed us. From our hiding place we don't have to wait long before he stands up, shoes tied together, and pretends to fall over, shouting and cursing at us. Nick is the worst kind of traitor and jumps up, points at me lying on the floor and shouts, 'It was William, he made me do it!'

And there he goes again: 'It's that Bloody William Miller! Get out of here now!' Nick howls with laughter, and Freddie, having taken off his shoes, stomps over in his socks, grabs me by my arm and marches me onto the landing. Then Dee comes out to the landing above and shouts down the stairs,

'Jesus H Christ, Freddie, don't be so goddamn anal. They're kids having fun.' She tries to get me to come back upstairs, but I feel awful and can't bear the look of anger on Freddie's face. It's obvious he thinks I'm the ringleader. I know running to Dee would only make everything worse. So I slip quietly through Freddie's bathroom, out of the back door and over the garden wall.

11

HYPOCHONDRIA

When I was really young – like, five or six – I never saw Dad working anywhere else except at home in his study. He went away quite a bit to America and to places outside London, so I guessed he was doing something else. He talked a lot about working in theatres with actors and making films for the television, but I hardly ever got to see him doing any of these things. When I was really small, we would sometimes walk across Regent's Park on Sunday mornings to the BBC, where he would be on a radio programme. As far as I could tell, that wasn't actually work because he sat in a room with other people who just talked and laughed together.

Afterwards, we would walk back home across the park in time for lunch. A few times we dropped in to see Grandad, as he lived in a flat around the corner from the BBC. He once gave me some horrible mint chocolates from a drawer in his desk, which I think had been there since the war because the chocolate had gone a bit white and the mint was really dry. One time, after a visit to the BBC with Dad, we took Grandad up the Post Office Tower for lunch. It had a brilliant restaurant right up at the top that went round and round and you could see all of London. It was so high up that the planes were almost at the same height as us and the people on the streets looked like ants. Not long after we went there the IRA put a bomb in the restaurant and blew the windows out, so they shut it for ever.

When I was a bit older, Dad starting taking me to the other BBC, where they make television programmes. It's called Television Centre, and you have to drive there, but Dad is allowed to park his car right outside the front door and a man then parks it for him. I really like going there, as I get to see people I know from the telly. It's a huge round building with lots of studios where you can see the programmes being made. The first time I went, Dad was on *The Parkinson Show*. They were also making *Top of the Pops* in one studio and *Doctor Who* in another. There are rooms with windows where you can look into the studios and see everything that's going on. A lady who was supposed to be looking after Dad took me off to a café to buy biscuits. It was next to the studio where they were making *Doctor Who*, and there were all these men dressed as green monsters. It felt sort of out of place because I knew all these monsters from watching them on the TV, but here they were at the table next to me and instead of trying to kill the Doctor they were drinking cups of tea and talking about how to get home from Shepherd's Bush.

My favourite programme on television is *Blue Peter*. The next time Dad was on *Parkinson* I went with him and they were making *Blue Peter* in the next-door studio. I was taken to the room with the windows to see what was happening, but none of the presenters were in the studio. I was really hoping they would have Lulu the baby elephant back, because last time she peed all over the studio floor and pulled John Noakes through it. They didn't, but later, when we were leaving, someone shouted, 'Hold the lift.' Suddenly, there they were, standing right next to us – Valerie Singleton, Lesley Judd, Peter Purves and John Noakes. I'd met famous people with

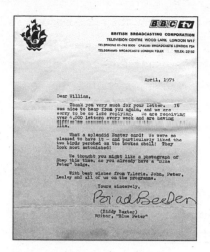

BLUE PETER

SHEP

Dad before, but no one as famous as the four presenters from *Blue Peter*. I saw them every week on television and it felt like I knew them as close friends, and now they were standing next to me in a lift. They really wanted to talk to Dad, who they were strangely excited to meet, and asked him loads of questions about what he was doing. They were looking up at him like he was their hero, which really surprised me as they're so much more famous than him. Then the lift stopped, and they were gone. At that moment I decided I would write and introduce myself to them properly and say that I'd met them in the lift at the BBC with Dad and how much I'd wanted to talk to them.

They wrote back, or rather someone called Biddy Baxter did, who was the editor of *Blue Peter*, and sent a picture of all four of them sitting on a sofa. When I showed the letter and photo to Conrad, he thought maybe, if I wrote enough times, they would give me a *Blue Peter* badge. So I did, and I sent them a drawing to go with each letter. I had to wait ages for a reply but when the letters arrived they were always from Biddy Baxter, and she started every letter with: 'Sorry for taking so long to reply. As you know, we get over 4,000 letters a week. We thought you might like a photo of Jason this time.' That was Valerie's Siamese cat. Other times it might be a photo of Peter's Alsatian, Petra, or John's sheepdog, Shep. Then, finally, a brown envelope arrived, and in it was the *Blue Peter* badge I'd waited so long for. I wrote straight back to thank them, and they sent me another photo of Shep.

After struggling for several years with his book on the philosopher man, Dad actually finished it and was spending more time out of the house or was away directing plays. One time he went to Los Angeles to do a Shakespeare play. He seemed to be gone for ages, and when he came back he had all these presents from a cowboy shop for me and Tom, and a ridiculous sheepskin coat for himself that made him look like he'd been searching for gold in the Klondike rather than directing a play.

I'm not sure if anyone read Dad's book, but I was sad when he finished it because Sue then went off to work for someone else. Although she came back so see us a lot, the house felt empty without her. She carried on taking me to Stanage to see Guy and Stella, and one time, when Mum and Dad went on a trip to America, she moved in to look after us. That was pretty amazing as it was like having Sue as a mum. She made our breakfast, took us to school and was there when we got home, and she read to us when she put us to bed.

It was around this time that our latest nanny came to work for us and, like the others, she moved into the flat at the top of the house and brought her husband with her. She's Spanish and is called Marina González, and her husband, who works as a waiter, is called Julio. He often gets back late at night and has to creep through the house and up the stairs. I think the

Spanish must be much stricter with their children because quite early on Marina made it very clear that she wouldn't put up with any cheekiness or bad behaviour from us. One night she decided to show us exactly what she meant by this. Mum and Dad were out and Marina was trying to get me and Tom to settle down and go to sleep. Every time she left our bedroom we would burst out laughing, and she would run back into the room shouting at us in Spanish. It didn't do any good and just made us laugh more. In the end she got so angry that she reached for the nearest of us, which happened to be me, and pulled me out of bed by my ear. She dragged me off to the bathroom, locked me in and left me there crying hysterically until I fell asleep. After what must have been hours, Julio came in and carried me back to bed.

Marina would have certain mornings off, and now that Sue wasn't working in the house, if one of us was off school Mum would have to take us with her to work. Mum's a doctor in a health centre in Kentish Town, so going with her to work is very different from going with Dad. It's pretty boring as we have to sit in an office and stamp prescription pads or help the receptionist put files back on the shelves. One day I convinced Mum I had a sore throat, so she took me to work with her and I was left in an office. From there I could see her talking to one of the other doctors, who was asking what was wrong with me. I saw Mum shaking her head and looking worried as she told the other doctor that I had an illness. Until that moment, I didn't think I was sick at all. In fact, I just wanted a bit of time off school, but now it turned out I really was ill and it had a name. I felt the blood drain from my body. What if I never got better, or worse, died from it? Terrified and sitting in total silence, Mum drove me home and left me with Marina, who had come back from her morning off, and I went straight to bed to die. I was well enough to answer the phone when it rang, hoping that I'd get some sympathy from whoever was calling. As it happened, it was Dee and the conversation went something like this:

'Hey, kiddo, I didn't expect to find you home. No school? What's wrong?'

'I'm ill,' I replied, 'very ill in fact, and it's got a name.'

'Goddammit, poor guy, you sound OK to me, so what's the name?'

'Hypo-something-chondria,' I replied, knowing that now I had a name for this disease I was going to get a lot more attention for it.

'No shit,' Dee snorted, 'that's bad. Well, we all get that sometimes. Hey, we're having French toast and milk shakes later if you think it might help.'

'I'd better not, I wouldn't want anyone catching it,' I said, trying not to cry.

I could hear her laughing at the other end of the phone as she put it down. I was a bit shocked that she thought my death from hypo-what-ever-it-was was so funny, but then I knew Dee could be cruel, even about people close to her dying. I didn't go for French toast that day, but when I did, it was Dee who explained what hypochondria really was. She'd already told Nick and Gully about it, and on my next visit it had become the house joke. Even Freddie shouted from his study as I went past, 'I thought you were dying of hypochondria!'

12

FANNY CON TUTTE

After years of doing plays Dad started directing operas as well, and has been taking me to watch his rehearsals. It's so interesting seeing him work with the singers and hearing all the lovely music. I've heard some of it before on records, but never sung by people who are only standing a few feet away. Even when doing operas with all that beautiful music Dad still gets depressed and says his life is terrible and that he wishes he could be a doctor again so that people would take him seriously. I know that he's always been tortured by his work, but it was usually because he was stuck in his study and not getting anywhere with his typing. He's always saying to Mum or his friends how much he despises the theatre and everything that goes with it, and now he feels the same about opera too. I don't know why he says this, because whenever I've seen him rehearsing he looks really happy, and he loves all the people he's working with and they love him back.

I know that what he hates more than anything are the critics, who he calls 'spineless shits' or 'poisonous inverte-brates'. Sometimes when he answers the phone he says things like: 'Hello, Home for Sick Critics, which one would you like to speak to?' Then he pauses before saying, 'Irving Wardle? No, sorry he's dead, how about Sheridan Morley?' I think it's the critics that ruin everything for Dad. If the rehearsals are going well, he comes home at the end of the day and is so happy he says, 'I think this is probably the best thing I've ever done', and then when the play or opera opens he can't wait to tell us about the bits he's most proud of. Then the reviews come out, and it only takes one bad one and this dark cloud comes over the house and his life is over and he's calling his agent to tell him to cancel everything he's going to do in the future. He comes out of it eventually, so it's a good thing his agent has learned to ignore him.

I've only been to a couple of rehearsals for Dad's plays, and they aren't nearly as much fun as his opera rehearsals. In the theatre there's a lot of standing around with the actors thinking and having serious conversations. Then, when the acting starts, it's hard to understand what they're going on about. It's even worse when it's Shakespeare and they speak all that old English that sounds like gobbledygook. Opera is so much easier as they act and sing at the same time, and if you don't understand what's going on you can just listen to the music. They still do a lot of standing around talking to Dad, and he tells them what to do and where to go. But then he steps back, the conductor takes over, a piano starts playing and the singers sing, and it's what I imagine it would be like if you believed in God and were about to enter heaven. I think going to Dad's rehearsals is what made me interested in music.

Dad directed an opera called *Così fan tutte* and it's my favourite. It's by Mozart and is about two young men who think their girlfriends, given half the chance, will run off with someone else. Since he was rehearsing it in a hall in Primrose Hill, he took me out of school one morning so I could come and watch. At lunchtime we went to a restaurant with the conductor and some of the singers. The owner came over to talk to Dad and asked him how his rehearsals were going for *Fanny*

Con Tutte. I don't know if he realised he'd got the name wrong, but he looked very embarrassed when everyone laughed.

I got to know the opera really well after Dad bought me the record for my birthday. We have a record of another opera called *La Traviata*, which I also like. Mum listens to it a lot, especially when she's reading a book on her own. The only thing is it makes her cry. I know it's a sad story and the woman dies in the end, but seeing Mum cry always worries me. I don't know if she's crying because the story in the opera is sad or because something else has happened that I don't know about. I don't like to think there are things I don't know about that make her cry.

Jeanie likes classical music too and now plays the piano really well, although she does like to practise in the middle of the night, when everyone has gone to bed. Mum and Dad say it drives them nuts because the sound of the piano coming up the chimney from the basement wakes them up. Before she plays anything nice, she starts with an hour of scales that go up and down, over and over again. I think it's the scales that wake Mum and Dad up. When she finishes those, she plays something nice and calming like Bach's *Goldberg Variations*. She plays that brilliantly, and it's so lovely it would send anyone to sleep.

It's not surprising Jeanie likes music so much. She has a cousin from Jamaica called Patsy who went to live with the Roebers for a while as their nanny. Patsy is married to a man called Stephen Preston, who plays the flute, likes classical music by Vivaldi and Bach and is in a small orchestra. When Jeanie isn't playing her own music, she goes to the Wigmore Hall or Royal Festival Hall to see Stephen playing in his orchestra. I love going with her as we have a fun night out and I like that kind of music.

Jeanie's not the only musical person in the family. Mum plays the flute really well, Tom plays the cello, and there's me with my violin and oboe. Then there's Dad: what surprises everyone about Dad directing operas is that he doesn't play a musical instrument and can't even read music. I don't think I've ever heard him sing along to anything other than country music, and when he does that he can only do the twanging and whining noises. My grandfather Bob is a concert pianist and music teacher. He sometimes comes over and helps Jeanie with her piano-playing. He also tries to help me, but I don't like it when he gets bossy about music and complains that I haven't practised enough. I know he's right, but I don't like being told. He makes me get my oboe out after lunch and sits at our piano and plays along with me. He doesn't smile, he just scowls and shakes his head when I get the notes wrong. Once he got so cross his false teeth fell out onto the piano keys when he was trying to tell me off. I thought that was hilarious, but he made me carry on playing – laughing and playing the oboe at the same time can be a bit tricky.

13

SON-OF-A-BITCH

Something I've been thinking about a lot recently is that I won't be at Primrose Hill for much longer, and when I go to my next school I'll be there until I'm 18, and that's nearly grown up. I think a lot about what it will be like being a grown-up and all the things I'll be able to do. I could leave home, get a job or even get married to someone I really like. I know I think about who I might marry quite a lot, but I also think about what I want do when I'm old enough to get a job. Only recently I wanted to be a farmer, and before that an airline pilot, and before that an astronaut. But whenever I tell Dad what I want to be he just laughs, shakes his head and tells me I should think seriously about being a doctor or a scientist like he had once been, and his father before that. I am not sure I want to be either of those, although I did once tell him I might like to be a surgeon. He got so excited by this news that he went off and got me all these fat books about it which I didn't understand.

Tom has a job delivering newspapers before school for the newsagent in Inverness Street, but that's just to earn a little money. Now he has his own money, which he adds to his pocket money and likes to show off about the things he can buy without having to ask Mum and Dad. I might try to do that when I'm 13, but I also like the idea of a Saturday job.

I'd like to have my own money to do what I want with and I could save up for a racing bike, or make my train set even bigger.

School seemed to be going well, or at least I thought it was until Mum and Dad were called to have a talk with my teacher, Miss Appleby. When they got back from the school, Mum and Dad were very cross, but decided to save it until the morning, when they would have one of their 'serious talks' about what had happened. It was on my way down to breakfast the next morning that I was called into their bedroom. I walked up to the end of their bed and stood there fiddling with the corner of the bedspread. They had the sheet pulled up to their chins. They always do this when they're trying to be serious and think they might laugh. It never works as the sheet starts shaking as they disappear behind it.

Mum came straight out with it – Miss Appleby had called them into the school because she was concerned about the bad language I'd been using.

'Like what?' I said.

It turned out Miss Appleby had a list she'd put together with some of the other teachers. On her list were 'goddammit' and 'son-of-a-bitch', and even 'motherfucker'. I stood in silence, not quite sure how to respond, then Dad said he knew exactly who I'd picked these up from: 'Dee bloody Ayer.'

'Nick uses them too, pretty much all the time,' I mumbled.

'That's hardly surprising, bearing in mind he lives with his mother and his foul-mouthed sister. The thing is, Dee comes from America, where this kind of language is very common, especially in films – even some good films.'

I tried to think of an answer that would impress Dad and make this less hard on both of us. 'The Marx Brothers don't speak like that and they're from America.' It was a risky tactic, as they're Dad's heroes. I've discovered that it's always good to get something in about the Marx Brothers if you can.

Dad looked impressed. 'Yes, that's very true. But the Marx Brothers made those films a long time ago, when no one spoke like that. Well, certainly not in films.'

The sheet on Mum's side of the bed had now gone up over her head and was shaking. I could hear her trying to say something to Dad, 'I think Groucho might have said "son-of-a-bitch" in *A Night at the Opera*.'

'Your mother seems to thinks Groucho might have used it once or twice; however, it's highly unlikely Harpo did.' It was Mum's turn now, and she warned me that most of the people they knew would be shocked by my language and that I wouldn't be invited to people's houses, birthday parties or weekends away.

Dad finished off with 'The bottom line is, you have to stop speaking like Dee or we will have to ban you from going over to the Ayers' altogether.'

That wasn't entirely the end of it as I was made to wash Mum and Dad's car as a punishment. Since my telling-off, my use of American swear words has got a little better. I suppose if you spend as much time as I do with Dee you're going to end up speaking like her, but I don't think Mum and Dad would ever have banned me from seeing the Ayers.

Dee is definitely the worst of all the grown-ups I know when it comes to swearing. Keith McNally never swears, but he certainly likes to shock people. He's back at Alan's house and I've been going over to see him a lot. One evening he asked me to come over to help him get Miss Shepherd out of the house.

Earlier in the year Camden Council decided to put

residents' parking in the Crescent, and some men turned up one day and painted parking bays and yellow lines along the whole street. For the first time it looked like it was all over for Miss Shepherd and she would finally have to move on. As Alan had an empty driveway, she knocked on his door and asked if she could park her van there for a few weeks. It's now been a few months and there is no sign of her ever leaving, so it looks like Alan is stuck with her van in his front garden.

He strung an electric cable from his house to her van so she could have electricity for a light and a radio. He told her that if he was away and no one else was there and it got too cold she could come into the house and watch the television and warm herself up. Although Keith was staying in the house, she was still letting herself in and making herself at home. What she liked best was to sit in Alan's special chair, with the lever on the side that makes the back go down and the front lift up for your legs. When Keith came back from work, she was in the chair, watching a documentary about penguins. She still had her coat and headscarf on, and her legs were sticking straight out with a pair of old slippers on her feet. By the time I arrived, she was watching the news and shouting at the television because of something Harold Wilson was saying.

Miss Shepherd doesn't like any of the children in the Crescent. Conrad once tried giving her some money he'd collected at school for starving children in Africa. He'd forgotten which day it had to be handed in, and when he did, Miss Appleby told him it was too late. Then he thought Miss Shepherd might need it, so he knocked on the van window and waited for her to stick her head out. When she did she shouted, 'I haven't got time for this, I'm a busy woman, what do you want?' Miss Shepherd never likes to be seen to be given anything as then she thinks it's 'charity', and charity is something the tramps get around the corner in Arlington House. She'll happily accept things if she can make out it had been her idea in the first place then it doesn't look like charity. Anna Haycraft is always trying to give her food, but even she gets shouted at and told to go away. The funny thing is Miss Shepherd will shout and make a fuss and tell you she doesn't want something and then at the last minute grab it out of your hand. She then quickly winds the window up and disappears into the dark inside of her van like a fish grabbing something to eat on the surface of a lake.

With Miss Shepherd comfortably settled in Alan's favourite chair, Keith stood in front of the television and asked her very nicely if she minded switching it off and going back to her van so he could get on and make his supper. It didn't work. There was now a story on the news about President Ford visiting the Pope in Rome, and she was leaning to the side so she could see past Keith. Miss Shepherd is a Catholic and very keen on the Pope, so there was no way she was going to stop watching now. Then he tried talking very loudly to me, but that didn't work either, and just made her shout at us to shut up. It was then that I remembered once seeing Alan's electricity box in the cupboard under the stairs. Without saying anything I pointed to the cupboard. I opened the door and climbed in over the brooms and buckets and flicked the big red switch on the box. Along with the television, every light in the house went off. Keith lit a match and, holding it up to his face, walked over to Miss Shepherd. She was still looking at the television, waiting for it to come back on again.

'Well, that's that, Miss Shepherd. Another power cut I'm afraid. It's the coal miners again, you know what they're like.'

I don't know what this had to do with the coal miners but it worked. When she realised the television wasn't coming back on, she pushed the chair lever forward, the leg rest dropped down, the back of the chair shot forward and lifted her body off the seat into a standing position. As soon as she'd gone I climbed back into the cupboard and switched the electricity back on.

Keith then went upstairs to fetch his little brown suitcase, which is the one he uses to keep his money in. He told me that when he'd filled it to the top he was going to buy an aeroplane ticket to America and go and live there for ever. I hoped he wouldn't, as I really like having him around. He now has two jobs to help him make enough money to fill the suitcase. The first is doing the lights for a musical called *The Rocky Horror Show*. He took me to see it one night, and I got to sit next to him at a big table up on a balcony with loads of switches that he uses to turn the different lights on and off on the stage. It was a very peculiar show, with everyone walking around in their knickers and bras. Every five minutes or so Keith has to jump up and grab a big spotlight, which he points at someone on the stage.

In the middle of the table is a big switch with a label underneath that says 'Fuck Light'. I pointed to it and asked what it did. Keith didn't explain but said he would let me work the switch when the time was right. About half-way through the show he suddenly switched off all the lights on the stage and everything went dark. He turned to me and whispered, 'OK, after three, flick that switch.' The music started, and he counted down and I hit the switch. At that very moment a bright light came on behind a giant screen on the stage. On it was an enormous shadow of a naked man lying on top of a naked woman on a table. He was moving up and down on her in a funny way and kind of moaning. 'There you go, that's the Fuck Light!' Keith said. I think I got it, but as far as

I could see the shadow of the man on top was trying to kill the shadow of the girl underneath him, but Keith said it was something else. I'm sure Mum and Dad have never seen *The Rocky Horror Show*, as I don't think they would have let me go if they'd known what it was like. It was definitely a show for grown-ups.

14

MOVING ON

My final term at Primrose Hill School went faster than any I could remember, and I wanted to enjoy every last minute of it, such as a big project on the Romans, which included a school trip to Northumberland so we could see how the Romans really lived in Britain. We did a school play about the Romans where at least the horrid Miss Crosby didn't make me dress up as a woman. Having already got into the secondary school I wanted to go to, there were no more exams or interviews to worry about. At home things were about to change too. Our nanny and housekeeper, Marina González, decided it was time to return to Spain. She told Mum that a man called Franco was going to die soon, and that was the reason she wanted to go home. Mum and Dad decided not to find another live-in nanny, which would free up our top floor for separate bedrooms for me, Tom, Kate and Jeanie. With everything else going on, Dad was spending his summer in Sussex at the Glyndebourne opera, where he was doing a production called *The Cunning Little Vixen*. He was staying in the main house at Glyndebourne with the Christie family, and we got to spend weekends with him there and go horse riding with the Christies' children.

Throughout all of this I felt an excitement that my life was about to change with my move to secondary school in

September. It's a big and proper change which I thought would never happen, but I think I am ready for it now. Of course I am nervous about leaving Primrose Hill Primary as it's always felt protected, and being only a short walk from home, it was so much part of growing up in and around Gloucester Crescent.

Tom and the Roeber triplets have been at secondary school for two years, and they seem very different now. Tom went to Acland Burghley in Tufnell Park, which is so rough someone punched him in the face and broke his nose just because he looked at them. The Roebers' mum thought, as triplets, it would be a good time to split them up, so they've been sent to Pimlico, Hampstead and Haverstock schools. Hanging out with them isn't like hanging out with the children from Primrose Hill Primary. They know real stuff and are doing real subjects that will get them ready for life. They do science and have Bunsen burners in their classrooms, and do maths that I don't understand but hope to when I'm at secondary school. I really liked learning about the Romans with their togas and underfloor heating, but Tom has been doing the Second World War and now knows about Hitler and the Nazis, which is so much more interesting and the way he's been taught seems less frightening than when Dad tells us about it. Tom and the Roebers now travel to school on their own, on public transport, and come back and tell us about all the things they've done and seen. Tom has even started reading Mum and Dad's copy of *The Times* and, as far as I can tell, understands it. When Tom and the Roebers get together, they talk about the news and politics, and they didn't do that before.

Most of the boys and girls in my year at Primrose Hill are going on to Haverstock, which is up the road in Chalk

Farm. The really brainy ones are going to William Ellis, which is a grammar school. I don't know why, but Mum and Dad didn't even think about William Ellis for me. I wish they had because it seems like a good school and I would quite like to be somewhere for brainy kids so I can talk to Dad about things like science and evolution and maybe go on to do the kind of job he would approve of.

One of Mum and Dad's friends told them that the best comprehensive in London is Pimlico School, which is big and in a massive glass and concrete building near the River Thames and is famous for its music. Because it's not a local school, the only way I could go there was to get a music scholarship. I went for an interview in January and had to play my violin and oboe to a man in a really small room. The heating was on full blast, and the man was sweating so much he smelled like those old suits you get in a charity shop. I got in, which really surprised me as I didn't think I was any good at either the violin or the oboe. So that's where I'm going, along with three other boys who got music scholarships as well – Conrad, Simon Elms and Neal Halling, whose dad works in the Post Office.

One of the other things I had to do before the end of term was go with Mum to John Lewis to buy my new uniform for Pimlico. She took me out of school for the day, so I got her all to myself, which made it feel like a special day out. After we bought the uniform she took me for lunch in the café at the top of the department store and we got to chat properly about school and all the things I was looking forward to. Mum said I was likely to grow over the summer, so everything we bought was a size too big, which made me look like my body had shrunk in the wash. She looked so proud when I came out of the dressing room and even cried a little when she said I looked so grown up. She got me to put it on again that night to show Dad and Alan when they were having supper. I'd never worn flannel trousers, a tie or a nice jacket before, but I loved all of it because it felt so special being dressed smartly for once. I felt like my days of looking like a ragamuffin were finally over.

On the weekend before school broke up, James Roeber took me and Conrad up to the top of Primrose Hill so we could see how much of London we would have to travel across to get to school. James, who had already been at Pimlico for two years, got us to find Westminster Cathedral and then the four chimneys of Battersea Power Station, and said that the school was somewhere between the two.

I'd been looking forward to taking the bus to school: travelling without grown-ups would feel like a big adventure. This was before our walk up Primrose Hill with James, when he told us about a family called the Frasers who lived on an estate near Pimlico. According to James, they'd all been expelled from the school, including the oldest, who was now in prison for putting an axe through a man's back. The youngest Fraser, called Kevin, who was too young to go to prison, enjoyed beating up anyone from Pimlico who looked weak or he didn't like. At the top of his list were posh boys from Pimlico and then anyone black or Pakistani. Thanks to our uniforms, Kevin would know exactly who we were and was likely to come for us first. I realised that the big colourful logo on our blazers, which I'd liked so much, now just screamed 'Hello Kevin, I'm at Pimlico, come and kill me!' James said the best thing to do was hide your blazer when you got on the bus and sit downstairs, where the conductor could keep an eye on you.

Up until now it had never crossed my mind that a school

might be a dangerous and frightening place, or that something terrible could happen on the journey there. Primrose Hill was so easy to get to and had always felt safe. The excitement I'd felt about finally going to big school was now overshadowed by this new information from James. It found a place in my head where it would pop up every now and then to remind me just how unfamiliar and scary everything was about to be. It was also a reminder that I really didn't know much about what went on in the streets and areas beyond the safety of Gloucester Crescent and Primrose Hill.

The summer term soon came to an end and, even with the worries I now had about the Frasers, I left Primrose Hill School excited about closing a door on a whole part of my childhood that I would never see again. I've been very lucky so far and have had a life that's felt safe and at times even magical, but now things are going to be very different and that's something to look forward to, even if there are people that are starting to worry me.

Within hours of finishing school, we were at Kensington Olympia Station. The summer holidays had started, and as I climbed into my bunk on the sleeper train I slipped in to a deep sleep, dreaming about my first day at Pimlico, my new school uniform and an angry boy called Kevin Fraser.

15

SUMMER VISITORS, 1975

There is now a new person over at the Ayers'. His name is Hylan, and he's been around, on and off, for some time. Everyone says he's Dee's boyfriend, which I didn't really understand at first as she's still married to Freddie. Hylan makes Dee happy, and since he turned up things over at the Ayers' have rather changed. Unlike with Freddie, Dee seems to do everything with Hylan; they go out to the theatre and parties, they cook meals together and even take Nick on holiday with them. Now, when Freddie goes to Oxford on a Tuesday morning, Hylan turns up as soon as he's gone and stays. Then, when Freddie comes back on Thursday, Hylan leaves. When Freddie's around, it's as if nothing has changed. Dee puts his lunch on the table like she's always done, and he sits at his desk, smoking and writing as he plays with his silver chain. Hylan is much younger than Freddie. I heard Mum telling some friends that she thought he was 'really quite handsome'. Like Dee, Hylan is an American, except he's tall and black and has a moustache. He's a fashion designer for women and he wears really fancy clothes which make him look like a film star. Nick likes him, so when he's around everyone seems happier, the house comes alive and Gully has someone else to flirt with. He has a daughter too, called Alex, who is 13 and sometimes comes with him to hang out with Nick.

Hylan Booker with Antonia Fraser

Many years ago the Ayers bought a house in the south of France, which they go to for their holidays. Like we do with Scotland, they pack up their car and head to France for the whole summer. This has all changed since Hylan turned up. Freddie has a girlfriend as well, but she never comes to Regent's Park Terrace. She's called Vanessa Lawson and has four children of her own. The deal now is that Dee and Nick go to France with Hylan for the first part of the summer and Freddie stays in London with Vanessa. Then, in the middle of the holiday, Freddie arrives with Vanessa and three of her children, Nigella, Horatia and Thomasina. Everyone spends the day together, and then Dee and Hylan get on the train and go home, leaving Nick to spend the rest of the summer with his dad.

This summer Dee took Tom with them to France, so he wasn't with us in Scotland for the first half of the holiday. Keith came to stay with us, which I had a feeling might be his last time. Before we left for Scotland, he called me over to

Alan's house to have a look at the suitcase he keeps his money in. It was now pretty full, and I knew straight away that it meant he had the money he needed to go to America. He told me he was going to buy a one-way ticket to New York and then go on to Los Angeles and Hollywood. There was enough money in his suitcase for the tickets and for him to live off before he had to get a job, which would give him time to work out what he really wanted to do in America.

Since Keith was keen not to spend any of this money, he decided to hitch-hike all the way from London to Archiestown. He didn't tell us he was coming, and then one evening in the middle of supper there was a knock at the front door and there he was. Keith likes surprises, and this was a big one. Everyone was so pleased to see him, especially me – I'd really wanted him to come and stay as I needed his advice about girls. He'd had quite a few girlfriends and he talks about them a lot, so asking him about girls seemed like a good start. It would be better than asking Dad, who I know would have felt incredibly uncomfortable talking about it. I don't think he dated any girls when he was my age, so I'm not sure he would have had much to say on the matter.

The thing was, I'd been having these thoughts about girls since my last term at Primrose Hill Primary. They were thoughts that seemed more grown up, and having them made me feel like I was growing up. Before this, I hadn't really thought about girls – everyone I have ever loved or wanted to marry was a proper grown-up, like Sue, Miss Laing and even Margery. I'd wanted to marry them for some time, but after a while they just seemed like fantasies that would never come true. Then, in my last term, I found it was quite nice talking to girls my own age.

Whenever we went to the local town, Keith started

pointing out girls I might like. I was embarrassed at first, but also worried that he might be teasing me and was trying to get me to say things for a laugh. Either way, it made me realise that there were loads of nice girls my own age who I just hadn't noticed in that way before. He also explained that some girls were not just nice to look at but could also be sexy. Since I'd only just worked out what being sexy was, I hadn't ever thought about girls like that before. I'd always thought they were pretty or sweet and would be nice to be married to. Keith explained that it meant something very different. The first time he showed me this was when we went to buy lemonade for supper from the saloon bar in the village hotel.

I'd been to the saloon bar a few times with Dad to buy lemonade, and I really didn't like it. The men in the village go there every night except Sundays and stand at the bar in their distillery work clothes shouting at each other. The inside of the bar was never meant to be cosy and is painted a cold and shiny blue, with a row of fluorescent lights hanging from the ceiling. I hadn't ever noticed before, but on one wall is a big calendar for Tennent's Lager with a half-naked girl on it. It was this calendar that Keith pointed to when we went to get the lemonade. He nudged me and asked what I thought of the blonde girl on the page for August, who was dressed in a see-through nightie. I could see quite a lot of her breasts, and she seemed to be looking straight at me from the calendar. One of the men at the bar turned and grinned at me. He pointed to the calendar and said, 'Aye aye, Wully, that'll be Shona. She's our "August Lovely".' She *was* lovely, and what's more, she was properly sexy. I also liked the way her eyes followed me as I looked over my shoulder when leaving the bar.

The next day Keith took me to the village shop. While I was looking through the penny sweet tray, he asked the lady

The lager can girls

behind the counter if she had any cans of Tennent's Lager. She went into the back and returned with a big box, which she placed on the counter. Keith took his time as he carefully selected several cans from the box. I'd always thought a can of Tennent's was like any other can of Tennent's, but it turned out they weren't at all. When we got home Keith showed me why he had gone to so much trouble as he set the cans out on the table. There, printed on each can, was a different picture of a girl, dressed in the same way as Shona was in the saloon bar calendar. They had names like Heather, Sally, Lee and Sylvia, and each one was looking at me in that same sexy way. Of all of them Heather was my favourite. She was more like the kind of girl you might marry one day, but she also had that new sexy thing that I was starting to like. She was wearing a very tight shirt and you could see quite a lot of her breasts in her half-opened shirt. At that moment Dad came into the kitchen and picked up the can. Looking at Heather, he shook his head and said, 'trollop' and walked off. I think it was Dad being so rude about Heather that made me like her even more.

Keith stayed for the rest of the summer, and Dad went back to London a few weeks before the end of the holiday. A neighbour had been checking on the house and feeding Kate's budgie, Chippie. Now Dad was going back to London, Kate gave him very strict instructions on how to feed Chippie. He'd flown into our back garden one day and Tom managed to catch him with a fishing net. He had a ring on one leg, so Mum thought he might have escaped from London Zoo. Dad bought him a big white cage, and he'd been living in it quite happily in Kate's bedroom for over a year. Back in London and getting on with his work, Dad completely forgot about Chippie. He remembered eventually, but it wasn't until the day before we were coming home and, fearing the worst, he raced upstairs to see if Chippie was all right. He wasn't – he was lying on his back with his little legs in the air.

People often tell me that Dad is one of the cleverest men in the world, but the Chippie incident wasn't Dad at his best. Thinking he was being clever, he put Chippie in a box and went straight to Palmers pet shop on Parkway. He opened the box and showed it to the lady behind the counter and told her he needed to replace the dead budgie with an exact lookalike. The thing is, Chippie was a handsome bird with smart blue feathers with neat white dashes across them. Between Dad and the lady in the shop they managed to choose one that might have looked like Chippie had he been blue and then dropped in white paint and shaken very hard. Clearly being a bit smarter than Dad about these things, the lady pointed out that Chippie had a ring on his leg. Everybody knew about this ring because they always pointed to it whenever Kate took anyone to look at Chippie. There was no way Dad could get away with the new budgie not having a ring on its leg. Dad smiled at the lady but 'No' was her answer when he asked her

Mum, Kate, Tom and me at the Old Manse, August 1975

nicely if she'd remove it for him. She told him to try Bucking-ham's the jewellers on the high street. So Chippie went back in his box and Dad took him down to Camden High Street. The man at Buckingham's scratched his head and told him the easiest thing to do was simply cut the leg off and remove the ring. He could then open the ring and Palmers could put it on the new bird. So off came Chippie's leg along with the ring and Dad ran back to Palmers so the lady could put the ring onto the new budgie with the splodgy feathers.

Feeling very pleased with himself, Dad headed back home, put the new bird in the cage and waited for us all to return from Scotland. The next morning we arrived very early on the overnight sleeper. Kate went straight up to her room to see Chippie and Mum went to talk to Dad, who was still in bed. Suddenly a scream came from the top of the house. Kate ran down the stairs to Mum and Dad's bedroom crying out,

'Chippie, where's Chippie?' By now Dad was hiding under the bedcovers, having already confessed to Mum what had happened, but he was leaving it to Mum to break the news. By the time the house settled down to just another day in the Crescent, Kate had decided the new bird wasn't all that bad, and after much discussion she called him George and soon started a game of playing her recorder to him. He always sang back, which, along with Jeanie's piano-playing and Dad's typing, became just one of the many familiar noises that filled our house.

PART TWO

August 1980
(Age 16)

Dad and me in the Cotswolds, 1978

16

PIMLICO SCHOOL – SEPTEMBER 1975

What I thought was going to be my very first day at Pimlico actually turned out to be the night before. Having gone to bed as early as I could, I woke up in the middle of the night and sat bolt upright. Although it was still dark outside, I grabbed my uniform, got dressed and ran downstairs for breakfast. Sitting around the kitchen table with Mum and Dad were Alan and a couple of other friends.

Holding my spotless new briefcase, I suggested we skip breakfast and get going straight away. Dad, trying not to laugh, said, 'I think you're about nine hours too early.' At that point everyone else started laughing and Mum got out of her chair and led me back upstairs to bed.

The next time I woke up the sun was streaming through the narrow gap between my bedroom curtains and it really was the start of the first day at my new school. The night before I'd carefully laid out my uniform on the chair at the end of my bed, ready to put on as soon as I woke up. I couldn't remember waking up and putting it on in the middle of the night, but now I stood and inspected myself in front of the mirror,

Pimlico School, London

taking in every detail: the crease down the legs of the grey flannel trousers, the crispness of the white shirt, the smart school tie and the embroidered logo on the breast pocket of the black blazer. I was so glad to have ditched the scruffy hand-me-downs I'd worn to Primrose Hill Primary.

This uniform would be part of the new me – an older, wiser and more experienced me. I would be a person who got homework to do every night and had a briefcase with books and a pencil case in it. I would be coming home having learned real subjects like geography, biology and chemistry, along with something called humanities. This was the school that would get me ready for life. It would take me right up to being an adult who would be able to make his own choices in the real world.

When we pulled up outside the gates that September morning in 1975, I realised I'd forgotten how big Pimlico School was. I'd been before when I did my interview, and with Mum and Conrad to look around, but it now seemed so much bigger. The school sits on Lupus Street like a huge concrete and glass battleship waiting to set sail with all sixteen hundred pupils on board. At each end of the school are the entrances, which are connected through the inside of the building by a long and busy concourse. Staircases go up and down from the concourse which lead to all the classrooms, workshops and sports halls. At the far corner is a modern swimming pool that I couldn't wait to try out. Between the low concrete walls on the street and the school building are tarmac-covered playgrounds and football pitches.

Conrad and I were driven all the way to Pimlico by his mum. My mum came too, and they dropped us off at one of the main gates. Smiling and waving, they drove away, leaving us standing on the pavement. I had never felt so proud and so terrified at the same time. As hundreds of boys and girls of every size and age, dressed in the same uniform as Conrad and me, streamed past us, I felt a sense of real belonging. Everything about Pimlico was huge and so unlike my primary school, and it was going to be my world for the next seven years. Once inside, we were guided along the concourse and up to a big hall at the top of the school, where all three hundred of the First-Year students were to be welcomed by the headmistress. There were almost as many pupils in a single year at Pimlico as there were in the whole of Primrose Hill Primary.

Mrs Mitchell, the headmistress, walked onto the stage. The hall fell silent, and she started a long speech about the importance of youth, doing something with our potential and our responsibilities to each other and to our parents. Next to me and Conrad, and looking as nervous as us, were the other two boys from Primrose Hill, Simon Elms and Neal Halling. The whole year had been divided into ten forms, with the fifteen music scholars in our year spread across two of these.

As our forms were called out, we were led out of the hall by our new form teachers to classrooms scattered all over the building. The two forms with the music scholars were based in the music department. My new form teacher, a Welsh woman called Mrs Roberts, was the deputy head of music. Since my form had so many music scholars, it didn't feel that different from the forms we had at Primrose Hill, which was why we all settled in quite quickly and got on together. It was when you stepped outside the form room and the music department and moved around the school to other lessons that you realised just how different the rest of the school was. For the headmistress, Mrs Mitchell, the music school was everything. Even though only a handful of the pupils were involved in it, she felt the musicians gave the school its reputation. We were her pride and joy, and she thought we walked on water. But it also meant the rest of the school didn't and wished we'd walk on water and die from drowning.

To begin with I really enjoyed being at Pimlico. I got up early every day, stopped by the Roebers to collect James and Conrad and got on the 24 bus with them. For the first few months I looked forward to walking into the school and feeling part of it, and I still liked my uniform, even though my shoes quite quickly lost their shine and my white shirts went a bit grey. I was in the school orchestra and choir, and because my voice was still a long way from breaking I got to sing solo parts in productions like *Dido and Aeneas*. Mrs Mitchell's best friend was the composer Benjamin Britten, so we were invited to perform *Noah's Flood* at the Aldeburgh Festival with Peter Pears. He played God, which he did by standing in a cupboard at the back of the church with a microphone. Every time God spoke to Noah this big voice boomed out over the church, like the man behind the curtain in *The Wizard of Oz*.

I already knew from James Roeber that there were gangs at the school who wanted to kill you, or at least make your life as miserable as they could. They seemed to leave me alone in the first term, but as I started to settle in I somehow came to their attention, and when that happened, everything started to change. It turned out the people they were most interested in bullying were what they called the 'posh musicians', who they hated more than anyone else. If only we could have been more invisible, but because we were usually carrying a case with a musical instrument in it we stood out wherever we went, and the gangs picked us off whenever they wanted to. We were known as the 'Melons' and their favourite sport was 'Melon-bashing'. They named us this because, having turned our noses up at the school meals, we went out to an Italian shop on Lupus Street that sold spaghetti bolognese and watermelons. It was often the case that you'd never make it to the Italian shop without your money being taken off you by one of the gangs, so you'd end up going hungry.

I soon discovered that there were two types of gangs at Pimlico, and they had their own particular methods. The first were the white gangs. They'd never hit you or hurt you physically – they knew that threatening you and leaving you in fear of what *might* happen was so much worse. They'd push you into a dark corner, stand within an inch of your face and tell you that they knew where you lived and how you got to school. They wanted you to know that at any point, when you were least expecting it, something terrible would happen to you, either on the bus or outside your own home. They planted the fear right there in your head and it stayed there, day and night, eating away at you. Quite early on, one of these boys told me he was going to spend years 'fucking with my head'. He wasn't joking and did it as often as he could. The worst part was knowing that they might get me at home. They said they would be outside my house waiting in the street, and I lived in fear of this for the rest of my time at Pimlico.

The black gangs were somehow better than the white ones. They only wanted one thing, and that was an instant moment of entertainment so they could prove to us and to each other who was boss. This often happened on the concourse, where they would surround you and beat and kick you to the floor. I don't think they even knew who they were beating up – anyone would do as long as they looked weak and weren't going to fight back. Once they'd finished, they would laugh with each other and walk off. It also happened a lot in the changing rooms of the swimming pool, where, standing shivering in your swimming trunks or underwear, they would turn their towels into a 'rat's tail' and whip your feet as they shouted, 'Dance you honky bitch, dance.'

I was really happy to have Simon Elms in my class. He was a trumpeter on the music course and lived in a flat around the corner from Gloucester Crescent. We'd known each other a bit at primary school but hadn't really been friends, and this changed as we settled into Pimlico. At the age of 11 he had the luck of looking like he was 16. He also happened to be good-looking, which meant all the girls, from our year up to the sixth form, wanted to know him.

Break times were always frantic and noisy. As no one was allowed back into the classrooms, the different groups in the school made a claim to an area or corner of the school where they could hang out. There's a big common room at the top of the school for the sixth-formers, and another in the basement for the fifths, with pool tables and a small canteen. Everyone else claimed a bit of the concourse where there were radiators and a long window ledge to sit on, while others headed to the playgrounds. That's where I hung out with the other music scholars, and a few friends from our form. The gangs preferred to roam around the school and intimidate whoever looked vulnerable. As a group we felt safer together and would spend all our breaks talking about who was going out with who, what we'd seen on telly (*Space: 1999* or *The Sweeney*) or which pop groups we liked (Queen, Earth, Wind & Fire and Hot Chocolate) and didn't like (ABBA and the Bay City Rollers).

Simon always held court in our group, with the girls hanging on to his every word. There was Sally, whose dad played the clarinet in the Royal Opera House orchestra, Abigail, whose sister Susannah had been in the film of *Swallows and Amazons*, and Philippa. Her dad was a composer called Wilfred Josephs, and they lived in a big house in Hampstead. Then there was Lena, whose dad was a union official at the Post Office. It was always good to have Simon around at break times, as he would step in at the first sign of trouble between anyone in our group and the gangs. He knew how to throw a punch in a way that would knock anyone straight to the floor, and he frequently put this to good use if someone so much as threatened us. I think some of Simon's confidence also came from having an amazing wingman called Jimi Keyede, who was in our form but not a music scholar. Jimi's family were from Nigeria, and he was as tall and fearless as Simon. Although he was the kindest and most gentle person you could meet, the gangs knew not to get on his bad side.

We bonded early on over him accidently setting my hair on fire in the middle of a maths lesson. While the teacher was busily writing something on the blackboard, Jimi thought he would see how close he could get the naked flame of a lighter to the back of my neck before I felt the heat. To his surprise, my hair caught fire before I felt anything. The first I knew about it was when Jimi started smacking my head with his huge hands as he desperately tried to put out my burning hair. He was put straight into detention but, knowing he had been stupid rather than deliberately trying to set me on fire, I chose not to take it further. From that day on we became close friends, and with him and Simon I had two much-needed bodyguards. By my fifth year it felt like the school had lost control of the more violent kids. They even put security guards on the school gates. This wasn't to keep us in but to stop boys who'd been expelled from coming back into the school to attack anyone they had a grudge against.

The worst thing about the threats from the white gangs was the absolute fear that Gloucester Crescent might no longer be the safe and secure place I'd grown up believing it to be. This wasn't helped by the fact that no one at home, except for Tom, understood what it was like to be threatened with so much physical and psychological violence. At first I thought they would get bored with it and go away. But as each year became another it carried on, and my constant state of fear started to wear me down. It left me exhausted to the point that when they threatened me, I wanted to say, 'Just do it and let's be done with it.' For the first few years there had been lots of good days at Pimlico, and it seemed like I could get past the bullying with the support of my friends. There were even lessons that were stimulating and I felt like I was being taught interesting and important things that would make a difference. But those days became fewer and the ones where I was truly miserable started to take over my life. Everything seemed hopeless, and I'd stopped learning anything as I was spending more time worrying how to get through each day, get home safely and wonder what the future held.

One morning, as if out of nowhere, when I was 14, I broke down in a way that I'd never done before. I think it started with my telling Mum and Dad that I wasn't sure how much more I could take and Dad nervously laughing it off saying he was sure I would be fine. As he tried to reassure me with one of his 'it'll be all right' smiles, I could feel the tears welling up in my eyes. Then when Mum reminded me that I needed to set off or I'd be late I snapped and told them this time they had to take me seriously. The next thing I knew it I was curled up in the corner of the kitchen crying uncontrollably and begging them not to send me back to school. To begin with they didn't seem to know how to respond – they stood there looking at each other and then back at this sobbing mass on the floor. It was Mum who finally knelt down and tried to console me, but I could tell she was as upset and confused as Dad. I can't really blame them as they didn't know how to protect me from what was going on or have any concept of what it was like. All they could do was promise to make some phone calls and start looking at a way out. By the end of the day they'd called several schools, but they all said the same thing – I was too old to change schools now, but could try

Stanage Park: Stella, Deborah, me and Kate

again for the sixth form when I was 16. Knowing that there would be a way out in the end helped, but that would be two years away.

With its distance from London, as well as the warmth and love from everyone there, Stanage had started to replace Gloucester Crescent as the one place where I could feel safe again. I went there whenever I could at weekends or half-terms. Nothing ever changed at Stanage, and I never stopped loving that moment when the house slowly appeared as I came up the drive. Stella was always there to greet me with the dogs, and the smell of wood fires and azaleas filled my mind as I entered the front hall. These were now more than just nice things to remember – they were what I connected with the new sense of security that Stanage gave me. Whenever I was pushed up against a wall and threatened, I just closed my eyes and thought of Stanage and walking into the hall and it would get me through it. I counted the weeks and days between each

Deborah and me

visit, knowing that, once I was there, I would be safe and no one could touch me.

As time went by, Stella became even more of an influence on me. Everyone assumed I was her grandson, but couldn't figure out how our families were related. She eventually decided it was easier to tell anyone who asked that she was my godmother. Without further discussion, even with Mum and Dad, that was what she became. On each visit I got closer to Stella, but at the same time I noticed Guy's health getting worse. He was no longer sitting on the big sofa in the library or cracking jokes at lunch. He had pretty much retired to his bedroom, where he would watch the races on television with an oxygen mask over his mouth. I would sit with him as he strained to breathe. Every now and then he would pull it off his face so he could shout at a fallen jockey or when his favourite horse had won a race.

Then, one Sunday morning when I was at home playing in the garden, Dad came out and told me that Sue had called from Stanage to let me know that Guy had died in his sleep. It was a call I'd been expecting for some time, but it didn't make it any easier. Other than Grandad, who I didn't know that well, Guy was the first person I was close to who had died. I don't think Mum or Dad knew how close we had become, so it was a surprise to them when I ran upstairs and hid in my bedroom. I sat on the floor and cried for hours, too embarrassed to show them how much I loved him.

17

THE LONG HOT SUMMER OF 1976

I think the man who designed Pimlico School really loved windows because he put them everywhere. He must have realised that with so many windows it would end up costing a fortune to clean them. So he made them all slope, and when it rained the water would run off them and that would make them clean. It sort of worked, but he forgot about the sun. When it was sunny, it was like being a tomato in a greenhouse and you couldn't sit at your desk without overheating and turning bright red. He must have then thought, 'I know, I'll put roller blinds in all the windows.' Another good idea, but I don't think this man had ever met the type of kids who went to Pimlico School. If he had, he would have known that if you put blinds in a classroom full of these kids, the first thing they do is swing from them until they fall down. So now all the blinds were either broken or had to be removed.

During the last month of the summer term of 1976 we had a fierce heatwave – the sun shone every day and the temperature rose to well over 90 degrees. Thanks to all those sloping windows with no blinds, the sun shone right down on us as we sat at our desks, with the temperature in the classrooms rising to over 110 degrees. Someone in the Inner London Education Authority decided that with temperatures this high it was too dangerous for us to stay in the classrooms. So they came up with a brilliant idea: open the school an hour earlier and close it at one o'clock and send everyone home for the rest of the day.

At one o'clock on the dot we poured out of the school into the searing London heat and headed home, where we would start our long lazy afternoons by climbing over the garden walls to get to each other's houses. Back doors were thrown open, and as the afternoons wore on we would wander in and out of each other's houses and gardens. We moved across the walls until we found a shady spot and then spent hours sitting around chatting about school, the summer holidays and who fancied who. Above the gardens, as we played and gossiped, the clatter of typewriters carried on from the open windows as the grown-ups struggled with their deadlines. Eventually, a mum or a dad would call us in for supper. By then the typing had stopped and the gardens started to fill with the noise of adults laughing and clinking glasses. Every now and then there would be the louder sound of a party coming from one of the gardens.

I've always liked going to the grown-ups' parties in Gloucester Crescent, whether I get invited to them or gatecrash. That summer, with all the good weather we were having, there were lots of parties in the Crescent. There was a big one at the Haycrafts' which I went to, as did many of Mum and Dad's friends. It was for a book that Colin Haycraft was publishing by a man called Professor Dover – I remembered his name only because that's where we got the ferry from to go to France. I heard Dad tell Mum that the book was all about homosexuality in ancient Greece, so I knew it wasn't a book I was likely to read. The Professor was very drunk and sitting in the corner of the room, where people were patting him on the back and congratulating him. He looked a little alarmed and like he'd been locked away in his study for years trying to finish his book and had forgotten what it was like to be around so many people. My godfather, an American poet called Robert Lowell, was at the party too. I'd only met him a few times, so Dad brought me over to say hello. He seemed very shy and wore little round glasses and had a twangy American accent like the men in *Gone with the Wind*. I don't think he knew what to say to me except 'I'm so sorry, my boy', and keep telling me how hopeless he'd been as a godfather. He'd given me a present once, when I was four, which was a box of coloured plastic tiles which you could lock together to build shapes with. This time, as he stood there apologising, he started searching around in his jacket pockets and pulled something out which he pushed into my hand, saying, 'Please my boy, go and buy yourself something nice.' I waited until he was out of sight before I opened my hand to take a proper look at what he'd put in it. It was a very crumpled and slightly damp bank note, which I carefully unfolded and held up to the light. It didn't look like anything I'd seen before, and when I showed it to Oli Haycraft he decided it must be Dutch. The next day Dad took it to the bank and changed it into British money, but it didn't turn out to be worth very much.

Claire Tomalin likes having parties too, but hers seem to be a bit more serious. The food's a lot better than the Haycrafts', and everyone stands around talking about things they've written about or read in the newspapers. There's a lift in the Tomalins' house as their son Tom has spina bifida and has to get around in a wheelchair. I'd been in lots of lifts, but never one in a house. The Tomalins' lift goes to each floor of the house and is only big enough for one person and Tom's wheelchair.

That summer they had a party and Mum and Dad said I could come along to the beginning of it to say hello to my uncle Karl and aunt Jane. They're good friends of Claire and had been at university with her and her husband, Nick.

I'd always wanted to have a go in the Tomalins' lift, even if Claire had told us never to play in it. She explained that if it ever broke they wouldn't be able to get Tom up or down from his bedroom on the top floor. With a busy party going on, I felt certain no one would notice if I had a go in it. I waited until I thought no one was looking, then slipped down to the basement, got into the lift and shut the door. Not sure which buttons to press, I decided to try all of them at once. From somewhere high above the lift came a terrible grinding noise and then the lift started slowly going up. I could hear the chatter and laughter from the guests as I passed each floor. Thinking it must have finally reached the top of the house, I hit the buttons again. The grinding noise came back, but this time it was closer and the lift came to a sudden halt. I tried the door, but it wouldn't open. I tried pressing the buttons again, but nothing happened. I waited, but the longer I waited the more I could feel myself starting to panic. After some time I heard the voice of a small child somewhere below me. It was clear I was stuck between two floors and I needed to get help. If I was going to be rescued it was now or never, so I started shouting to attract the attention of the child below.

'HELP!'

'Hello lift, who's there?' came the voice of a little girl.

'It's not the lift, it's William. Can you get my dad?'

'Who's your dad?'

'Jonathan, tall with curly hair and a big nose. He'll be the one talking.' I waited and eventually heard the child's voice again.

'Sorry, lift, I can't find your dad, would you like me to get Claire?'

'No! Don't get Claire! Please find my dad, or a man with a Scottish accent called Karl.'

I was now desperate for her to find my dad or Karl. I knew neither of them would be able to fix the lift, but they might get someone who could. But the girl decided to go straight to Claire and tell her someone was stuck in the lift. The next voice to come from below was Claire's.

'Who completely disobeyed me and went in the lift?'

'It's William Miller, I'm so sorry, Claire. I was, umm, looking for Tom's wheelchair. Can you get my dad so he can get me out?'

Silence again, and after a while I could hear voices coming from right above me. The first one was the familiar but angry Scottish voice of my Uncle Karl, who had opened a hatch door and was half hanging into the lift shaft as he shouted down at me.

'For Christ's sake, man, what a squalid circumstance. What were you thinking? Claire is not a happy woman.'

'Don't worry, I'm here, we'll get you out,' came the more concerned voice of Dad. Somehow, I didn't feel comforted by his words. He could barely change a light bulb, let alone mend a lift.

After another half an hour, a crowd of know-it-all dads had gathered at the top of the house, and I could hear them debating how to wind the lift down to the basement. It was obvious that no one knew what to do. In the middle of these voices was Claire instructing Karl on how to use a winch handle to wind the lift down. An hour later, with a lot of cheering, I was released. Standing at the door was my dad, looking relieved, and Claire, who was furious and banned me from ever going in the lift again. At that moment I was upset with myself for letting Claire down. I felt terrible that she could end up hating me like Freddie Ayer did. The last thing I needed was for the Tomalins to start thinking of me as that 'bloody William Miller'.

Mum and Dad had a small family party for their wedding anniversary which was mostly relatives, but I was allowed to invite the Roebers. There were also parties we weren't allowed to go to, but we got to see some of those from our hiding places in the gardens, like bushes or hanging out of trees. From here we could get a good look at what our parents did when they got together without their children. I could always spot Dad at these parties as, being taller than most people, he stood out, and it was no surprise to see that he did most of the talking while everyone else stood around him nodding and laughing.

When the Mellys were still living in the Crescent, they had lots of parties. As they didn't have a tree or any bushes in their garden, there was nowhere to hide and watch them, but Mum and Dad would go and then we'd hear about them the next morning over breakfast. What I most liked hearing about was George Melly's favourite party trick, which he called 'Man, Woman and Bulldog'. According to Dad, what George did was take all his clothes off and stand in the middle of the room and tell everyone he was a 'Man'. Then he'd push all his bits between his legs and squeezing them together shout 'Woman!' Finally, he'd turn around, bend over and bark 'Bulldog!' For a long time I didn't know why that was funny,

Our back garden at Gloucester Crescent, 1976:
Alan Bennett, Karl Miller, Dad, Mum

but I do now, and I'm glad Dad hasn't ever done that trick at a party.

One thing I've noticed is that there has always been a big difference between the parties in the Crescent and the ones in Regent's Park Terrace. In the Crescent, the mums and dads spend ages getting them ready, moving furniture around, making salads and putting out the taramasalata, French bread and cheeses. Then the dads walk around holding bottles of wine, filling glasses and making conversation with all their guests. In the Terrace they get special people in uniforms to work at their parties. These people take the coats at the door, serve the drinks and make the food, which is handed around on shiny trays. I think I prefer the parties in the Crescent as they seem less uptight. Something I've noticed about the people who live in Regent's Park Terrace is that, although they're all pretty much the same kind of people as the ones in the Crescent – with similar political beliefs and doing the same kinds of job – they think they live in a smarter street, and in a better area. Everyone in the Crescent says they live in Camden Town, whereas everyone in the Terrace, which is one garden away, says they live in Primrose Hill. I think that says a lot about them.

18

FOR YOU, THE HOLIDAY'S OVER – SUMMER 1976

After our long and lazy summer term of afternoons off school, I went to the south of France with the Ayers. I'd always longed to go with them, and this was the first year I was invited. I was going with Dee, Nick, Hylan and his daughter, Alex, for the first half of the summer, and would then go off to join my parents in Scotland when Tom came out with Freddie and the Lawsons for their half. The Ayers' house, La Migoua, is in Provence, on the edge of a hill surrounded by woods and vineyards. It isn't a very big house, and as it doesn't have that many windows it's dark and cosy inside. It felt good to finally get away from the heatwave in London, which by now had been going on for six weeks or so. France was hot, but a least we were in the countryside, high up in the hills, where there was a breeze. I'd only ever been to France in the Easter holidays, but in the summer it felt completely different. When we got out of the car at La Migoua, the first thing that hit me was the constant noise of the invisible cicadas and the intense dry heat, which filled the air with a wonderful smell of pine trees and herbs. As you looked out across the valley towards the vineyards below, everything seemed to shimmer in the heat.

We soon settled into a routine of long, leisurely meals on the terrace along with visits from old friends of the Ayers.

There was the Guirey family, who we all knew from London, as well as friends of both my parents and the Ayers, like Bill Deakin, who did lots of exciting things in the war, and Nicky Kaldor, who Dad says is a famous economist.

It was a few days after we arrived, on our first trip to the beach, that Nick decided my enthusiasm for being on holiday needed to be knocked on the head. The journey to the beach was along winding roads, which made it one of the most uncomfortable ever. The car wasn't really big enough, with Dee and Hylan in the front and me, Nick and Alex squeezed into the back. The rest of the car was filled with cold boxes of food, towels, beach kit and skateboards, which would all be required for a lazy day at the Ayers' favourite spot – the Bikini Beach Club at Les Lecques. Even with all the windows open it was unbearably hot in the car, and being squashed between Nick and Alex, the skin of our bare arms was starting to stick together. Nick has this mean pinch he likes to use when he wants to get his own way and started doing it on my legs to get me to move over. Once he'd got me to squeeze half onto Alex's lap, he started talking about his plans for another holiday he was going on with friends later in the summer. I felt like we'd only just arrived in France, and I was surprised by his lack of interest in the holiday we were on.

'We've only just got here,' I said. 'Shouldn't we be talking about *this* holiday, when there's so much to do and it's only just started?'

There was a pause before Nick said, 'For *you*, the holiday's over mate.'

He kept a completely straight face, but everyone else in the car burst out laughing. This soon became the most over-used phrase of the holiday, with Dee and Nick reminding me whenever they could that for me, the holiday was over. As she often does, instead of defending the person Nick was attacking, Dee took sadistic enjoyment in his bad behaviour, and encouraged it. He seemed to feel this gave him the right to be as mean as he could to anyone who didn't play by his rules. My other friends sometimes asked me why I bothered being friends with someone as nasty as Nick. Maybe the answer is that the two of us grew up together, and for most of that time I felt close to him and we had fun. I also felt sort of protective of him, knowing that his mum didn't seem to give him the kind of love and support that mine did. I could see why sometimes he might want to get her attention by being cruel, and I was an easy target. It didn't mean it hurt any less.

As fond of me as Dee was, she obviously felt that, for an easier life, it was better to be on Nick's side while on holiday. It was also part of the 'sink or swim' strategy that she had towards most children. At that moment, squeezed like sardines into the back of the car, I felt like I was sinking and that Nick's spitefulness was getting close to the kind of bullying I was used to at school. It was clear that no one was going to support me and that I would have to develop a thick skin to get through the next few weeks. This proved to be harder than I thought, as I was now very sensitive to any kind of bullying wherever it came from, and the last place I'd expected to find it was on holiday with friends.

After two weeks of relentless teasing from Nick and Alex, I decided to teach them all a lesson. One afternoon I took myself off to the edge of a wood on the other side of the valley, where I sat on a rock in the shade of a large cypress tree. I felt a calmness come over me as I breathed the warm herb-scented air into my lungs. I also had a perfect view of the front terrace at La Migoua. As the time passed, I could see the situation slowly go from a casual 'Has anyone seen William?' to serious concern and then to panic mode: 'Jesus, where the fuck has William gone?' First Nick and Alex came out of the house and I could tell they were laughing together. They looked up and down the terrace and behind the bushes and then went back inside. Hylan appeared next and searched the car and the lane up to the house. The next time Nick and Alex came out, they were looking worried and clearly arguing with each other. Finally, it was Dee's turn and I could just about make out the words 'Jesus fucking Christ' echoing across the valley. One by one, they all came out, and like a camp commandant Dee had them lined up in front of her. I couldn't hear what she was saying but it was obvious with all the arm-waving that she was giving them a dressing down.

Over supper the night before I had casually said to everyone that if Nick carried on being such an arse I would leave and make my own way back to London. Now, out on the terrace, this had started to sink in and was no doubt the cause of all the panic. When I finally strolled up the lane they'd all gone into the house, where Hylan had taken control of the situation. I could hear him shouting and telling everyone off for their bad behaviour, including Dee.

Through the kitchen window I could see Dee, Nick and Alex standing in front of Hylan as he carried on telling them off. They were all looking at the ground and trying not to laugh, but the more their shoulders shook, the angrier Hylan got. When I came through the door, Hylan went silent and then everyone's eyes followed me as I walked past. Not a word was said about my disappearance, but for the remainder of the week Nick and Alex decided to back off and Dee went back to being kind and paying me some attention.

When the changeover day came, Freddie, the Lawsons and Tom arrived from the station in a taxi, having taken the overnight train from Calais. Vanessa Lawson's two very cool and beautiful daughters, Nigella and Thomasina, came with her. They are a little older than us and considered themselves to be young women, whereas Nick, Tom and I were just kids who should be ignored. By the end of the day I had failed to make any impression on either of them and gave up, but I knew Nick and Tom would carry on showing off and making complete fools of themselves as they tried to impress them. By the time we drove away from La Migoua, it was clear that Nick had met his match with Nigella and Thomasina – and that, for him, the holiday was well and truly over.

The changeover day also gave me the interesting opportunity of seeing Freddie and Hylan together for the first time ever. What surprised me most was how nice they were to each other, but it did make me wonder how Dee could have been in love with two such different men. Those differences became more obvious as the day wore on. By the afternoon Freddie was dressed for the beach like a character from *It Ain't Half Hot Mum* – khaki shorts pulled up over his stomach, a cotton shirt and long grey socks. In stark contrast, Hylan had changed into his travel wear for the overnight train, which was a light brown suede suit with tassels on the arms and knee-high black boots. As he walked to the car, Nick burst out laughing and told him he looked like the black sheriff from *Blazing Saddles*, which he didn't seem to mind at all.

On the overnight sleeper to Calais I had one last chance to see Dee at her best before heading off to join my family in Scotland. Sharing a six-berth couchette with an elderly French couple, the heat and smell of sweaty bodies in the compartment was awful. The French couple, who were worried about suffocating, wanted the door left open to let some fresh air in. Dee, however, was worried someone would steal all our luggage and wanted the door closed and locked. In the middle of the night I was woken by a lot of shouting and saw the French couple trying to pull the door open and Dee trying to push it shut.

'Non, fermez la porte,' said Dee, then 'Goddam it, let go!'

'Non, s'il vous plaît, madame.'

'Let me shut the fucking door!'

'Non, madame, arrêtez, s'il vous plaît.'

Then Dee finally exploded, 'Oh Jesus H Fucking Christ. Do you think the Americans went to all that trouble to save your sorry asses in the war so you could treat us like this? Let me shut the goddamn door.'

The old man said something back to Dee that I hadn't learned at school, and it was Hylan, as usual, who had to step in and calm everyone down. Still wearing his sheriff's outfit, it really was like a scene from *Blazing Saddles*. I think the problem was that Dee always felt certain types of French people owed her one. This might have had something to do with the fact that she believed Freddie had been personally responsible for the liberation of France in 1944. The truth was that Freddie had been posted to Paris as an SOE officer just after the liberation. He hadn't been part of the liberation itself but had instead cruised around Paris in a chauffeur-driven Bugatti with an army radio installed so he could report back on how it was all going. From what Dad told me, Freddie spent most of his time drinking champagne, chasing women and hobnobbing with other philosophers in a place called the Café de Flore.

Exhausted, we arrived back in London the next day with plenty of time for me to catch the overnight sleeper to Scotland that evening. As a parting treat, and perhaps to make up for being so mean, Dee took me to Bayswater for a Chinese meal and a trip to the American Food Store on Queensway. She then put me on the Inverness train as I hauled a lifetime's supply of Marshmallow Fluff, Kool-Aid and Lucky Charms breakfast cereal into my sleeper compartment and settled down in my bunk. As I was rocked to sleep by the rhythm of the train, I breathed a sigh of relief knowing I was on my way to the Old Manse, where I wouldn't be undermined or have my confidence kicked into the dirt by bullies like Nick or the gangs at school.

19

THE MAN FROM THE BBC

From my bedroom window on the top floor of the Old Manse I can see all the way to the end of the Green Road. It's exactly one mile long and goes from the village war memorial to the bottom of a hill before turning off towards the River Spey. The Green Road is so straight you'd think it had been built by the Romans, but it means you can see any car approaching the village long before it arrives. This is something I've done many times when I've been excited about the arrival of a visitor. On this occasion the whole house was excited about the arrival of a man from the BBC. He was flying up from London to see Dad and talk to him about making a television series that he claimed could change his life. Apart from the time Dad had gone back to London on the same day we'd arrived, no one had ever come all the way from London just for the day, so it must have been a big thing.

'I can see him, he's nearly here!' I yelled as soon as I saw the white taxi turning the corner onto the Green Road. 'Five minutes at most!'

I raced down the stairs and burst into the kitchen, where Mum had already started making the coffee. From the kitchen window I could see the taxi coming through the square and pulling up outside our gate. A man with messy black hair and thick-rimmed glasses got out, walked up the garden path and

The Green Road, Archiestown

knocked on the front door. He was carrying a briefcase and was dressed like someone who'd clearly come from an office. Dad took him straight into the kitchen and shut the door. They were in there for hours, and when they finally came out they both looked really pleased and asked us to join them for a walk. They carried on talking about what Dad wanted to do in this television series and the things that interested him. The man with the glasses seemed just as enthusiastic as Dad.

As soon as the taxi headed back down the Green Road, Dad started telling us what they'd talked about. He started by saying how there had been only two big and important series on television: *Civilisation,* with a man called Kenneth Something-or-Other, and *The Ascent of Man,* with a man Dad liked, called Dr Bronowski. I remembered this man because he had a strong Polish accent and Dad sometimes mimicked him when he was explaining how something worked or had been built in a particular way. The series the BBC wanted Dad to do was to be called *The Body in Question,* and it was going to be as big and important as *Civilisation* and *The Ascent of*

Man. Dad was so chuffed, and said that after all these years of doing work he called 'fatuous and loathsome' he was finally being asked to do something serious that he could feel proud of. It would be something where he could, in a way, go back to medicine and at the same time teach people about everything he had loved about being a doctor and talk about what he knew about the human body. The man from the BBC said it would be the biggest science project the BBC had ever made and would be seen all over the world.

Soon after the BBC man left, Nick and Caroline Garland arrived with their two children, Alexander and Theo. The Garlands are Mum and Dad's closest friends and come to stay with us every year. Dad is always happy to be in Scotland when Nick is there because they're best friends and they can talk together about their lives, which is something I think Dad needs to do. His life might have been quite different if he'd had a brother to compete with and – like Tom does with me – tell him when he's being an idiot. Nick is probably the closest he'll ever get to having a brother, and when he's around it makes a big difference to Dad's mood and outlook on pretty much everything. He's one of the few people who can bring Dad round from whatever's making him unhappy and get him to see all the positive things in his life. The most important thing is that Nick and Dad make each other laugh.

Dad basically thinks his life has been a total waste of time. According to him, everything he's done has amounted to nothing, which I've never understood because I don't know anyone else's dad who's done as much mine. And it doesn't matter how many times everyone tells him this, he still falls into these depressions and then finds it hard to get out of them. He does in the end, but getting there can be hard on all of us, especially Mum. She says it often starts in the middle

Dad and Nick Garland, Scotland, 1976

of the night, when he wakes her up to tell her how his life has been worthless. At other times it's because he doesn't like what he's working on and wants to get out of it and feels trapped. Someone told Mum it could be something to do with his blood sugar, which might get low in the middle of the night. So she bought a fancy box to go by his bed and filled it with his favourite biscuits. That didn't work, but what usually does is his having Nick Garland around.

Dad told Nick about his big new television series and how

Dad playing Dr Bronowski, with me, Duffus Castle, Moray

making it was going to be like having a magic carpet. All he
would have to say is, 'Do you know, there's a fascinating tribe
in Africa with a witch doctor?' and whoosh, off they'd go to
Africa to meet the tribe. He might mention an important
painting of a man having his leg chopped off by surgeons,
which happens to be in a museum in Italy, and whoosh again,
off they'd go to Italy. Nick, like all of us, only wants Dad to
be happy – and for the first time in ages it really seemed like
he was. For the rest of the holiday it was like he was on some
kind of happy pill, and it felt as if the sun shone brighter
every day.

A lot of the time, when Nick and Dad are together, it's like
watching a comedy sketch unfold in front of you. On a trip
to the beach that summer we stopped off to look at a ruined
castle. All that was left of it were the walls, and you could
see the empty doorways on the upper floors that now led
nowhere. Dad started climbing over the ramparts and then
disappeared. We were worried he might have fallen down a

gap between the walls and everyone started searching for him. Then he suddenly reappeared in one of the doorways on the first floor, where there had once been a staircase. Looking out over the ruins he started telling us, in a Polish accent like Dr Bronowski, how the castle had been built before the invention of stairs, which made life very difficult for its occupants.

Always, within days of the Garlands returning to London, a big fat envelope turns up in the post. Inside the envelope is a letter from Nick made up of ten or more pages of thin white drawing paper. Nick is a cartoonist for a newspaper and writes these brilliant letters filled with cartoon scenes from the holiday.

Garland car being repaired in Scotland after a crash

The Garland family returning from Scotland without their car

The Garlands and the Millers

Because Dad was in *Beyond the Fringe* some people only seem to know him for being a comedian and actor, so I often get asked what it's like living with a joker. They say things like 'It must be a right laugh all the time at your house!' I don't know why they think comedians spend all day telling jokes. I know Dad can be funny but he's never 'comedy funny', like the Goodies or Monty Python. We have a record of *Beyond the Fringe* at home, which Tom and I tried to listen to and pretended to laugh at, but we didn't really get the jokes and it just sounded very old-fashioned. I suppose it didn't help that we couldn't see what they were doing on stage.

Dad doesn't want to be known for being funny; he wants everyone to see him as a serious person with serious thoughts and ideas. He says he was so happy when he was a doctor, and that he would have been a really good one had he stuck at it. He'd done lots of comedy shows at university, and when he was at medical school someone asked him to come to the Edinburgh Festival and be in a sketch show for two weeks. He thought he could take a short break and be back in London, working as a doctor, before anyone noticed. That show was *Beyond the Fringe*, and he never went back to being a doctor ever again. He said it was as if he'd been tricked into going through a door that was slammed shut behind him and he was trapped on a stage and never allowed to go back to what he really loved. He says he's been trying to find the key to that door ever since. Now he'd been given this series for the BBC, it was clear that *The Body in Question* was his chance to go back through that door.

I think Dad likes making people laugh because he loves having an audience, especially when he tells one of his mad jokes. They're nothing like the ones I know, as his are all quite complicated and hard to remember. When I tell him one of my jokes, he doesn't even try to laugh. He just sighs and says, 'You do know why that joke isn't funny, don't you?' Then he starts explaining in detail exactly what makes a joke funny, and then ends up telling his 'Skinner and Tupper' joke as an example. Alan must have heard that one a hundred times but it still makes him laugh. He has this deal with Dad that, when one of them dies, the other has to tell this joke at their funeral. I know why the 'Skinner and Tupper' joke is funny: it's about someone who is given a joke to tell, which he then can't remember and gets completely wrong and it ends up being really rude, and that's what's funny about it. So, basically, it's about how *not* to tell a joke. So Dad tells it for two reasons: to make you laugh and to show you why you should never tell jokes unless you're very good at them. He warned me that if I ever tried telling any of his jokes I would hear him in my head screaming, 'For Christ's sake, don't tell that joke!'

I've only once broken Dad's golden rule. It was with Simon Elms's mum and dad, when I went for supper. Dad was right and I wished straight away that I'd listened to him. As I was telling the joke it was as if he was at the back of the room staring at me and shouting, 'Stop now before you make a complete fool of yourself!' I didn't stop, and just as Dad had warned me – I even got the punchline wrong. Simon's mum and dad didn't laugh, and we all sat there in excruciating silence for what seemed like ages.

I did actually meet some real comedians a few years ago when Dad did a show called *The Secret Policeman's Ball*, which John Cleese had asked him to direct and perform in. It was for charity and had all these famous comedians doing their best sketches for three nights in a West End theatre. Monty Python were there, as well as the Goodies along with *Beyond the Fringe* and others like Eleanor Bron, John Bird and John Fortune. Barry Humphries was in it as well. He was doing another show in the West End and had to walk from the other theatre to do his sketch still dressed as Dame Edna.

Dad, Alan and Peter Cook rehearsed their sketches from *Beyond the Fringe* in our sitting room at Gloucester Crescent. Terry Jones and John Cleese from Monty Python came too, because Dudley Moore was in America and they were standing in for him in two of the sketches. Mum and Dad's friend Roger Graef was making a television programme about the whole thing, so there was also a film crew. And I was allowed to sit and watch them rehearse. It was pretty crowded. Seeing them all work together was when I first realised how hard it is to be properly funny. They didn't just come up with a joke and tell it. They spent ages discussing each line, how they'd act it out and then dissecting the jokes and working on them until the whole thing was perfect. They also did quite a bit of sitting around chatting and laughing about the old days. I am used to seeing Alan and Dad together, but it was strange to see them actually working together like they would have done before I was born. They were good together, so I was surprised when Alan asked Terry Jones how Monty Python had managed to stay together for so long and then casually told him that he didn't think he could ever work with Dad again. I thought this was sad, especially as they're such good friends, but then maybe that's why.

The Secret Policeman's Ball was the first time I'd ever seen Dad on stage, and he was brilliant. I felt so proud of him as he was so funny and, as it turned out, a really good actor too. I realised it was likely to be the first and only time I'd ever get to see him perform sketches from *Beyond the Fringe* – and this time I got the jokes. They did one I really liked called

The original 1961 *Beyond the Fringe* sketch 'So
That's The Way You Like It': Jonathan Miller, Peter
Cook, Dudley Moore and Alan Bennett

'So That's The Way You Like It', based on Shakespeare. The
four come on wearing these mad medieval hats and speaking
in a silly rhyming Shakespearian way. Terry Jones had a bit
where he sings to Alan with a violin. He'd borrowed my violin
for the sketch and plucked it very badly while singing like a
whining cat. I was impressed by the way Dad was still able to
remember all his lines. There's a bit where he has to say them
very fast without pausing and then finishes off with

I most royally shall now to bed,
To sleep off all the nonsense I've just said

which made me really laugh. Peter was drunk on the night and had trouble remembering his lines, but he was still very funny and it didn't seem to put the others off. Dad did his philosophers' sketch with John Cleese, and Peter managed to do his one about the miner who wanted to be a judge. Then at the end of the night everyone came on stage and sang the Lumberjack song, which I wasn't sure Dad knew the words for.

20

THE MAGIC CARPET

Dad had got his magic carpet from the BBC and was travelling everywhere with it, filming for *The Body in Question*. He'd been all over the world visiting so many of the places he'd always wanted to go to: Bolivia, Peru, Greece, the Sudan and more. He went to meet a tribe who live in the jungle in the Sudan and have a witch doctor. According to Dad, they live a very simple life with none of the modern luxuries we have at home, and he thought it would be interesting to be like Dr Livingstone, the explorer of the Nile, and introduce them to some of the things we take for granted. The man from the BBC thought cardigans from Marks and Spencer would be good, so he filled two suitcases with them. Dad had a more old-fashioned idea. He went to the newsagents in Inverness Street and bought loads of Old Holborn tobacco and Rizla papers.

The children from the tribe loved their cardigans, but when the crew met the chief of the tribe the first thing he did was offer Dad a Marlboro cigarette. The chief also had a big fridge he'd been given by a charity to store medicines. Seeing as how they had their own witch doctor, he decided to use the fridge to keep tins of beer cool. I think Dad was a little disappointed as he really had gone with this romantic idea that he would be one of the first Westerners to meet the tribe, but clearly this wasn't the case.

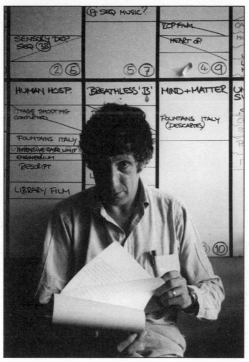

Dad, production office at the BBC for *The Body in Question*

Besides all the travelling, a lot of the filming took place in a studio in Ealing, in west London. The producer told the designer that he wanted a set that looked and felt like the inside of Dad's head. It needed to be filled with all the kinds of things that interested him. Things to do with science and medicine, as well as things from the world of art. He ended up building a big circular room with a round table in the middle. Like the sitting room at Gloucester Crescent, they filled it with animal skeletons, souvenirs collected from Dad's travels, medical instruments, a microscope, sculptures, paintings, an African pot and hundreds of other objects. This was the equivalent of Dad's dream garden shed. It was a place where he could hang out, play at being a doctor and teach the world everything he knew.

One day Dad and his film crew came to Gloucester Crescent and interviewed me. He wanted to ask me about what
I'd felt when I was ill and became delirious with a dangerously
high temperature. This had happened a few times, and when
it did, I'd have these waking nightmares where my hands felt
enormous, even though I could see they were normal. Dad
thought this was fascinating and wanted to use me to talk
about how your brain can feel different things from what you
see. I was a bit nervous at first as the idea of talking about
something that only happened when I was delirious, and
which I didn't fully understand, might make me look like I
was mad or talking rubbish. Dad assured me people would
find it interesting and I'd get a day off school and it would be
exciting to have a film crew come to the house just to film me.
In the end I wasn't sure what convinced me: the chance to be
in one of Dad's television programmes and seen by millions
of people, or getting a day off school.

For the last few years at Pimlico the white gangs continued
telling me that they knew where I lived and that they would
come and get me when I was least expecting it. They never
did, but I carried on believing they were outside the house,
hiding in the shadows. I was worn down and stressed out
from worrying about it, and every night I would switch off
the lights so I could check outside to see if anyone was out
there. For me, this meant Gloucester Crescent stopped feeling
like the place where I felt safe and in my head was split into
two different zones: there was out front on the street, which
was as dangerous and frightening as school, and then the
back, with its safe and protected gardens where no one could
get to me and where I felt I could relax and breathe. In the
end, the obvious thing to do was to plead with Mum to let me

move to a room at the back of the house. When Jeanie moved out to live with her boyfriend, Robert, Mum let me have her room. It's a quiet and sunny room that looks out across the gardens of the Crescent. It's also identical to Conrad's room two doors down. Being on the same floor, we were able to run a wire between our two houses so we would talk to each other on a radio and send coded messages.

The view from this room opened up a whole new world and often feels like the Hitchcock film *Rear Window*. It's calm and peaceful, and I can spend hours watching life go on in the houses in Regent's Park Terrace. I can see the back of Freddie Ayer as he works at the large round table in his sitting room. A few doors from the Ayers' is the writer V. S. Pritchett, who I occasionally see wandering around naked before getting dressed and settling down at his desk. Next door to him are the two Harrison sisters, who'd been at Primrose Hill School with me and would occasionally wave from their house. This is without doubt my favourite side of Gloucester Crescent, and I felt calmer, safer and happier once I'd moved to the back of the house.

The other thing I look straight into from my room is a small conservatory that comes off the back of the Ayer's house. One weekend Dee asked me to help plant a small bag of marijuana seeds that Hylan had given her. We sat in the kitchen and chatted while she carefully laid the seeds out on damp tissues. By the following weekend the seeds had sprouted with these little green shoots, and we moved them one by one into pots of earth and placed each one in the conservatory. Every day from my bedroom window I could see Dee in the conservatory watering and looking after these little plants. Within a few weeks the seeds had grown into small bushes, and by the following month they were enormous and completely filled the conservatory. Every now and then Dee would appear between the bushes, clip off a few stems and disappear back upstairs. It was around this time, on a visit for French toast and milk shakes, that Dee presented me with one of these plants. 'Here,' she said, handing me a pot with a four-foot marijuana plant in it. 'You helped me plant this little guy. Take it home and enjoy it.' More excited by my gardening skills than the fact that I was now the owner of an illegal drug, I carefully carried it over the garden wall. I took it up three flights of stairs and placed it on the table by my bedroom window. The smell, I noticed immediately, was overpowering, but I liked the way this enormous plant added colour and life to my bedroom. I didn't know what I was going to do with it, other than let it grow bigger, as I had no desire to chop it down, hang it up to dry and smoke it.

As it turned out, I wasn't given the chance to do any of these things. As soon as Mum walked through the front door, I heard her yelling my name from two floors below. I ran onto the landing and innocently called down the stairs. There was no fooling my mother. 'I can smell that plant from Inverness Street,' she said. 'Take it straight back to Dee's before the police show up.' My plant and where it came from clearly needed no introduction. Everyone on our side of the Crescent, including my mother, knew about Dee's marijuana plantation as it was right there in the conservatory for everyone to see. So that was that – back across the garden wall we went, and the plant was returned and put back with the rest of Dee's crop.

Dee called later to apologise to Mum, who seemed more concerned that our family could have been arrested than that I might have spent all summer off my head. But things soon settled down and Dee went back to pruning, drying and giving cuttings from her plants away to friends as presents.

The Miller family at the wedding of Gully
Wells and Peter Foges, 1978

Nick managed to pilfer a few stems for himself and spent
much of his time lying on his bed smoking joints and reading
comics.

While Dee was busily attending to her marijuana plants,
Gully had finally found herself a boyfriend she considered
worth marrying. He's called Peter Foges, and he works as
a producer at the BBC. Dee wasn't at all sure about Peter,
believing he wasn't good enough for her daughter. I think she
had this fantasy that Gully would marry an Austrian prince
with a castle in the Alps, and she and Hylan, or even Freddie,
would get to spend Christmases drinking schnapps, dressed
in Lederhosen and schmoozing with royalty. But Gully was
certain Peter was the right man for her, and within months of
meeting they were married. The wedding party was at a restaurant in Chelsea. With the film of *Grease* having just come
out, I'd learned a bad version of rock 'n' roll dancing and
spent the whole evening on the dance floor making a fool of
myself in front of Gully's somewhat alarmed girlfriends.

A few months later Peter was offered the job of running
the BBC's offices in New York and they left London for ever.

I don't know what it is about New York, but it seems to have this effect on people. When they get tired of Gloucester Crescent, they just pack their bags, go to New York and never come back.

21

HOPE - SUMMER 1978

I've never seen Dad cook anything other than coffee or tea, and that doesn't really count. The only time I've seen him near the cooker is when he's reading something to Mum while she's making supper. So I was quite surprised to see him standing over the cooker, alone, trying to boil peas in a saucepan. It also seemed to be the only thing on the menu for lunch. Mum had gone into hospital that morning, and up until this point no one had told us why. I knew she'd had a pain in her stomach for some time and was going to see someone about it, but I never thought it would mean she would actually have to stay in hospital. Tom, Kate and I sat quietly watching Dad as he stared down at the peas.

The silence was broken by him shouting 'FUCK!' The saucepan had tipped over, and the peas were now rolling in every direction across the kitchen floor. I couldn't bear to see Dad's hopelessness and frustration as he crawled around the floor trying to pick up the hot peas with his hands. I ran over and joined him and, having grabbed the dustpan and brush, made a better job of clearing them up than he did.

'I don't know how we're going to cope without your mother,' Dad said. At that moment my body went completely cold and I felt sick.

'Mum's coming back, isn't she? She's not that ill?' I asked.

'I'm afraid she's very ill and I'm not sure what's going to happen, but either way it's a disaster.'

Tom and Kate hadn't moved from the table and were now looking down at both of us on the floor. They started to cry as they talked over each other, asking Dad for any information. Picking himself up off the floor, all Dad was prepared to tell us was that they'd found a large lump in Mum's stomach and they weren't sure what it was. Unlike most people, Dad always prefers to err on the side of catastrophe than caution. At this moment I was trying to decide which one he was going for. If he was right, it was more than a disaster; it was curtains for our family and everything that was steady and stable in our lives. My head was spinning as a million thoughts ran through it. Mum was not the sort of person you ever expected to die. At least not until I was a grown-up with my own children and she was a grandmother. As much as I dreaded it happening, with his smoking and talk of killing himself I always felt I'd be ready for Dad's death. Mum, however, was the rock in our family: always there, always well, *and* she's a doctor. Doctors didn't get sick.

My next question came with the answer I had most dreaded. 'What do they think that lump in her tummy is?'

'Cancer,' Dad said without a pause.

Other than the gangs at school, who might or might not be outside waiting to kill me, there were two other scenarios that really scared me. They were ones that I knew I had no control over and which could take me or those close to me without any debate: nuclear war and cancer. Both had been described to me in detail on many occasions by Dad. Nuclear war was terrifying for all the obvious reasons and, as Dad liked telling us, would create panic everywhere, and there would be nothing we could do to stop it. It would be the end of the world and we'd all be dead, which, in a strange way, seemed better than the second scenario – cancer. Cancer could creep up out of nowhere and grab one of us at any time. With cancer, we would all be left to grieve and deal with that one person having gone. Now it was about to come and take my mother. I asked Dad if there was any good news, but he said, at the moment, no.

He at least had the good sense to call Jeanie, who by teatime had come over, so there would be proper food for supper and we weren't going to starve. When Dad was out of the room, Jeanie explained that no one knew what the lump in Mum's stomach was, and until they did, it could be anything.

The hospital Mum was in was the National Temperance, a somewhat shabby Victorian building on Hampstead Road. This happened to be on the 24 bus route from school, and there was a stop right outside the front door of the hospital. The next day, without telling anyone, I made a plan to get off the bus and see if I could find Mum and hear about it from her.

She had her own room, which looked out over Hampstead Road and the side of Euston Station. The whole place smelled of boiled cabbage, sick and disinfectant. I had only ever seen Mum lying in her own bed, so seeing her pale and ill in a hospital bed was really frightening. I did everything I could not to cry as I came out with what I'd been waiting to ask all day: 'Dad told us what you have is serious and that you might die.'

'Oh God, did he? Silly arse, that wasn't how I suggested he put it.'

'He told us when he was trying to make us lunch when he dropped the peas all over the kitchen floor.' I don't know why I told her this detail and I immediately regretted it. She now looked concerned about what was going on at home, and what Tom, Kate and I were being told, and fed.

I could barely bring myself to ask the next three words, which had been screaming in my head since the peas incident. 'Is it cancer?'

'I don't know. And the doctors won't know anything until they remove the lump and take a proper look at it.'

'So you mean it might *not* be cancer?'

'That's right, it might not be, and we can only hope it's not.'

At this point I couldn't hold back any longer and burst into tears. I think I was partly crying with relief that cancer wasn't a definite but also because I hadn't thought about anything else all day and had struggled not to cry at school. As I rested my head on Mum's side, I sobbed into the covers on her bed. She stroked my hair as she tried to soothe and comfort me. The word 'hope' was comfort enough. It was the word I'd been waiting for and that I could hang on to. I couldn't pray, as I don't believe in God, but I could at least hope.

I couldn't bear the idea of leaving Mum on her own in this awful, lonely hospital room, but I could see she was tired and trying to stay awake for me. In the end, it was the nurse who told me I needed to leave and let her sleep. At home, Jeanie would be doing what she could to hold things together. Dad would be on the phone calling their friends to tell them everything he knew about the worst possible scenario. If Mum was going to die, we would need someone to look after us who could do a better job than Dad. There was no way he would ever be able to cope – not unless he married someone else, and right now that idea was unthinkable. I'm sure there were plenty of women waiting in the wings, but no one could ever replace Mum.

Back on the 24 bus, in spite of the hope, I started to think about which of Mum and Dad's friends or families could take us all in: the Garlands might be good, or Uncle Karl and Aunt Jane. Now that Gully was married and living in New York there might be room at the Ayers. Then again, I wasn't sure how having that 'bloody William Miller' living in his house would go down with Freddie. Another possibility crossed my mind: the three of us could all be split up and we might each be sent to live with a family of our choice. If that was going to happen, I would need to choose someone who really loved me and would look after me as well as Mum did. That evening, when Dad left the house to visit Mum, I called the only person I knew who would fill the role: Stella Coltman-Rogers.

Obviously it was much too early to come out with my plan, and, should the worst actually happen, then the suggestion would have to come from Stella rather than me. I told her everything Mum had told me in the hospital, as well as Dad's less positive take. In Dad's scenario there would be months of brutal cancer treatment, followed by inevitable death. Stella's immediate response to this was 'Rubbish. Your mother will get through this and everything will be fine.' Stella's optimism gave new life to the word hope. She also made a suggestion that added a layer of icing to this cake and would be something to look forward to. Mum had told me that if she was all clear after the operation she would need to convalesce for several weeks. This would coincide with the beginning of the summer holiday. There was no way we could get Mum to Scotland, but she would need fresh air and a lot of looking after. Stella suggested that the best place for this would be Stanage – and I could hardly have agreed more.

A few days later they operated and removed the lump from Mum's stomach. And to everyone's relief, not least Dad's, they confirmed that it wasn't cancer and Mum was given the all-clear. After everything we'd been through over the last week or so, it was as if we'd all been given a second chance. I felt like I'd been taken right to the edge of a cliff and forced to look over the edge at what life would be like without Mum and the safe and secure world we'd grown up in.

Now I knew she wasn't going to die I longed for life at Gloucester Crescent to return to normal. There would be a summer of Mum convalescing and then we would go back to school and Mum to work. She would always be there when we got home, and meals would be cooked effortlessly, with Alan coming over to eat them with us. Dad would come and go and finally finish making *The Body in Question*.

Before Mum went into hospital I'd gone with her to a garage in Euston to buy our new family car. She'd chosen an enormous brand-new estate car, which we'd seen advertised on television. In the advert there was a woman in a flowing blue dress throwing herself over the car and running her hands over its body. An unseen chorus kept singing 'Peugeot 504', followed by the woman in the dress looking into the camera and whispering words like 'Luxury', 'Ultimate' and 'Refinement'. I wasn't sure if it was the ad that swung it for Mum or the salesman, who was going overboard with his pitch. We'd driven to the showroom in our beaten-up Volkswagen Variant, and the man did his best to impress Mum with the things he could see we'd never had before: a built-in radio-tape player (brilliant), an electric aerial and three rows of plush velour seats (also brilliant, though I didn't know what plush velour was). Mum wrote a cheque and we left to go home with her half-joking that Dad was going to kill her. At the time she probably didn't think she'd live to see the car anyway and thought she'd be doing him a favour by at least leaving him with a reliable family car to drive us around in when she'd gone.

Now Mum wasn't going to die, but she was still in hospital recovering from her operation when the garage called to say the car was ready to be collected. This meant I was the only other person who knew where the showroom was, so I went with Dad to collect it. With the house in Scotland and weekends at friends in the country, a large family car was essential. In spite of this, Dad thought buying any kind of car was foolish and unnecessary. Getting him to collect our brand-new car from the showroom would only be a terrible reminder that money had left his bank account. Dad wasn't a miser, but he had a constant fear of ending up broke, and he was determined to prove that Mum had bought this car in a moment of madness. This time he was in luck, and his theory was about to be helped by the man in the showroom.

Being very small, the man had moved the driver's seat as far forward as possible so he could reach the pedals when he drove the car to the front of the showroom. He then forgot to move the seat back when it was time for Dad to get in. When Dad tried to get in the car, he could barely get one leg behind the steering wheel, let alone the rest of his body. He got out and tried again, but whichever angle he tried to position his legs at, he just couldn't get in the car. Stepping back out again, he slammed the door shut. 'That's it. Another waste of bloody money. Your mother has managed to buy the biggest car in the world, and it was built for a midget.' The salesman was trying to apologise for leaving the seat forward, but Dad was having none of it. He'd been delivered a gift on a plate and was clearly thrilled to have it in order to prove that this car was a complete waste of money. He told the salesman that Mum would be in touch for a full refund, and we walked off leaving the car where it was.

Several days later, after I explained to Mum what had

happened, she managed to persuade Dad to calm down and give it another go. Much to his disappointment, it was proved that the seat could be moved back and that there was more than enough room for someone as tall as him. This was a great relief, as it was crucial for Dad to be able to drive our enormous new car. He had to get us to Stanage so he could leave Mum, Kate and me with Stella and get himself back to London for work. Before he did this, he also had to drive Tom to Heathrow and put him on a flight to New York. Tom was spending the summer with old friends of Mum and Dad's called the Aldriches, who had five daughters, an apartment in Manhattan and a farm in Connecticut.

Stella had done an amazing job getting Stanage ready for Mum, and had prepared one of the nicest rooms in the house for her to convalesce in. It was filled with flowers and had an enormous and very comfortable bed. Mum could sit up in it and look down the drive and across a distant valley towards the Clee Hills. A large handbell had been placed by the bed, which she was told to ring whenever she needed anything. Sue came up for our first weekend, and Kate and I were left to run wild as Mum got better and her strength returned. I knew I would have been happy living at Stanage with Stella for the rest of my childhood, but now I didn't need to think about that. Hope had won the day, and I had my mum back. By the end of the summer we would all be in Gloucester Crescent and our lives would be back to normal, and Stella and Stanage would always be there.

22

IT'LL BE ALL RIGHT
ON THE NIGHT

Sometimes, when something big and brilliant happens, you forget the bad times you went through to get there. I think for Dad *The Body in Question* is one of those. Once he'd finished making it, and it was finally on the television – with a big a book in the shops to go with it – he forgot about all the bad stuff. Dad's problem has always been that when people say nice things and ask him to take on a new project or, as Mum calls it, 'ask him to come out to play', he always says yes. He never says, 'Great, but here's the deal: I'll do this bit, but someone else will have to do the others.' In the case of *The Body in Question*, the man from the BBC flew all the way to Scotland to tell him they were going to give him his own massive television series, which would be as big as Dr Bronowski's. He would get to talk about all the things he loves and interest him the most. When the man said, 'Oh, and by the way, you're also going to have to write the whole thing, and did I mention a book to go with it?' Dad should have said, 'Hang on a minute, Mr BBC Man.' Before suggesting this, the man from the BBC should have come round to Gloucester Crescent, sat in our garden and listened to Dad's slow and painful typing and watched him lying on the floor of his study telling us all how he was going to kill himself.

Once Dad started making the series, it quickly became clear that he'd taken on far too much and it was all starting to fall apart. He felt that part of the problem was that they didn't get what he was all about, or the way he wanted to do things. Soon everything was running way behind schedule and the people at the BBC were starting to panic. On top of all this he had the book hanging over him, which he realised he didn't have time to write, and people from the BBC and his publishers kept calling up to ask how it was going. When Dad feels trapped like this, he gets desperate and just wants to escape. It was made worse knowing how big the whole project was and that jumping ship would let so many people down.

We could all see how much pain he was in. Every night he would come home from the studio and tell us he was living in hell and that he wanted to die. We all found this distressing, especially as there was nothing we could do or say to stop him feeling like this. Before long he was telling Mum the only way out was to kill himself. Although I'd heard this all before, I'd never seen him this low, and it frightened me more than ever. It wasn't helped by a recurring nightmare I was having where he would try to throw himself out of the top-floor window of our house but it didn't work and like a madman he would frantically keep running back into the house and up the stairs again to give it another go.

Then, just when we thought there was no way out, two amazing people came along who made Dad feel like everything might be possible. The first was a nice man called Patrick Uden, who Dad then made the BBC put on the project to produce the series. Patrick changed all sorts of things, but the most important thing was that he understood how Dad's mind worked. He knew how to bring together all of his wild and crazy ideas about science, art and medicine and make something exciting out of them all. It was Patrick's idea to make the set like the inside of Dad's head, and he also knew how to write the scripts so he took that off his hands as well. He could see that letting Dad be himself was going to get the best results. The other person who helped Dad and cheered him up was his friend Susannah Clapp, who's a writer and an editor. She would meet Dad every night at a Greek restaurant in Camden Town and work with him on the book. Although he was completely exhausted after the day's filming, he would spend hours working with Susannah over taramasalata and kebabs as they wrote the book together. So, with Patrick and Susannah, Dad was a lot happier, and stopped going on about killing himself as a way of getting out from doing the series.

By November 1978 it was all over; the series was finally coming out on television, and everyone was so relieved that it had turned out so well in the end. Every Monday night, for the next thirteen weeks, people all over the country were glued to their televisions as Dad took them on a journey of both the human body and what was going around in his head. He hooked himself up to electrodes, made himself sick flying in a biplane pretending to be a red blood cell, made himself faint in a pressure chamber and was the first person ever to dissect a human body on television. The newspapers loved him too, with one calling him the BBC's new Dissector-General – we all thought that was pretty cool. For Dad, it finally gave him the chance he had wanted for so long, to show everyone he could be serious and explain science and medicine to millions of people.

My appearance in the series, talking about my experiences of being delirious, turned out not to have been the smartest idea. I'd been doing everything, over the last year or so, to be as invisible as I could at school, and being on telly only made me stand out. This gave several of the gangs a reason to ratchet up the bullying. Maybe when I agreed to be interviewed I thought they'd all be out mugging people or watching *The Sweeney* or *Cheggers Plays Pop* on a Monday night. But I was wrong – *everyone* was watching *The Body in Question*, which was great for Dad but not so good for me. For weeks afterwards they would stop me in the corridors at school, waving their hands around, shouting, 'Oi, Miller, you tosser, let me tell you about my hands – it's my hands, they're huge!' Then they'd turn their thumping great hands into fists and hit me as hard as they could.

The start of *The Body in Question* also meant we got to have a television back in the house again. The old one had gone a couple of years before when, in a moment of complete fury, Dad unplugged it, took it round the corner and gave it to Arlington House, the place for homeless men. He claimed Tom, Kate and I had stopped reading books because we were too busy watching 'mind-numbing rubbish' on the telly. I'm sure there was some truth to this, but Dad had to take some of the blame. The three of us found that whenever we did 'prise open the covers of a book' (as Dad liked to put it) he always told us we were reading the wrong book. When he discovered I was reading *The Catcher in the Rye*, he said if I was interested in American literature I should read *The Grapes of Wrath*. He'd then ask, every five minutes, if I'd read it. The thing is, I wasn't interested in American literature but I liked J. D. Salinger and I had to read *The Catcher in the Rye* for my O-levels. Dad did this with every book we ever read, so the three of us just stopped reading altogether. Getting rid of the TV didn't stop us watching it, as we just went over the garden wall to the Ayers or the Roebers, where we spent many hours watching theirs.

The week before *The Body in Question* started, I saw Dad walking up Inverness Street carrying a brand-new TV he'd bought at Rumbelows on the high street. It wasn't long before we were back watching endless hours of rubbish and he was furious about the television all over again, despite the fact that he was on it once a week for three months.

Even though we all drove Dad crazy, I was still so proud of him and found it amazing that he could be on the television one day, talking about blood, human organs and chopping up bodies, and the next day be back doing another opera. He was out at the weekends doing book signings for *The Body in Question* and appearing on chat shows to talk about it, but during the week he was rehearsing *The Marriage of Figaro* at a big opera house in central London. Then, after Christmas, he went straight to Frankfurt to do an opera called *The Flying Dutchman*.

When the half-term came in February, I flew out to Germany to stay with him and watch his rehearsals. This was the first time I'd ever stayed on my own with Dad and not had Mum there to look after us. I was curious to see how he coped without her, and my conclusion was: not well. He had a small flat around the corner from the Frankfurt opera house, and the only food he'd bought was a box of an inedible cereal called Fru-Grains, a pint of long-life milk and a grapefruit. Dad's assistant at the opera was a lovely woman called Renate Itgenshorst, who, after asking me one morning what I'd had for breakfast, realised I was going to starve if left with my dad. Renate came over to the flat, packed up my things and took me home to stay with her and her husband in a town outside Frankfurt called Darmstadt. There I would wake up in the morning to a full German breakfast of rye bread, cold meats and cheeses, and then take the train into Frankfurt and watch the rehearsals.

By Easter, Dad was travelling all over America promoting *The Body in Question* and taking Mum and Kate with him. Tom went skiing with friends, and I went to stay at Stanage with Stella for the holidays. The other person staying there was Stella's grandson Jonathan, who had inherited the house and the estate when Guy died but was living most of the time in London. I hadn't met Jonathan before, and although it was obvious Stella adored him, I could see how difficult it was going to be to hand over control to someone else. Guy had always insisted that, when he died, Stella would be allowed to stay at Stanage for ever. Now that Jonathan was taking charge, things were starting to look very different, and none of it was going to be easy for Stella. For over forty years, with Guy's support, she had done a brilliant job running everything. She had managed this through the difficult years of the war, and when they had plenty of money and when they didn't. Guy and Stella never spent money on fancy things, preferring to let the faded sofas and curtains become part of the slightly shabby feel that made the whole place so nice. The house hadn't changed in decades, and even though it was big and grand, one of the things that made it so special was that there was nothing flash about it.

Jonathan is in his twenties and he wanted a place he could fill with grown-up toys and have fun with his friends. He was also talking about spending money on smartening up the house. I could see Stella was going to find this hard to accept. In spite of Guy's wishes, Stella told everyone that once Jonathan got married, she would move into one of the cottages on the estate. There were plenty to choose from, but the idea of Stella leaving Stanage was unthinkable.

When I first met Jonathan, I thought he was different from anyone I'd met at Gloucester Crescent, or school or anywhere else for that matter. He has a relaxed confidence, which I assumed came from having been to public school. He'd actually been to Eton, the poshest public school ever, and a world away from Pimlico, which was probably why I instantly liked him. I knew Stella wanted us to get on, and fortunately, even with a ten-year age difference, Jonathan seemed happy to take me under his wing and let me hang out with him. As the days went by, he took me to explore every corner of the estate and we helped the men who worked on it to clear the woods and put up fences on the farms.

The peace and quiet I loved about Stanage, along with our happy routine, were soon disturbed when a group of Jonathan's friends turned up for the weekend. They arrived in their fast cars, had the same cool confidence as Jonathan and, like him, were friendly and accepting of me. The men seemed to know him from Eton, and their girlfriends were like Gully: well dressed, sexy and a bit intimidating. I discovered that some of the men had also inherited big houses and estates after losing their fathers when they were young. I decided never to tell Dad about Jonathan's friends, as he would have used it to prove one of his favourite so-called theories about the upper classes – that they drink too much and kill themselves driving their cars into trees or falling off their horses. Then, he goes on, their 'dreadful' children get everything before they can read or write and sooner or later end up running the country.

Although they were the kind of people Dad despised, during the time I spent with them they opened my eyes and I found I could see things about myself that I now wanted to change. They all knew with absolute certainty who they were and what they wanted to achieve in life and seemed pretty confident that they could have it. I wanted to be like them and to feel happy and confident about my future. Their world was full of opportunities that I didn't seem to have at Pimlico. I realised I'd been treading water just to survive at school, and that if I stopped I would sink and drown. As I left Stanage and returned to London I knew something had to change. Somehow I had to try again to persuade my Mum and Dad to get me away from Pimlico and send me somewhere else as soon as they could. I had the whole summer to convince them that, when I went back to Pimlico in September, it would be for the last year. After my O-levels I wanted, more than anything, to spend what was left of my school years in a place where I felt at ease, where good things were possible and where I could make anything happen.

23

A VISIT TO AMERICA – JULY/AUGUST 1979

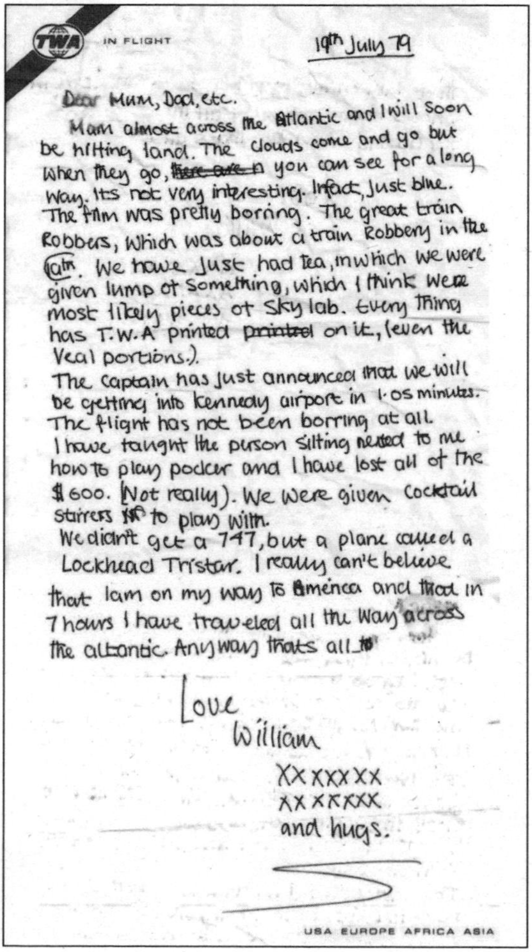

TWA IN FLIGHT

19th July 79

Dear Mum, Dad, etc.

Mam almost across the Atlantic and I will soon be hitting land. The clouds come and go but when they go, in you can see for a long way. Its not very interesting. Infact, just blue. The film was pretty boring. The great train Robbers, which was about a train Robbery in the rain. We have Just had tea, in which we were given lump of something, which I think were most likely pieces of Sky lab. Every thing has T.W.A printed on it, (even the veal portions.)

The captain has just announced that we will be getting into Kennedy airport in 1.05 minutes. The flight has not been borring at all. I have taught the person sitting next to me how to play pocker and I have lost all of the $600. (Not really). We were given cocktail stirrers to play with.

We didn't get a 747, but a plane called a Lockheed Tristar. I really can't believe that I am on my way to America and that in 7 hours I have traveled all the way across the atlantic. Anyway thats all to

Love
William

XX XXXXXX
XX XXXXXX
and hugs.

USA EUROPE AFRICA ASIA

Two of the Aldriches' five daughters had been to visit us in London in the past, and Tom had been to stay with them in New York and Connecticut the summer before. Now, finally, it was my turn to go to America. For me, it was a massive adventure as I hadn't been back to New York since I was born there, fifteen years earlier. I'd always longed to go back and see it for myself – the place of my birth, which Dad talked so much about.

As I was staying for a month, Nelson and Anna-Lou Aldrich decided I'd go to their farm in Connecticut for most of the holiday, and would be with their daughter Nonny, who is my age. Nelson and Anna-Lou would return to New York during the week, leaving me and Nonny with an au pair they had hired to look after us. We would all then come back to New York for a few days at the end of my trip.

Tom had told me a little bit about Nonny from the summer before, so I thought I knew what to expect, although girls at that age can change a lot in a year. One day they're a bit pathetic and immature and they drives you nuts. Then you don't see them for a while, and when you do, they've changed into a woman and you're the one looking pathetic and immature, left behind waiting for your voice to break. So, using this theory, the Nonny that Tom got to know last summer was likely to be very different from the Nonny I was about to meet. The thought that we were going to be thrown together for a month, and that we might become friends, made me both nervous and excited. What's more, I'd be able to get to know her without having other boys, like the Roebers, Simon Elms, Nick Ayer or Tom, breathing down my neck. I wouldn't have them undermining me or pushing me to the back of the room. The trouble was, I still wasn't that confident with girls my own age. I knew I'd have my work cut out, with the first challenge being to keep my cool and show her I was different from American boys and someone worth getting to know.

As I pushed my trolley through customs towards the big metal doors leading to the arrivals hall, I knew Nelson and Nonny would be on the other side, standing by the barrier waiting for me. This was going to be my big arrival moment, and I needed Nonny to think I was everything she'd hoped I'd be. I'd worked out the details of my grand entrance and played them back over and over again in my mind. The automatic doors swung open, but to my surprise Nelson was the only person standing waiting at the barrier and he was grinning back at me. As we made our way through the crowd I tried to show I wasn't bothered and to hide my disappointment at Nonny not being there. For one awful moment it dawned on me that the plan could have changed without me knowing; Nonny had gone elsewhere for the summer and it was going to be just me, Nelson and Anna-Lou in Connecticut. Trying not to show my horror of the possible situation I casually dropped the question: 'Where's Nonny?'

To my relief, Nelson informed me that she was on her way from Los Angeles and flying into the same terminal an hour later. A thought crossed my mind: if I was the one now casually waiting at the barrier, the roles would be reversed and I would be the one looking cool and relaxed. I seriously thought this plan might work, until Nelson and I settled down in an airport café to wait for Nonny's flight to land. I've always liked Nelson, with his Robert Redford film star looks, but the picture he painted of Nonny's trip to Los Angeles did not look good for me, and he was enjoying telling me about it: it turned out she'd been to visit her big sister, Bibi. That's nice for Nonny, I thought at first – sisters together sightseeing and swimming in the sea. Then Nelson went on: 'Those Californian boys will have thought Nonny a real sweetie.' He followed this with a forced laugh then a hard suck on his cigarette and raising of an eyebrow to say 'you know what I mean?' I did, and my heart sank with this news. How was I ever going to compete with Californian boys? I'd seen them in a documentary about skateboarders and I didn't stand a chance. I'd just flown in from a hotbed of corduroy-wearing intellectuals in Gloucester Crescent and she was flying in from one of the coolest cities in America, where she'd been hanging out with tanned skateboarders with muscles where every other word would have been 'Cool, Man' or 'Dude' and they would have all had sun-bleached long blond hair. Nelson must have seen my fear, and he carried on. According to him, it was more than likely Bibi would have taken Nonny out clubbing and introduced her to older boys with jobs and cars and cool tastes in music.

Eventually, we returned to the arrivals hall and took our place at the barrier and waited. My mind was spinning when the doors finally swung open. There she was, with her tangled curly hair falling over her shoulders, looking like she'd just got out of bed. She had the swagger and maturity I had both hoped for before and dreaded now. She might as well have been holding a sign that said: 'I've been in LA with older boys and I've been having sex.' My plan now had failure written all over it. What little confidence I'd arrived with had vaporised into the ceiling of the arrivals hall and I was now feeling dull, English and no more than a little boy.

I had a whole speech worked out with witty jokes about my flight from London along with updates about my family. Instead, now faced with this confident and sexy young woman, I could hardly find the words to put a sentence together. I was trying to work my way towards saying something useful when I was ambushed by something completely new and unexpected: an incredible heat and suffocating humidity which hit me as we stepped out of the air-conditioned TWA terminal. I felt like a lobster that had been taken out of a fridge and dropped into a pot of boiling water. I hadn't experienced anything like it before. The south of France was really hot, but that was a wonderful dry heat that made you feel completely alive. As we searched for the car, Nonny was excitedly telling us all about her trip. With each story I could feel my self-esteem sinking into my shoes. Now, with bright sunlight in my eyes and the feeling that my clothes were melting into my skin, I had become completely mute and depressed. I just wanted to go home.

As soon as we got onto the freeway, with all the windows open and a warm breeze starting to blow around the inside of the car, the heat and humidity began to feel bearable. In the front seat, Nonny's mass of curly brown hair was blowing wildly around her face as she laughed and chatted to Nelson. She was looking so relaxed and pretty, which reminded me of a fantasy I'd had about being older and driving in a sports car with a beautiful girl. As my mind and body started to cool down, the panicky suffocation started to disappear and my spirits lifted as a glimmer of hope returned.

Everything around us was so much bigger than I'd ever imagined: the freeway was enormous, and the cars were like huge boats floating effortlessly on their suspensions. And the drivers were slouched back in their seats, one hand on the wheel and an elbow resting on an open window. In spite of the heat, everyone seemed laid back and untroubled. The vast freeway swept in long curves through the suburbs, past factories, shopping malls and cemeteries. Finally, it rose up onto the Triborough Bridge, and as it did so, the Manhattan skyline came into view. Here were the buildings I knew so well from photographs: the Empire State, the Chrysler and the Twin Towers of the World Trade Center. On the other side of the bridge the road spiralled down onto a slipway that took us south on the FDR Drive, which clung to the edge of the city with the East River on the left-hand side. Before long we turned off and headed into the heart of Manhattan.

We drove through the city, crossing avenues that stretched up- and downtown like canyons, and then through Central Park and out the other side towards the Aldriches' apartment on the Upper West Side. Everything I'd seen in films and on the telly and in the picture books we had everywhere at home was there right in front of my eyes: the sweltering heat, the yellow taxi cabs and streets filled with people of every nationality coming and going in every direction.

The city felt so alive, and I loved everything about it. Thanks to something as simple as my place of birth, I felt a true sense of belonging – I was as much an American citizen as I was British, and that had always made me feel different from the rest of my family. America was my country, and New York was my city.

I would get to spend time in New York properly later on, but a plan had been made for us to head up to Boston the next day to stay with another of Nonny's sisters, Alison, whose boyfriend had managed to get us tickets to see Bob Marley and the Wailers at the Harvard Stadium. I'd never been to a pop concert before, but my hope was that by going to one as massive as Bob Marley I'd get the chance to show Nonny that I had the edge on the boys from LA. I wasn't entirely sure what that edge would be, when there was also the nagging question of having to dance. I'd once made a complete fool of myself to some grown-ups at a wedding, so I knew that dancing to impress a girl was a risky strategy. I'd therefore decided beforehand that if I stuck to some safe but gentle swaying from side to side, maybe with a little foot-tapping, I might just be able to give off the right vibe.

There was no protection from the heat on the stone terraces of the Harvard Stadium. Before the concert started, a tall black man with a long beard and a fancy white suit came onto the stage. Nonny's sister Alison told us he was a famous comedian and civil rights campaigner called Dick Gregory. He gave a long speech, which no one seemed to be listening to, about apartheid in South Africa and the murdering of American Indians. Just as the heat was getting unbearable, Bob Marley came on and kicked off with 'Positive Vibrations'.

It wasn't long before my simple dance plan had gone up in flames. I quickly realised that if you don't get up and dance at a reggae concert, you're going to look and feel pretty stupid. There is nothing that stands out more than a white boy swaying like a moron and tapping his feet. Nonny wasn't holding back, and by the time Bob Marley was singing 'Buffalo Soldier' she'd been adopted by a group of ageing Rastafarians standing next to us and sharing an enormous joint.

By now I had only been in America for three days, but the more time I spent with Nonny the more relaxed I felt around her, and I was beginning to think she might be feeling the same about me. I was even making her laugh, which, as Keith had told me, was the best way to make a girl like you.

On Sunday evening Nelson drove us from Boston to their farm in Connecticut. As the sun went down on the freeway and I sat in the back seat of the car, I noticed Nonny's arm fall between the two front seats and her hand reach back towards me. I wasn't sure if this was my moment. Was she reaching out to take my hand? What if I took it and had misread the signal? Either way, I knew it was now or never and slowly slid my hand into hers and held it. She didn't pull back. I'd never held hands with a girl like this, and my heart was beating so fast I thought I would faint. My terrible jokes and our easy chatting had paid off. This was it: she liked me and I liked her – I had got myself a real girlfriend.

I don't know why the Aldriches call their house a farm. There is nothing farm-like about it, other than it's in the middle of the countryside, next to a field of melons and surrounded by low scrubby woodland that goes on for ever. The house, a mile up a dirt track, is modern, with brown wooden shingles covering the outside walls. On one side are large sliding doors that open onto a deck that wraps around the house. It was here that I stood the next morning, trying to get my bearings, as a beaten-up car came bouncing up the track towards the house. A slim girl in her twenties, with a tight T-shirt, cut-off denim shorts and long red hair, got out of the car and dragged a duffel bag into the house. A few minutes later she reappeared on the deck with Nelson and Nonny. Her name was Doreen, and she had been hired by Anna-Lou as our au pair for the summer. Doreen looked like Daisy Duke from *The Dukes of Hazzard*. This left me wondering if she'd been hired to look after us or to help get Nonny and myself into trouble. If Anna-Lou had hired her, she must have done it over the phone and without ever meeting her, and I could tell Nelson had doubts about her suitability for the job. As he walked back into the house, I saw he was shaking his head and mumbling, 'Oh Jesus Christ, Jonathan and Rachel will kill me!' Had Anna-Lou been there, I'm not sure she would have left the three of us alone, but five minutes later Nelson's car was heading down the track on his way back to New York. Whatever our au pair's qualifications were for the job, or even her lack of them, I liked her straight away.

We soon settled into a chaotic but happy routine eating junk-food meals and picnicking and swimming in a local lake. On the weekends, when Nelson and Anna-Lou returned, we hung out at the yacht club in Stonington and took the family's dinghy out across the bay for sailing lessons. It was probably down to Doreen's lack of sailing knowledge that she then let us go back to the yacht club during the week, where, with no experienced adults around, Nonny would take charge of our days in the dinghy. On one trip we attempted to cross a two-mile stretch of open water to Fishers Island. As you would expect when two kids and their au pair head out to sea unprepared, the weather decided to teach us a lesson and turn nasty. On this occasion we had to be rescued by a fishing boat, which towed us, by now shivering and wet, back to the yacht club. A man from the Coast Guard turned up to give us a serious telling-off for heading out to sea without notifying anyone, checking the weather or wearing suitable clothing. Having thought we were going to die out there in the storm, I felt he might have had a point.

Perhaps it was because of our near-death experience that things started to heat up between Nonny and myself. It began with us kissing when the au pair wasn't looking. This moved on to a fair amount of lying in each other's arms on the sofa as we read or listened to music. Doreen was fine with this as it usually happened when her boyfriend, who had only recently been let out of prison, turned up in his pick-up truck. They would then disappear into her bedroom for an hour or two and make noises like cowboys at a rodeo.

Left by Doreen to entertain ourselves, Nonny and I had soon moved on to lying on my bed together, late at night, talking until we fell asleep. Then one night, out of nowhere, she asked if I thought it might be time to try something else. Surely this was the moment I'd been building up to, waited for and talked about so many times with friends like Simon and the Roebers? I'd had to listen to one or more of the Roeber triplets going through every detail of how it's done. Simon had bragged about it every time he took a girl out. Now I was being offered that very thing, by a girl I really liked, who was right there next to me on my bed, thousands of miles from all the people I most worried about judging me. But in the confusion of the moment I panicked and my first instinct was to say, 'Can I think about it and get back to you?' As soon as I did so, I felt stupid and a coward. Nonny smiled nervously at me, rolled over and soon fell asleep as I lay staring at the ceiling with a zillion thoughts going through my head. Why, after all the talk, was I so scared and unsure that this was the right thing to do? If I was ever going to lose my virginity, hold my head high and join Simon, Nick Ayer and the Roebers' special club, this would have been the moment.

When I woke up the next morning, I'd forgotten Nonny was there – I wasn't used to having a girl in my bed. I watched her as she slept, lying naked next to me with the covers half over her legs. I lay there for some time just staring: her hips, her breasts and the smoothness of her tanned skin. It was the body of a woman and, what's more, a woman who had offered herself to me, and I'd said, 'Can I get back to you?' There were so many thoughts racing through my head, but the one that worried me the most was: was I physically mature enough to do it? I just didn't know if I was or not, but not knowing was holding me back, which I was hardly going to admit to Nonny. Somehow I was going to have to get over it, take the risk and do it or I'd have to keep making excuses for the rest of the holiday. I also knew that if I didn't man up and do it, I'd never be able to live with myself. To top it all, how would I ever explain my bottling out to someone like Simon? 'Yes, Simon, we spent several nights together naked in a bed, and no, Simon, we never had sex. I just didn't want to do it because, look at me, I'm still just a boy.' Surely saying that to any of my friends, let alone Simon, would be worse than being laughed at by Nonny.

Nonny eventually woke up, and after a slightly awkward conversation about breakfast she went downstairs to look for Doreen. When I finally made it down to the kitchen, it was obvious I was walking in on a private conversation between the two of them. The conversation stopped, and Nonny and I both sat in silence as Doreen attempted to make pancakes. Watching her burn our breakfast and set fire to a tea towel felt like a good distraction. She looked at us and smiled knowingly, which I found a little uncomfortable.

'I think what you guys need is something to help you chill out a little. I have a friend over in Rhode Island who can get us some of New England's finest weed.'

I turned to Nonny and she looked back at me with a smile. Looking straight into my eyes she said, 'Great idea, Doreen. I think William has some cash.'

Nonny's eagerness to get stoned was another side of her I wasn't ready for. I was also pretty sure my parents hadn't intended the money they'd given me to be used to buy drugs, and I still had a long shopping list of gifts to buy and bring home with me. But maybe Doreen had a point, and if this was what Nonny and I needed to help move things forward, I was prepared to give it a go.

Setting off in Doreen's Ford Pinto, we headed across the state line to Rhode Island to meet her friend. He was waiting for us around the back of a supermarket car park in a town called Westerly. We pulled up next to a battered pick-up truck. A man with a goatee beard and a greasy ponytail wound down his window. There was no small talk, and the deal was done in seconds. Doreen handed over my cash and the man gave us a sandwich bag stuffed with the same leaves I'd seen Dee drying and handing out to her friends. Before we knew it, we were on the road back to Stonington.

After a lazy day of picnicking and swimming at a nearby lake, we returned to the farm and settled down on the deck to watch the sun go down. Doreen rolled three small, neat joints and handed one to each of us. It wasn't much of a surprise to find that Nonny knew exactly what she was doing, while I tried my best to look as if I did too. As I lit mine up and took a timid drag, I coughed and spluttered, but soon got the hang of it and sat back in my deckchair and pretended getting stoned was an everyday event.

Did you know, if you stare long enough at the Moon, there really is a face on it? I'd never noticed it before, but as the sky got darker and the Moon brighter, there it was, looking back at me through the white and grey patterns of its surface, and it was definitely smiling at me.

'Hey, Nonny, can you see the face on the Moon?' I said.

'What face?' she said, staring at the Moon with me.

'There, look, can't you see those two big eyes and the grinning mouth?'

'I think you might have had a bit too much of that weed, Mr Miller.'

She was right, no more weed for me. I was also beginning

to think again about the inevitable bedroom situation later that night.

Dee had always joked about having the munchies after smoking marijuana, and after getting stoned she would dance around the kitchen with Hylan, making elaborate Asian stir-fried meals for everyone. While I was trying to show Nonny the face on the Moon, Doreen went off to the kitchen to cook us all a big bowl of pasta. By the time we'd polished it off I was feeling a lot less high, but at the same time nicely mellow and relaxed and certainly less freaked out about the inevitable challenges of bedtime. At least, I was, until we actually went to bed and Nonny slipped out of her clothes and stood there naked in the middle of the room. Suddenly the panic returned.

'Can you excuse me for just one minute,' I said as I bolted into the bathroom, locking the door behind me. I stood in front of the mirror, gripped the edge of the sink and took deep breaths.

'OK,' I said to myself, 'this is it, no more messing around. It's now or never.' To calm myself down, I fixed my gaze on the tiles on the wall and found myself starting to count them one by one. It was at this moment that I came up with an idea, or maybe more of a deal with myself. I reckoned that the width of a single tile, from one edge to the other, might be about the same as someone would consider acceptable for the length of a grown man's penis. So, the deal was this: if mine was close in size to one of these tiles, or even more, I was man enough and it had to be a go. Any smaller and I would tell Nonny it was never going to happen and I would have to live with the consequences.

When I finally returned to the bedroom, Nonny was lying

on top of the covers waiting for me to join her. We started off with some slow and gentle kissing – and the rest I'm not sure how much I can actually remember, but Nonny was definitely taking charge. I know there was a lot of fumbling around and things started to move faster and faster, but it was quick and seemed to be over before it had even started. Nonny pulled herself off me and without saying a word left the room. I lay back on the bed with a mix of confused feelings. I'd done it, I had finally lost my virginity and clearly she had lost hers too, but it all felt like a big let-down. To add to it, she'd run out of the room without saying a thing. I felt completely crushed.

We didn't do it again. In fact, during the days that followed we didn't return to sleeping in the same bed together. For Nonny, our brief moment of chaos had been enough, and in her mind she'd done what she'd set out to achieve and it had clearly been something of a disappointment. To my relief, the affection and jolly joking continued, but we chose not to discuss what happened that night. I remained confused; much of what my friends had told me about sex and the glorious and intimate moments of doing it had clearly been exaggerated. What I was certain about, for now, was that I was in no hurry to try it again any time soon. In a way, the build-up and anticipation of losing my virginity felt rather similar to trying to get my Blue Peter badge. It was something I'd talked about for so long and had planned for, and when it finally arrived it turned out to only be any good for wearing on my jacket so people knew I'd got it. With losing my virginity, I had the badge and could tell my friends – as long as they didn't ask too many questions about how I got it.

Being stuck on the Aldrich farm in Connecticut meant there

was no one I could talk to about what had happened. Unlike Nonny, I certainly wasn't going to talk to Doreen, who had apparently been filled in on all the details and was now smiling at me like Mum did when I only got a pass in my oboe exam. I would just have to wait until I got to New York, where I could talk to Keith. In the past, he was always the one I turned to for advice about girls, and I knew he would be thrilled, if not a little proud, to hear my news. I knew, if I was honest with him about what had happened, he wouldn't judge me in the way my friends at home would.

As soon as we were back in New York I went to see him. Of course, Keith was thrilled for me, but it was in a way that made me wish I'd kept my news to myself. I knew it had been a disaster, but he was treating it like I'd scored the winning goal at an FA Cup Final, and had done it with skill. Even as I heard the words coming out of my mouth I felt like a fraud. I got carried away with his excitement and I never got to tell him how terrible the whole thing had been and or ask for his advice. He told me everything was going to change for me and, to kick it off, he was going treat me to a complete makeover so I could show the world I was no longer a child.

Our first stop was a trendy hairdresser's in the East Village for what had to be the most expensive haircut I've ever had. Then to a clothes shop, where he bought me black jeans and a pair of white Converse boots. Keith now seemed satisfied that I was ready to return to London and announce to everyone that the old William Miller was no more. The new one was now a real New Yorker who went to bed with girls. I looked good, but there was no getting away from it – I still felt like a fraud.

Keith was now the manager of a successful restaurant on

Me on my return from America, August 1979

Fifth Avenue called One Fifth. He suggested, to complete the transformation, that on my last night in New York I should take Nonny out to dinner at the restaurant. I'd never taken anyone out to dinner, let alone a girl. Nonny was impressed that I could get a reservation at one of the best restaurants in her city. For our last evening together I managed to put aside any feelings that I might have let her down. Everything about our date was cool and sophisticated. Standing on the corner of Broadway and 94th Street on a warm summer evening and hailing a cab felt so glamorous, as if I was starring in my own film, and then walking through the doors of the restaurant with a girl on my arm made me feel like a man of the world.

As we sat down at our table the waiter offered us drinks, and then asked straight out, 'Are you the Shit from Camden Town?' I didn't know what to say, but Nonny thought it was the funniest thing anyone could have asked. It gave her English boyfriend a punk rock status that no New York or LA boy could ever dream of. It was a title that put me up there with some of Britain's finest: 'The Shit from Camden Town' would for me be what 'Sid Vicious' was to John Simon Ritchie or 'Johnny Rotten' to John Lydon. I had made it and was no longer just the kid who had arrived to stay for the summer – I was *The Shit from Camden Town* who she could tell everybody she'd lost her virginity to. The next day, to celebrate my new status, Nonny presented me with a gift before I left for the airport – a purple T-shirt with 'USA' printed across the back and on the front the words 'The Shit from Camden Town'.

24

JE PRÉFÈRE UNE BANANE

When I got back to London, I managed to push all the embarrassing parts of losing my virginity to the back of my mind.

At some point I knew I would have to tell my close friends, if only to set the record straight. The Roeber triplets were a good start. They are as close as brothers, and part of me wanted to tell them so they could make a fuss and celebrate with me. But that strategy came with the risk that they would ask questions that would need answers. In the end I told them while sitting around their kitchen table having tea. I waited for the right moment to bring it up. We hadn't seen each other for the whole summer, so there was the usual chatter as everyone caught up with their news. My opening came as one of the them mentioned a girl he'd met in France, and there was a lot of talk about what had happened. In an attempt to compare notes, I slipped my bit of news casually into the conversation. There was a pause as everyone turned to look at me. It was followed by a chorus of 'Really?' And that was it! Without having to explain a thing, I was in the club and could move on.

By the time school started again, I'd told a handful of friends, which turned out to be plenty. I had already started to feel quite different about myself – I had grown up over the summer, closed one door and I now had a mission and wanted to go back to school and start looking to the future. For that, I needed to come up with something of a life plan. The first steps in this plan were to finish my O-levels and get the grades I needed to move to another school. By now I hated everything about Pimlico and knew I wouldn't have it in me to make it through the sixth form there. It was no longer about the bullying or the meaningless threats, which had more or less stopped; the whole school had become a war zone and the bullies had bigger battles to fight elsewhere.

When it came to the moving schools part of my plan, I was way ahead of Mum and Dad. They had probably forgotten all about it, hoping my urgent need to leave Pimlico had gone away. It hadn't, and Conrad and I were out there searching for alternatives and doing all we could to make plans for our escape. It was Conrad who first mentioned Westminster School, when he said that he'd looked into it and was thinking of applying for the sixth form. We had passed it hundreds of times on the bus but hadn't realised it was there, tucked away behind Westminster Abbey. In the mornings we'd seen confident-looking uniformed boys disappearing down an alleyway off Parliament Square, but we didn't know where they were going.

Conrad's mother called the school for a brochure, which we looked through together, and I then borrowed it to show Mum. When I thought about going to a private school, this was what I'd imagined it would be like – and from what I could tell it was exactly like the schools our parents had been to. Westminster was the kind of school I wanted to go to. There was a problem, though – on the first page in the brochure was the bit of information I most dreaded finding: 'Every potential candidate will be required to sit Westminster's entrance exam before being considered for a place.' There was a time when I'd been good at exams and would always get results above 70 or even 80 per cent. But as one Pimlico year became another, my results got worse, until I was getting below 40 per cent. I knew the Westminster exam would be the stumbling block for me. Even though I knew it, and so did Mum and Dad, this fact was brushed under the carpet and never discussed. No one tried to find out what the exam would involve or how to prepare for it. No one suggested I sit practice papers or find a tutor to get me up to speed. We'd winged most things when it came to school, so why not the Westminster exam and my chance of getting away from Pimlico and into a better school?

For Mum, Dad and their friends, an entrance exam for a school is a 'competition', and that means there will be winners and losers, which, in their world, was unfair. They want everything to be equal and for everyone to have access to the same opportunities. Of course I want the same thing, but at Pimlico the idea of a fairer world wasn't working. If our parents had spent a day there and got to experience some of the classes I'd been in, they would have been shocked. They would have been horrified to see really good teachers who were unable to teach because they couldn't control a couple of psychotic kids who were ruining it for everyone else. They might also have got to experience what it was like to be thought of as different because they were 'posh' and then beaten up for it. If they'd spent a day at Pimlico, they would have realised it was going to be pretty hard to live up to any of the expectations they had for us.

As far as Conrad and I were concerned, we'd finally had enough. What we wanted now was to go to the sort of school our parents had been to, to enjoy what was left of our time at school and not to feel frightened any more. Maybe even pass our exams. We'd come to the conclusion that, if there was any chance of this happening, we were going to have to take control of the situation and make it happen ourselves. And that's why we went to the trouble of applying for Westminster. Even if we weren't prepared for the exam, we lived in hope.

One Saturday morning in January, Conrad and I were driven by our mums to the front door of Westminster School. Just like they'd done at Pimlico, nearly five years earlier, they pushed us out of the car with a kiss and a wave and left us to fend for ourselves. We walked through a low stone arch and, like Alice in *Through the Looking-Glass,* found ourselves on the other side, in a world we had never known existed. We were met by a serious-looking man in a black gown who led us across a paved courtyard and past ancient school buildings. Unlike the feelings of fear and hopelessness I've had when walking along the huge concourse at Pimlico School, I could feel all around me the centuries of confident boys who came here to learn and to be made ready for a life doing exciting and interesting things.

As I walked along the oak-panelled corridors, past the portraits and trophies, I knew this was the unfair world of privilege that Dad and his friends talked about and thought was wrong. But if coming to a school like this was what it was going to take to stop me feeling like my life was going nowhere, then I knew I was ready to be part of it. If this was the very same world our parents had enjoyed, then maybe with it we could be a little more like them when we were older. It had crossed my mind that with their knowledge and my experiences I might, one day, be able to find a way to help change things for the better.

Our final destination was a large hall with high windows and walls covered in fancy crests. We were each given a desk, where a thick exam paper lay waiting for us. As I stared down at the words on the cover, 'Westminster School Entrance Exam', the sense of history I'd originally felt had now turned to panic. As I looked around the hall, it was obvious who this exam was for. If I was overwhelmed by the school before, I was now feeling stupid and an impostor for being there. I opened the first page, and a cold sweat broke out across my forehead as I tried to focus on the questions. My mind had gone blank. The words on the page might as well have been in Greek, or Martian for that matter. I knew before I'd even started that I had failed and I was angry with myself, angry with Mum and Dad and angry with what the school represented and the fact that I would never be part of it, even if my parents did have the money.

As the sun shone through the high windows, I remembered it was a Saturday morning. Beyond the walls of this exclusive world was a city getting on with its weekend, without a care for the suffering and humiliation I was going through in this hall. Nick Ayer would be at home stoned and watching *Tiswas*, while Simon would be out shopping with his girlfriend of the moment and the Roeber triplets probably out on Primrose Hill riding their bikes. I'd taken the day off from my Saturday job at the local garden centre to do this exam and could have been earning money and stuffing it in an old suitcase like Keith had. Instead, I was here kidding myself that I stood a chance of getting into this school. My first thoughts were why was I putting myself through this, and why, if I'd really wanted it so badly, had I not pushed my parents to make an effort to get me ready for it?

When the letter finally arrived from Westminster, it was hardly a surprise to find I'd been turned down for a place, as had Conrad. It was short and to the point, but kind enough not to drag up how badly I had done in the exam. It wouldn't have mattered anyway, as my dream of escaping Pimlico was in ruins. Mum knew how furious I was with both myself and her and Dad for their total lack of support. She waited for a moment when the two of us were alone before explaining that she had a plan of her own. In her usual gentle way, she sat me down and took me through it. She understood why I'd wanted to go to Westminster, but she had felt from the start that it was the wrong school for me. Her reason for this was one I had never considered – my father. She'd watched me try too many times to please him, and it broke her heart to see how much it upset me when I failed. Like everyone else who wanted to impress him with things they'd learned or heard, he always came back with something he thought was bigger, more complex or significant and that just made everyone feel stupid.

Even if the teaching at Pimlico had been as good as West-minster's, Dad would have found a way of telling me that what I was being taught was far too simple or just not the bit that was most interesting. It wasn't because he wanted to put me or anyone else down or prove my teachers wrong, and it didn't matter what it was: why a fish didn't sink to the bottom of the river or why Brutus murdered Julius Caesar. If I'd been excited by these things at school, his response was to get carried away by telling me something he thought to be more interesting, even if it was likely to fly over my head and confuse everything. Mum pointed out that I was putting more effort into making Dad happy than into focusing on what I was being taught by my teachers, and that that was leaving me not knowing what to think or who to follow.

Mum's solution was very honest and straightforward: I

needed to get away from Dad. I needed to find a school where I would be happy, get a better education than at Pimlico and eventually get into university – and do it for myself and not him. She explained that none of this meant that Dad and I didn't love each other. What Mum wanted was for me to find a way of being my own person, and that would be better for my relationship with him.

She had it all worked out, which surprised me. I knew that before she went to ballet school and then St Paul's she had been at a school in the countryside called Bedales. Her father had been a pupil and a music teacher there. Mum, her sisters, her mother, aunts, uncles and all her cousins had been to Bedales. Before the war it was one of the few co-educational liberal public schools in England to accept Jews. This was one of the reasons why nearly thirty members of her family had gone there.

Bedales stands at the bottom of a line of wooded hills just north of Petersfield, in Hampshire. Unlike Westminster, the school isn't particularly beautiful or old, but the surrounding countryside makes up for it and that was good enough for me. There are 350 boys and girls, and they all call their teachers by their first names, no one wears a uniform and the parents of these children are pretty much like mine, so it would be an easy adjustment for me.

Mum and I were shown around by a sixth-form boy called Oli, who had unbrushed shoulder-length hair and wore torn jeans and a trench coat. But what I noticed first was the healthy glow on his face, his easy-going manner and that every person we passed, pupil or teacher, said hello and smiled. There were no security guards at the gate, no bullies or knife attacks, and everyone liked each other. It made me think that if Gloucester Crescent had been a school it would be Bedales. It was obvious that this was a place I would fit into easily and that I would be better off without the pressures of a school like Westminster or St Paul's, where I would have struggled to keep up. And there didn't seem to be any question of having to sit an exam. When Oli had finished the tour, I was handed over to the headmaster for an interview. He offered me a place there and then, although it came with a condition: I had to pass at least five of my eight O-levels. It was a challenge that I wasn't entirely sure I was going to be able to meet, but it was something to aim for.

The Bedales plan was put into action so quickly that Conrad wasn't initially a part of it. As soon as I got home I told him about Oli, the tour, how friendly everyone had been and how they'd made me an offer. Within days his mother took him to look around the school for himself. Just as they had with me, they offered him a place straight away. If he got the grades, he would be joining me in September. The whole plan was starting to come together, and Conrad getting an offer was exactly what I'd hoped for. At last it looked like our days at Pimlico were numbered, even if it did all hang on passing our O-levels.

Although I was feeling good about the future, I also felt guilty about leaving close friends, like Simon and Jimi. They'd made the last five years survivable and, at times, bearable. I knew that if, like them, you were able to stand up to the bullies, then Pimlico wasn't a bad school to be at. There were plenty of pupils getting the grades they needed to go to university, and if anyone could survive and make the most of the sixth form it was Simon and Jimi. I had come to appreciate that a lot of the teachers could have been really good if they'd had the time or resources to teach properly and didn't have to deal with the difficult kids. You could see the frustration and sadness in the faces of these teachers the moment you stepped into their classrooms and there seemed to be nothing they could do about it.

My French teacher was one of them. She was a really good teacher and was actually French, but we were the bottom-stream class, which I'd ended up in after failing a simple test at the end of the third year. Once I was in that class there was nothing I could do to claw my way out of it and into the top-stream class. Conrad was in that class, and he said the teacher had it under control and they actually learned to speak French. The problem in my class was that the teacher didn't know how to control the small gang of violent boys who sat at the back and made everyone's life a misery. From where they sat they would throw anything that wasn't fixed to the floor. Our teacher spent every lesson trying to get them under control and avoid being hit by flying furniture. I didn't get to speak a single word of French in two years, but at her suggestion I got my eyes tested after she noticed I was squinting from the back of the room. 'William,' she said in her lovely French accent, 'get ze glasses or sit in ze front.' Knowing that the front of the classroom was the most dangerous place to sit, I got the glasses and stayed safely at the back, where I wouldn't be hit on the head with a chair.

The bottom-stream course was something called *Smile French*. I discovered, from looking through the book, that it was all about terrorists who lived in somewhere called the Basque Country. As far as I could tell, these people spent their time either asking for directions to the Information Centre or talking about bananas as they went around on bicycles collecting machine guns off fishing boats. When I did the French oral exam, the only phrase I could remember was, '*Je préfère une banane*', which I wasn't sure would ever come in useful and certainly didn't impress the examiner. He kept asking me, '*Où sont les armes?*', and all I could do was shrug my shoulders and smile.

Soon enough our day of reckoning arrived, and the exams started. Every day for three weeks we sat in one of the school's big gymnasiums as we took one exam after another. As I ticked the exams off and counted them down to the finish, they soon became a blur. I realised that Mum's theory about how I should have listened to my teachers and not my father was looking more obvious than ever. Even if I did know the answer to a question, I often thought I had a better one which was likely to be a jumble of confused bits of information Dad had told me or that I'd got from a very serious and wordy book he'd forced on me. There were several examples of this, like a question that asked: 'Explain the importance of the swim bladder in a fish.' I knew the answer, but that didn't matter as I had a cleverer one that Dad had told me. But as the information had gone in one ear and half out the other and then got mashed up *en route*, my answer was a long and confused load of gibberish about how the evolution of fish began 530 million years ago. I wrote about something called the Cambrian Explosions and then went on to describe how fish had developed a skull and spinal column. It wasn't the answer they were looking for, and the person marking the paper must have thought I had brought a back issue of *Scientific American* into the exam with me.

After three weeks of spouting off all the half-baked facts I'd got from Dad, the pain of exams was over. I had no idea how I'd done, but the relief of no longer having to sit in a hot and airless gymnasium and perhaps never having to set foot inside Pimlico School again was enormous. I didn't have to turn up at school for what was left of the term, and for the first time in ages I had no revising to do. I could relax, go outside and breathe in the warm summer air and do nothing other than hope and pray. I would now have to wait six weeks to find out if my exams had been a disaster and my dream of going to Bedales was over. In a moment of panic one morning I admitted to Mum and Dad that we should all prepare ourselves for the worst. If that happened, I wouldn't be going to Bedales, but I also told them there was no way I would go back to Pimlico. For now, no one had a plan, other than to wait it out and try to enjoy the long holiday ahead.

I spent a restless summer worrying about my results. I lost count of the times I'd woken up in the middle of the night after dreaming about opening the brown envelope from the examination board. On some nights, the results were better than good and everyone was proud of me. On other nights, it was a story of complete failure. Many of my dreams were filled with the shame of letting everyone down, the look of disappointment on my father's face and my mother crying as she blamed him for everything. In every one of these dreams I found myself trying to comfort him. There was also a recurring dream about turning up at Bedales with my trunk in the back of the car. The headmaster was standing at the entrance and telling me to leave. Behind him was a crowd of Bedales pupils shouting, 'Go home!'

We went to France for the first two weeks of the summer holidays. I tried to relax, and Mum did everything she could to help make up for the sleepless nights I was having. She had rented a house in a village near Clermont-l'Hérault. In the mornings we wandered through the village to fetch warm baguettes and croissants from the local boulangerie, and for the rest of the day we'd drive to Lac du Salagou, where we'd picnic on the shore and sail in a small dinghy. I even met a nice French girl, whose family took the same spot on the beach near us every day. We might have got together had I known more French than just '*Je préfère une banane*'. We returned to London and then travelled on to the Old Manse, where the usual stream of visitors came and went for the rest of the holiday.

Conrad came to stay during the week our results were due to arrive. When the day finally came, we sat in the kitchen doing our best to eat breakfast as we tried to work out what time the postman would arrive 500 miles away in Gloucester Crescent. I'd lost my appetite, whereas Conrad, who'd pretty much cruised through his exams, was feeling quietly confident and was managing to finish off a bowl of porridge and several slices of toast. I sat in silence, playing through my mind the scenario from my dreams.

For what seemed like hours we waited for our old Bakelite telephone in the sitting room to ring. When someone calls, it starts with a single loud ping that echoes throughout the house and makes everyone jump. Then there's a pause before the phone breaks into a continuous and deafening ring, which can be heard in every part of the house. As the predicted time got closer, Conrad and I sat at the kitchen table like coiled springs waiting for that initial ping. When it came, we burst into action and raced across the hall and into the sitting room, throwing ourselves at the phone before the ringing started. As we dived across the furniture, we both grabbed the receiver and pulled it between our heads. I could hear Conrad's mother on the other end, and I let go. Settling down on the sofa, I followed the expression on Conrad's face for clues as to what he was being told. As he put the phone down he grinned and punched the air. He had passed everything with A's and B's. Dad, who'd wandered into the room, looked thrilled and started clapping and patting him on the back saying, 'Well done, Conrad, that's brilliant. Your family must be so proud of you.'

Within minutes the ping sounded again. This time it was Jeanie calling to say she'd found the brown envelope on the doormat at Gloucester Crescent. I asked her to open it and read it out. She was so calm and nice as she tried to explain what each grade meant. Rather than talking about the ones I'd failed, she focused on what I'd passed. As I put the phone down, I tried to be like Jeanie and talk about the good bits. Unlike Jeanie, all Dad wanted to know was which subjects I'd failed. I had taken a total of eight and had scraped through with five grade Cs. In so many ways this was a terrible result, but as far as I was concerned a C is a pass and a pass gave me the five O-levels I needed for Bedales. I didn't need the other three, which I failed so badly it wasn't worth mentioning. Dad had gone back to congratulating Conrad as I pushed my way past him and out the front door. I didn't know why he was so pleased for Conrad and not for me. The fact that I had managed to get the five O-levels I needed to go to Bedales didn't seem to have crossed his mind. But I knew it didn't matter what he thought any more.

I left the house and got on my bike and with one shove let it freewheel down the square, picking up speed as I headed out of the village and onto the Green Road. As the wind blew through my hair I started to smile and then laugh. The waiting was really over and I had done it. Everything was now going to change in ways I could hardly imagine. The sun had come out and the purple heather on the distant hills was glowing in the morning light. I wanted to be alone outside in the fresh air to celebrate my victory on my own terms. My life was about to change for ever, and if I could, I would keep pedalling until I got to Bedales.

PART THREE

September 1982
(Age 18)

Conrad and me (second and third from left), Michael White's
son Sasha and Peter Hall's son Edward (bottom row right)

25

BEDALES, SEPTEMBER 1980

From occasional visits to the attic of our house in Gloucester Crescent I remembered that somewhere in the furthest corner was a large leather trunk that hadn't been moved or opened in years. It was exactly what I had in mind when I thought about turning up at boarding school on my first day. Clutching a torch, I ventured deep into the attic, making my way around cardboard boxes, broken furniture and long-forgotten toys. Covered in a thick layer of dust and cobwebs, the trunk was full of old magazines, film scripts sent to Dad but never read, and a collection of real human bones left over from when he was a medical student. The spinal column (held together with a length of rope), a hip bone and the left hand were now on display on a table in the middle of the sitting room. I'd once taken a couple of these bones to Primrose Hill Primary for a show-and-tell, which made the girls scream and won me valuable brownie points with the boys.

I'd got it into my head that going to boarding school required a proper trunk. I felt it made a statement, if only to myself, that I was leaving home and everything was about to change. Having a proper trunk was like a trophy of the battle I'd fought and won with my parents over leaving Pimlico and going to boarding school. The old trunk was perfect – thick black leather with wooden straps wrapped around its body to give it strength. The fact that Dad had completely forgotten it existed meant I could stake my claim. I emptied its contents into cardboard boxes and hauled it downstairs to the bathroom, where I washed it down. After polishing the leather, I wrote my name and address and that of Bedales in neat bold letters on the top with a silver marker pen. I packed everything into it that I would need for school, and then hid the things I valued most in my bedroom cupboard – I knew Tom would steal them, so I fixed a large bolt and padlock on the door.

When the day finally came to leave for Bedales, I dragged the trunk down to the ground floor and across the front garden to the street. There I was joined by Conrad, and we loaded our trunks into the back of the car, grinning at each other as if to acknowledge the symbolism of the moment. We knew how long it had taken to win our parents over to the idea, and now here we were, packing up the car and heading off to a new life at boarding school. We'd got what we wanted and it felt exhilarating, but we knew it was a bitter pill for our parents to swallow. After so many years of hoping they could make a difference, they'd finally had to agree that the route they had chosen had been something of a failure for their children who had ended up paying the price for their choices.

With Conrad's mother sitting next to her, Mum drove us out of London and down the motorway to Hampshire. The journey couldn't have been more different from the one we'd taken five years earlier, when they drove us to our first day at Pimlico. Once off the motorway we drove through a number of small towns and villages, past the home of Jane Austen at Chawton, then into the hills north of Petersfield. I couldn't believe how beautiful Hampshire was and wound down the window to breathe in the fresh air and feel the warmth of the late summer sun on my face. We carried on along narrow lanes bordered by steep embankments and impenetrable hedges and past woodlands that looked mysterious and ancient. When we reached the crest of the hill above Bedales, you could see for miles across an open plain towards the South Downs. Dropping down the hill, we drove along a winding lane which soon entered a dark tunnel of trees that canopied the road before bursting back into the sunlight as we approached the entrance to the school.

As we drove through the gates we were directed towards a large building where the dining hall and the boys' house were located. We got out of the car to be greeted by a laid-back man in his forties who looked like Bob Dylan and turned out to be my housemaster. As Conrad and I shook his hand, he made a point of reminding us that at Bedales you refer to all the teachers by their first names, and his was Harry. He announced this all-important school rule with an air of casual authority only to turn to our mums and shrug it off as if to demonstrate how cool it all was. He'd clearly won them over with the impression that we were being handed over to the spiritual leader of an ashram. Clearly comfortable with this idea, our mums wished us luck, gave us a reassuring hug and with that got back in the car and left. Harry then introduced us to two boys, who offered to help carry our trunks and show us to our dormitories. We stopped first at Conrad's, which was spacious, carpeted and had built-in beds and wardrobes, and three large windows that looked out over playing fields.

We continued down a maze of corridors until we found mine – which couldn't have been more different. It had six white-painted cast-iron beds, a cold linoleum floor and a single window that looked out over a kitchen yard with a collection of large rubbish bins filled with pigswill. Whereas Conrad's dorm felt like you were in the countryside, mine could have been over a takeaway off Camden High Street. My trunk-carrying assistant assured me that getting the worst possible dorm this term meant there was a good chance I'd get a good one the next.

Having deposited my trunk and reconciled myself to the idea that my bleak dormitory might only be for one term, I headed downstairs in search of the dining hall, where we were gathering for tea. By the time I found it, a number of small groups had formed and people were sharing news of their summer holidays. I was struck by the way friendships seemed to be so effortlessly picked up from where they'd been left off at the end of the previous term. Everyone was relaxed and affectionate with each other, with many hugging or holding hands as they talked. There wasn't any of the vicious gossip and frantic dissing I had become used to at Pimlico, with everyone talking over each other about who'd been beaten up or expelled from school, or who had slept with who over the holidays or might have got pregnant.

At Bedales, as we sipped tea and ate fruitcake, there was an easy-going air to the discussions as each group swapped stories about their holidays and caught up on news. As I looked around the dining hall, I tried to listen in on the conversations, keen to get a better feel for the new friends I might make. Next to me was a group discussing the many plays they'd seen over the summer. In another, three boys were holding court as they recounted their shared experience of travelling across France on an overnight train together. I could just make out a heated debate on the other side of the room about the political situation: unemployment having hit two million and the more surprising news that a Hollywood actor had been selected to run for President in America and, worst of all, he might be going to win. Although these conversations were so different from the ones I'd been part of when sitting around on the radiators at Pimlico, they were strangely familiar, similar to the ones my parents and their friends might have around the kitchen table or at parties in the Crescent.

I felt excited to be around people my own age who could have conversations of this kind, and with so much ease and confidence, and to think that I might get to participate in similar conversations myself. I did feel a twinge of embarrassment as I listened in on some of the other conversations in the room. These had an altogether different air to them: there was a girl boasting to her friends about being seduced on a beach in Mustique by an ageing rock star while somewhere else a loud, shouty boy was complaining about overcrowded beaches in Italy. Another was complaining that his first week of school would be a write-off because of his jet-lag. As those around him shook their heads in sympathy I felt a surge of guilt for having sold out and deserted my friends at Pimlico. It dawned on me that some of those old friends would have had a terrible summer by comparison, having gone nowhere more glamorous than a local park or a holiday camp in Kent. For a moment I thought about Jimi and Simon and what they might be doing back at Pimlico at that very moment. I wondered how I would have felt if things had gone differently for me, if I'd failed to get that all important fifth O-level and then had to return to Pimlico for the sixth form.

26

ANGRY YOUNG MEN

Conrad and I turned out to be part of a small group of new-comers in the Bedales sixth form and, with that, the only two to have come from a comprehensive school. We also discovered that our having come from one had created a certain mystique around us that led some to believe we were streetwise and not to be messed with. After all our years at Pimlico, where our status had been the complete opposite, we found this rather perplexing. Fortunately, there was an upside: people were keen to get to know us. This gave us the confidence we needed to feel accepted and helped us settle quickly into school life, although I had a constant worry that we'd be exposed for not being quite the tough guys they thought we were.

I soon discovered an important fact about all schools: no matter where you are, there will always be a group of boys who think they're tougher than you. This gets them the undivided attention of the prettiest and coolest girls in the school, but with it comes the need to be a bully and show who's in charge. Dad describes boys like this as 'the ones who drag their knuckles along the ground when they walk', and sure enough there was a small group of them at Bedales. The only difference being that these Bedales bullies could recite poetry and passages from Shakespeare, but they were still 'knuckle-draggers'. Pretty soon Conrad and I came to the attention of these boys, and they were looking for an excuse to show us who was in charge, in case we had ideas of taking over their patch.

It came after the school dance at the end of our first week. As we drifted out of the hall, I was still spinning with the excitement of my first school dance. Intoxicated with the idea that everyone at Bedales loved each other in equal measure, I made the error of introducing myself in a matey way to a boy called Billy. He was walking with two girls I'd got to know a few days before and had been friendly with since. This had obviously come to Billy's attention, and he wasn't happy about it. I'd clocked him from afar and was aware that he was the dominant male in a pride of lions that roamed the school – he was the ringleader of a group of cool but relatively harmless boys who thought they were the 1980s' answer to the Angry Young Men. Billy had evidently taken on the role of a young Harold Pinter, all dark and brooding in his long trench coat, and the only one who looked like he was suppressing some form of untamed anger towards everyone around him, which probably started with his parents. In Billy's eyes, my over-familiarity with 'his girls' meant that I'd already crossed an invisible line, and my ham-fisted introduction was all he needed to set things straight.

Something else Dad told me, which was sort of connected to his knuckle-dragger theory, was that if you stick your head in the mouth of a lion it's going to get bitten off. Suddenly, Billy was all roar and claws, and before I knew it he had me up against a wall as he snarled, 'I'm Billy and I don't give a fuck which school you went to.' Then he said that if I crossed him again he'd 'kick my fucking arse back to whatever shitty school I came from'. I didn't quite pee in my pants, but I might as well have.

As usual, I found myself spluttering a pathetic apology. I knew deep down that Billy was different from the bullies at Pimlico and that I should have kneed him hard in the groin, followed by a punch on the nose. I'd witnessed it done enough times, whereas Billy had probably only ever seen it in films or on stage at the Royal Court. My friends Simon and Jimi had spent five years trying to get me to understand that you only had to do it once, and that you had to make sure you were the one making the first move. That was all well and good for Simon and Jimi – they were built like a pair of mahogany wardrobes, and no one was going to mess with either of them. At Pimlico I feared that striking first was likely to go wrong and make me even more of a target, so I ignored their advice. Had I given Billy a good seeing-to, he would have probably cried and slunk off in his trench coat and never crossed my path again. Instead, I let him get the upper hand, which meant from now on I would be the fool who had to avoid him.

Before Billy destroyed my belief that Bedales was a thug-free zone, I'd been enjoying the school dance. However, like the end of the evening, the beginning hadn't gone well either, but that was to do with my horror of dancing. Apart from my over-the-top attempt at Gully's wedding, I had no dance moves that didn't come with the risk of ruining my reputation. Paralysed by this thought, I found a dark corner well away from the dance floor but close enough to observe the many and varied styles of Bedalian dancing. To my surprise, Conrad hadn't hesitated to get himself out there and dance with whoever. I had no idea where he'd learned his moves, but there was a definite and well-thought-out style to them. It involved moving his arms around as if he was doing kung fu while keeping the bottom half of his body completely still.

At the same time his head was moving up and down like one of those nodding toy dogs in the back of a car. You couldn't fault it: he was in his element, and the girls were lining up to dance with him.

From my dark corner I could see that no one cared if they were making fools of themselves. Eventually, a girl called Juliet lurched out of the throbbing mass, grabbed my hand and dragged me back onto the dance floor. It was no good protesting, and I realised I had to think on my feet about the style I was going to adopt. It turned out to be a combination of standing in one place, leaning forward very slightly and letting my arms swing rhythmically from side to side, along with a little head-nodding stolen from Conrad. There were no two ways about it, I was a terrible dancer, but the extraordinary thing was that no one seemed to be watching or laughing at me.

It wasn't long before I threw myself into songs like Billy Joel's 'My Life', the inevitable 'YMCA' and Gloria Gaynor's 'I Will Survive'. I was half-way through Kool and the Gang's 'Get Down On It' when the girl I was dancing with led me off the floor and straight up to another girl, who was standing in the shadows trying to avoid catching anyone's eye for fear of being asked to dance. This girl was pretty and sweet in an innocent way, with perfect teeth that came into their own when she smiled. Shy and rather too neatly dressed for a Bedalian, she shook my hand as my dance companion introduced us. 'William, this is Sarah, who I know would love to dance with you.' Her smile vanished and the look on her face turned to one of terror. I took her hand and pulled her onto the dance floor. As I resumed my new dance routine, Sarah moved her shoulders from side to side, obviously counting the seconds for the song to end and probably praying that the next number wasn't a slow one like 'Nights in White Satin'. When the song finally ended we thanked each other and she slipped back into her safe dark corner.

Later that evening, while I was in the communal bathroom getting ready for bed, a boy said, 'I see you were dancing with Sarah Armstrong-Jones.'

My immediate response was, 'Who?'

'You know, *Lady* Sarah Armstrong-Jones, Princess Margaret's daughter.'

I did know that Princess Margaret had two children at Bedales, but I hadn't given it any thought and didn't know what either of them looked like. Now, as I stood brushing my teeth in the bathroom, it started to make sense that Juliet, who I'd rather liked, had handed me off, in the middle of a dance, to someone else. She was clearly a friend of Sarah's and must have been looking out for her and thought the best way to get her out of the shadows and onto the dance floor was to use the innocent 'new boy'. Now, having been told who she was, it came back to me just how dreadful my dancing had been, and I wished I'd known who she was so I could have toned it down a bit.

It turned out that Princess Margaret's son, David, had left the previous term, and while Sarah was in my year our paths hadn't crossed until the night of the dance. I was also somewhat embarrassed about my ignorance, as Princess Margaret was someone Dad knew quite well and occasionally talked about. While he never stopped complaining about the royal family's 'complete irrelevance' and their 'responsibility for the rot in our class system', Princess Margaret was always very nice to him, even if he claimed she was more interested in him than he was in her. He also said that she was obsessed with three things: theatre people, intellectuals and Jews – the first two she was desperate to be part of and the third she found intriguing, though Dad wasn't entirely sure why. Dad ticked all three of these boxes, and she always sought him out at parties and occasionally invited him to dinners or other events. Mum was convinced Princess Margaret had a crush on him, and said she was even more certain after they were both invited to a party at Windsor Castle and she'd made Dad sit next to her while Mum was left chatting to some boring old man on another table. Then, after the dinner, Princess Margaret took Dad off on his own for a tour of the castle's private rooms. She was far from Dad's type, but flattery can go a long way with him.

My brief encounter with Billy had initially brought me down to earth with a thud; I was rattled by the unexpected realisation that physical violence might be lurking only a few rooms away while I slept, but fortunately my worries didn't last long. When I mentioned the incident to Conrad, he laughed and pointed out that the chances of my being on the receiving end of a serious beating at Bedales were slim. He said that the worst that might happen would be a loss of face, which was a lot easier to live with. He was right, and other than this momentary blip I was starting to enjoy being at boarding school – I felt independent for the first time, and there was something rather satisfying about being cut off from everything back in London.

It was easy to make new friends, and I quickly found a group who were bright, funny and stimulating to be around, and generally came from a similar background to my own. There was Remy, whose mum, Helaine Blumenfeld, was a sculptor while his dad, Yorick, was a writer; Joshua and his younger brother Sasha were the sons of *The Rocky Horror*

Show producer Michael White; a few others were connected to Dad's time at the National Theatre – I shared a dorm with Dan Nichols, son of the playwright Peter Nichols, and a few years below me were Peter Hall's son Edward and Laurence Olivier's daughters Tamsin and Julie Kate. Others who became good friends included Malcolm, the grandson of the politician Rab Butler, and a boy called Roddy, who proved to be a brilliant and hilarious writer.

I loved the new and unfamiliar routine of boarding school, which started with breakfast at 7.30 and then onto morning lessons. After lunch we had sports or general studies, followed by tea and then evening lessons and supper. After that there was prep or a range of activities such as play rehearsals or clubs. No longer having to travel to and from school saved hours in the day and allowed me to get so much more done. There were no more late nights watching telly, which at Bedales, oddly given its reputation for leading liberal thinkers, was rationed to shows like *Top of the Pops* and important events like *Miss World* and the *Eurovision Song Contest*.

When I was at Pimlico, everything seemed rushed, especially breakfast, which I'd grab before meeting up with Conrad to race across London at the mercy of the Tube or bus to get us to school on time. At Bedales all you had to do was get yourself out of bed, dressed and downstairs to the dining hall. After lessons we'd stroll back for lunch or supper. Each meal felt like a relaxed social event where we'd sit around talking and laughing with our friends. We chatted about things that happened in class or about the books we were reading; we debated politics, our fear of Ronald Reagan becoming president, nuclear disarmament and the CND movement.

The one thing I missed at Bedales was music, for the simple reason that is wasn't worth doing. At Pimlico we'd had a chamber and a symphony orchestra, and because of its famous music course they were known for being the best school orchestras in London. They could play pretty much anything from a Beethoven symphony to Purcell's *Dido and Aeneas*. At Bedales the orchestra could only be described as terrible. When I'd arrived, I'd wanted to give up the oboe and take up singing, but when the head of music discovered that I was an oboist, he begged me to keep it up and join the orchestra. I was truly shocked by the first rehearsal: the orchestra met in the school hall and the head of music began conducting while remaining completely oblivious to the fact that no one was playing in tune or keeping time. After the first term I walked out, put my oboe away and joined the choir, which was only marginally better.

I'd been interested in the usual political causes when I was at Pimlico, like CND and the Anti-Nazi League, but our involvement never went further than wearing badges or drawing their logos on our school bags. There were plenty of serious campaigns to choose from at Bedales, and each came with a lot of sitting around in classrooms and common rooms, where we'd discuss the issues and then take action. Along with the ones I'd been familiar with at Pimlico there were also others to get behind, like Greenpeace, the Anti-Apartheid Movement and Friends of the Earth. Partly because of Dad's involvement with them when he did *The Secret Policeman's Ball*, I chose to throw my lot in with Amnesty International.

Once a week Remy and Joshua got a group of us together in a classroom after supper to write letters on behalf of Amnesty International. These included a regular letter to the president of South Africa asking for the release of Nelson Mandela. Then there were letters to a number of notorious dictators, which Remy suggested ways to personalise with things like 'Dear

Mr Bokassa [or Mr Mobutu or Mr Gaddafi], on a recent and most enjoyable visit to your country I became aware of the imprisonment and torture of one of your citizens and leading intellectuals. In the interests of a better world my friends and I wondered if you might consider setting him free.' The hour and a half of letter-writing each week felt far more worthwhile than the times I'd spent writing to Biddy Baxter at the BBC asking for a *Blue Peter* badge, even though we never got a reply from any of our dictators. Maybe I half expected to get one that said, 'Dear Mr Miller, sorry for the slowness in replying, but we get over 4,000 letters a week, but in the meantime, we thought you might like a photo of one of our torturers.'

The disappointment I felt about my dorm was compensated for by being assigned one of the nicest studies in the school, tucked away in a large attic room in the science block. I shared it with four other students, who all turned out to be rather too laid back about their academic commitments. This probably had something to do with the fact that our remote location was far away from the prying eyes of our teachers, which allowed us to get away with sitting around for hours drinking coffee and gossiping. Conrad was doing English, maths and physics for A-level, and his study was on the other side of the school, in the English department. It was on the ground floor, with large windows, and was next to a busy pathway. This meant people were constantly walking past and could see whatever he and his study companions were up to. As a result, his study companions were a lot more studious than mine and spent more of their time working or discussing what they'd learned in class.

Owing to a constant concern that we might burn the school down, kettles had been banned from all the studies, but this

Conrad outside his study at Bedales, 1981

hadn't stopped one of the boys in my study hiding one behind a panel in the eaves. I'd discovered a deli in Petersfield that sold freshly ground coffee like we had at home, and I asked Mum to send a large box of coffee filters in the post, which she did along with a very large fruit cake that she'd made. This allowed my study mates and me, along with a steady stream of visitors, to sit around on two dilapidated sofas, brewing coffee, chatting and generally not getting on with our work. One of the boys had shown us how to make elderflower champagne in old lemonade bottles, which we hid with the kettle. But he forgot to tell us about the need to release the pressure from the bottles occasionally. Needless to say, one afternoon they exploded like a 21-gun salute. Everyone in the building assumed the noise had come from an experiment in the chemistry lab, so no questions were asked, which would have led to the discovery of our contraband kettle.

The obligatory A-levels for medicine are the three sciences: physics, chemistry and biology. The thing about the first two, and what makes them different from, say, English or history, is that they require you to know the answer to the question, and as my teachers were always telling me, there is only one answer – and that's the right one. To get the right answer you also need to have a pretty good grasp of maths, which quite frankly I didn't have. Biology is subtly different; there's no maths, but you need to understand what's actually taking place in a plant or animal and then identify all the parts and remember their names. You have to know the facts, but in biology you can also get away with having an opinion and writing about it, which you can't do in chemistry or physics.

The first project I did for biology A-level was anatomy and the dissection of a rat, which, thanks to all the lessons from Dad, I was able to do with precision. Anatomy was a pushover too, as I'd grown up with an enormous anatomical picture on our kitchen wall of a man's torso showing all the organs, and many meals were spent being tested on their names and functions. The thing about dissection is there's no right or wrong way of doing it – you're either good or bad at it, and thankfully I was quite good. We were each given a rat, which arrived in a plastic bag and was completely rigid, with fur that had turned a fluorescent yellow from the formaldehyde. With the skill of a surgeon I traced the nerves and blood vessels, in spite of their rubbery texture. I removed the liver, heart and kidneys and then cut off slices to examine under the microscope. By half-term the rat was no more than a head with a set of sharp teeth in a rictus grin. The expertise with which I'd dissected the rat and identified all its parts had initially impressed my biology teacher, but this didn't last long.

When it came to following the rest of the A-level syllabus, I found myself making the same old mistakes. Once again I'd let Dad's enthusiasm for my doing sciences get the better of me and, before leaving for Bedales, I'd accepted the loan of a collection of books that he claimed were essential for a budding doctor. Among these were several advanced and irrelevant books such as *Gray's Anatomy* for medical students and two volumes that Dad insisted I read straight away. These were on animal behaviour and written by a Dutch scientist who'd spent his life studying sticklebacks having sex. I naively tried to use these books to prove to my teacher that I had the makings of a serious biologist, but soon found it had the opposite effect. On one occasion he set the class the task of researching and writing an essay on the life cycle of the earthworm, which was right there in the A-level syllabus. It should have been fairly straightforward, but I felt the need to impress and decided to write a detailed account of the courtship and mating habits of the stickleback instead, which I copied almost word for word from Dad's books. Needless to say, I was asked to stay behind after class, where the teacher drew a red line across each page of my essay and then accused me of wasting both his time and mine. 'I don't know where you got this nonsense from,' he said, staring down at the essay with his head in his hands, 'but I think you'll find the stickleback bears no resemblance to the earthworm.'

As with my O-levels, side-tracking into topics I didn't

understand and which weren't part of the syllabus turned out to be the beginning of the end. I'd only just got away with it at Pimlico, but at Bedales it exasperated the teachers and led them to write in my first school report that I would do far better if I stopped talking in class and stayed focused – neither of which I seemed able to do. It had all started so well with the dissection of my rat and the idea that I only had to focus on the three sciences, which would set me on course to becoming a doctor and success in the eyes of my father. The trouble was, in biology I thought I knew it all, which I clearly didn't, and in chemistry and physics I was rapidly coming to terms with the fact that I knew very little. In both of them I couldn't do the maths, so it wasn't long before I found I was either missing the point or struggling to keep up. With that, a sense of drowning started to take over again and that generally led to panic. Maybe if someone had taken me aside and explained in simple terms how to study properly I might have been able to get on and finally ignore Dad's counterproductive suggestions, but no one ever did.

27

LIFE IS BUT A DREAM

After I left for Bedales, it seemed that life in Gloucester Crescent had carried on as if nothing had changed. I did wonder if it might have been like Freddie's explanation of philosophy – the one about trees falling in forests and whether they made a sound if no one was there to hear it. In the same way, I wondered if my not being at home meant life as I knew it would just stop. No comings and goings, no Alan, Eric, Oliver, Mary-Kay and others sitting around the kitchen table having interesting conversations – everything frozen in time until I came home.

It was one of those scenarios Conrad liked to debate when we were much younger. One of his favourites, which he liked telling me to freak me out, first came about when I was singing the song that went 'Row, row, row your boat, gently down the stream, etc. etc. … life is but a dream,' when he came back with, 'You do know life might actually only be a dream and we're all fast asleep and everything that's happening in your life is the dream and only happening to you.' Conrad was full of these philosophical conundrums. There was another when we went on a school trip to the London Planetarium when we were ten. The whole class sat staring up at a galaxy of stars projected across the domed ceiling as the commentator told us he was now going to take us back thirteen billion years to the

The kitchen, Gloucester Crescent – Alan Bennett,
Mum, my cousin Daniel Miller, Kate (with joke
teeth) and Dad getting on without me

beginning of the universe. As the man waffled on about the
Big Bang, Conrad, a bit too knowingly, whispered in my ear
that if we walked out of the Planetarium at that very moment
there would be nothing out there. All of London and everything we knew would be gone, replaced with swirling gases
and mega-volcanic explosions. I was completely convinced it
was true that we'd travelled back in time, until we stepped out
onto the Marylebone Road and found it was exactly as we'd
left it two hours earlier.

It was abundantly clear that life in the Crescent was carrying on as if I'd never left. I knew this because I could hear it at
the other end of the phone whenever I called home: whatever
space I'd taken up within our house and in people's minds had
been filled. This idea played into a fantasy I'd had for some
time about running away and letting everyone think I'd never
come back, and then secretly moving into a room in one of

the houses across the gardens in Regent's Park Terrace. From there I would watch my family getting on with their lives without me and see if my disappearance had made any difference or if they cared.

When I'd stood on the front steps with my trunk, I remember thinking, 'This is it. I'm moving on with the rest of my life.' I knew I'd come back for holidays and the odd weekend, but from this day on my relationship with my family would be completely different.

I called home most days in those first weeks because I was excited to tell Mum and Dad about school and my new friends, but it was always a challenge and the novelty soon wore off. The boys' house only had one telephone, a payphone in a doorless cupboard with no privacy, which made any kind of personal conversation impossible. Each night you took your place in the queue and waited your turn. When it came, you had to try to complete the story you wanted to tell before being cut off by the pips and the frantic shoving of coins into the slot. Mum wanted to hear my news and tried her best to take it all in, even though she was obviously distracted by everything going on around her, which sometimes left me feeling like I might as well be talking to myself. If Dad got to the phone first, he only wanted to know if I'd read his books and, finding I hadn't, lost interest and handed the phone over to Mum. Then there was Tom: if he answered, he was keen to let me know that my place in the family had been filled, that I wasn't missed by anyone and didn't need to bother coming home again. I never really minded Tom's digs as I preferred to stay at school and make the most of my two short years there.

I found it comforting that the metaphorical trees in Gloucester Crescent kept falling and continued to make all the familiar noises one would expect. I wanted to be more independent from my family, but knowing that life at home was carrying on as usual helped give me the confidence I needed to detach myself from my family. I had no back-up plan other than to return home if it all went wrong, so it was good to know that I could potentially slip back home if I had to, even if Tom had other ideas.

We had the option of going home at weekends, but I rarely felt the need and ended up not returning to London until the autumn half-term. When it came, I made a brief visit to Stanage to see Stella and then spent the rest of the holiday at home catching up with my friends. Dad was now at the BBC directing *The Taming of the Shrew* with John Cleese, so I spent a day with him watching the filming at Television Centre. It was part of the BBC's Shakespeare series, which had become a big project for Dad and one he was actually enjoying.

The BBC had asked him to take over the running of the series the year before, when he was in Vienna directing *A Midsummer Night's Dream* at the Burgtheater. I was staying with him at the time and we were sitting outside a famous old restaurant called the Café Landtmann eating these big creamy pastries. As we sat there in the baking sun, two men, holding their jackets over their arms and carrying briefcases, made their way across the Ringstrasse shouting 'Jonno!' For some reason only people in telly call Dad Jonno, which I've always hated. These two men came skipping over, sat down and asked him straight out if he'd like to come and work at the BBC and take over the Shakespeare series. He was never one to say no to a big project, and it also happened they'd turned up at the right time. Things had not been going well for Dad in Vienna; the German-speaking cast, who'd been forced on him, got off to a bad start by pretending not to understand a

Dad rehearsing with John Cleese for the BBC's
The Taming of the Shrew, London, 1980

word he was saying. To add to this, the lead actor walked out half-way through rehearsals claiming to have come down with a mystery illness. Dad got the cast together and told them 'Ich bin Arzt', which means 'I am a doctor', and informed them that this mystery illness didn't exist. By the time the two men from the BBC turned up he was desperate to get out of the production, although he knew he couldn't leave until the rehearsals were over. So he said yes to the men from the BBC, and before the curtain went up on the first night we were off.

When I came home for half-term, I discovered the padlock on the cupboard in my bedroom had been removed and my treasured belongings had all gone. The culprit, it turned out, was the actor Bob Hoskins, who'd been staying in my room when I was away at school. He was playing Iago in Dad's BBC production of *Othello*. Dad had been warned by Bob's agent that he might need a bit of supervision to keep him out of trouble, so he and Mum invited him to stay and gave him my room for the month. Having seen him rob, torture and murder people in *The Long Good Friday*, Tom had asked Bob if he knew anything about picking locks. It turned out he did, and on his first night he showed Tom how to pick the lock on my cupboard. Tom told me with some pride that it had taken Bob less than a minute to open it. He also pointed out how surprisingly boring everything in the cupboard had been, but that it had been worth it just to see the look on my face when I got home.

There was one big change in the Crescent that had happened in my initial absence, and it had happened without me being aware of it ever taking place. I only discovered it when I walked up the stairs to my bedroom and looked out across the gardens to Regent's Park Terrace and noticed something different about the Ayers' house. From my window I could see that all the rooms and the conservatory on the half-landing were now empty – gone were the marijuana plants, Freddie's desk, the big ornate mirror in the sitting room and all the pots and pans that hung across the kitchen window on the second floor. The Ayers had vanished, left the Terrace, and I hadn't had the first idea it was happening. I sat by my window and stared at their empty house for ages. I'd never seen one, but it was what I imagined a dead body would look like: from the outside it looked familiar, but somehow you could tell the person you knew had gone.

Other than the Mellys, the Ayers were the first of our close friends to sell up and leave. The Mellys had only moved up the road to Gospel Oak, but the realisation that the Ayers had packed up and gone hit me hard. Mum handed me a letter Dee had written for me to read when I came home from school. I pictured her sitting at the typewriter in her bedroom with cigarette smoke drifting from her mouth and into her nostrils as she thought about what to write. In her usual straightforward manner she explained how she and Hylan had finally fallen out of love with England and wanted to return home to America. She described England as 'a mean and shitty little country filled with snobs, and that includes Freddie'.

There was something spontaneous and crazy about the whole thing. Everyone knew Dee and Freddie's marriage had been a mess for years, but they put up with it by being constantly angry with each other. Now, finally, they were separating and had sold their house in Regent's Park Terrace. Eventually, they'd get a divorce and Freddie would marry Vanessa Lawson, but for now he was living with her in Fulham, so maybe they'd all be happy. Dee wrote that she and Hylan were about to board an ocean liner (which I thought a rather old-fashioned way to get to America) and were heading across the Atlantic to start a new life in New York, where she would be close to Gully.

The strangest and least-thought-out part of all of this was that Nick didn't feature in anyone's plans, least of all Dee's. When I asked him about it later, he said he'd come home one day and been told by his mum that the house had been sold and she and Hylan were leaving. They hadn't asked him to come with them to New York, and he hadn't been invited to live with Freddie and Vanessa either, though he said he wouldn't have wanted to anyway. Nick was now seventeen and had been desperate to escape the turmoil of his parents' fighting, and he saw this as an opportunity to get away from both of them. The more troubling problem was that Nick considered himself to be an adult and, having discovered the freedom of being independent, was now living with friends in squats where drugs were freely available. This worried Mum and Dad, who felt that Dee and Freddie had been somewhat irresponsible in abandoning him in the way they had, although there wasn't much they could do about it; had they been able to offer Nick a place to live, he wouldn't have given up the new-found freedom he'd been given by being dumped by his parents.

At the end of the half-term holiday I got to witness another form of irresponsibility when Dad had a go at taking the law into his own hands. I'd been dragged along with him and Mum to see an unwatchable French art film at a cinema in Bloomsbury. As we filed out of the cinema with the rest of the audience, who were now analysing the brilliance of the film, a woman across the road and screamed, 'Help! I've been mugged!' When I looked back, Dad had vanished, but then I caught sight of him chasing two very dangerous-looking boys who were holding the woman's handbag triumphantly over their heads. My only thought was, 'Oh my God, he's going to get killed', so I took off after him. As I ran, I became aware that the disorderly group of intellectual cinema-goers had now joined Dad in his pursuit of the muggers. When we all caught up with him, he was waving a plastic palette over his head which he'd picked up off the pavement and was shouting out the usual abusive lines about how he was going to rip various body parts out of them.

While Dad was bellowing words like 'spleen', 'oesophagus'

and 'thyroid', a small man with tortoiseshell glasses managed to get shoulder-to-shoulder with him and shouted breathlessly, 'I think we met once at Susan Sontag's.' For a split second Dad stopped shouting, looked down at the man and said, 'That's interesting, was it in New York or London?' Then he went back to yelling at the thugs. Eventually, the boys stopped running, and one of them took out a baseball bat from under his coat. The gang of arty corduroys came to a halt behind Dad, who dropped the palette, held up his fists like a boxer and shouted, 'Come on, then, I'll have you both!'

I knew it had gone too far, so I grabbed him by the collar and dragged him back while the boys made their escape. As Dad was patted on the back and led away by his new friends, he turned round and accused me of being a coward. I was shocked and hurt by this accusation – I was more than familiar with boys like that from my time at Pimlico and acutely aware of what they were capable of doing, but for Dad it was as harmless as a scene from one of his Shakespeare plays. I didn't think I was being a coward – I thought I was being sensible. I knew that if I hadn't dragged him away they would have cracked his head open like a coconut. It was one of those situations I've always dreaded Dad getting into, where, out of naivety, he'd stumble into dangerous territory and wouldn't know how to reverse out of it without getting hurt.

28

GIRLS VS. BOYS

Having acquired a little confidence from losing my virginity, you might have thought that being at a mixed-sex boarding school would have been the perfect opportunity for me to find a girlfriend. It turned out not to be the case. Every now and then I'd hear about a girl who was interested in me, but I was incapable of doing anything about it. Maybe it was shyness, a fear of being turned down, or maybe it was something else. I certainly spent a lot of time, when I should have been studying or revising, thinking about my ideal girlfriend and the kind of relationship I'd like to have. Sigourney Weaver in *Alien* came pretty high on my list. She was beautiful, independent, self-possessed, and I'd always wanted to travel through space. Then *Blue Lagoon* came along and I became obsessed with the idea of being marooned on a desert island with Brooke Shields and swimming naked in the sea with her. To add to this fantasy, there was a girl at school who looked quite like her. Through the grapevine I heard that she liked me too, but before I could pluck up the courage to ask her out she was snapped up by another boy.

In the school library was an enormous scrapbook, or *School's Record*, for everyone to browse through, which was put together by a group of sixth-formers who called themselves the Records Committee. Their job was to create an amusing record with photos and cuttings of the big things that happened over the school term: plays, concerts, events and the overall fun parts of school life. On the final page for each term was an 'official' list of who was going out with who, which could then be compared with the lists from the previous terms.

Top of the list were the couples who'd been together for years and appeared on it without fail term after term. I always thought those relationships were far too serious and grown up, but what alarmed me most was the way their friends treated them like surrogate parents. Personally, I didn't have time for any of them and wondered if they weren't heading for a massive fall. It had to happen sooner or later: school would end, off they'd go to their different universities, and then what? On the rare occasions that one of these couples did split up I couldn't believe how everyone got dragged into the politics of their separation. Wherever you went, there were people in mourning or dealing with some crisis the break-up had inflicted on everyone. You'd come across groups of their friends consoling one half of the couple, who would be sobbing uncontrollably in the back of the library or a common room. A girl in my year was even sent up to London to see a shrink because she'd been traumatised by the break-up of her two friends, who'd been together since the third year. Like the parents in a family, this couple were the glue that held her world together, and once they'd split up nothing seemed worth living for.

Next on the list were the short-term relationships. These started with a fanfare – everyone had to know about it, watch them snogging in inappropriate places around the school, and it would be very boring for everyone else. Then there'd be tears as they said goodbye on the last day of term. When they came back the after the holidays, it was like it had never happened, which made it easier for everyone else: there was nothing like the clean break of a holiday to stop the rest of the school getting caught up in someone else's messy liaison. This was the kind of relationship I most aspired to have, but for some reason it never happened.

I did go out with one girl, but it only lasted two weeks, which was long enough to get myself on that list. I was encouraged by her best friend to ask her out, even though I wasn't entirely sure about it at the time. Before I knew what was happening we'd become this boyfriend-girlfriend thing: I stopped functioning as William and we were suddenly an official couple with everyone getting involved, including the bloody Records Committee. The thing is, my fantasies about having a girlfriend were all about being alone with her, stuck on a spaceship or a desert island, and they didn't involve other people sticking their noses into our affairs all the time.

The final nail in the coffin of our flightless relationship came with the awkward ritual of walking one's girlfriend back to the girls' house at night. There was something I couldn't bear about the knowing look another boy felt he had to give you as you passed on the footpath with your girlfriend. Then there was the inevitable kiss at the front door, except my girl-friend insisted on dragging me into a yew hedge, where she would French kiss me with so much force I thought I was going to choke on her tongue. I began to dread these walks, and after two weeks I put an end to it. I'd never had to end a relationship before and spent the entire night and the following day torturing myself over what to say and when would be the best time to do it.

I played out several scenarios in my mind. I could do it over lunch, but then I pictured everyone in the dining hall dropping their cutlery and turning to stare at us as she broke down in tears. Then there was her study during prep time: I'd wait for her to be alone and then saunter into the room, sit down, ask her what she was working on and casually come out with it. Then I remembered she had one of those studies near Conrad's, where everyone could look in – if my plan didn't go well, she might start shouting or crying and a crowd would gather at the window like they do at the zoo. In the end I opted for the most obvious – the yew hedge outside the girls' house. I would time it for the exact moment when she started to lunge at me for the kiss, then I'd stop her and make my announcement before it went any further. If things became difficult, I would have the hedge to hide in.

Much to my relief, she was remarkably calm about it. She said it was a shame, but she'd sensed I wasn't that into her and hoped we could still be friends. And that was that. It all seemed a bit too easy, and as soon as I'd said it I felt liberated, with a new-found lightness in my step as I skipped back to the boys' house. I felt like a man who'd been released from jail, and I made the decision that for now I needed to remain single – no more girlfriends. The thing is, lots of boys in the school fancied this girl so, unsurprisingly, by the following week, she'd found a new boyfriend and I was starting to ask myself if I'd been a bit too hasty breaking up with her. I also started to ask myself if there wasn't perhaps something altogether bigger going on with my fear of relationships with girls.

It was around this time that the idea of being gay started to cross my mind. I hadn't stopped fancying girls, but for the first time it felt like homosexuality was a road I could explore or go down if I wanted to. Thanks to Mum and Dad's friends, there have always been gay people in my life, and these fall into two categories. First there are the older ones, who never talk about it, live on their own and don't seem to have boyfriends. Then again, Alan once told a journalist who'd asked him if he was gay that that was a bit like asking a man crawling across the Sahara if he'd prefer Perrier or Malvern. Then there's the other set, who are very open about it; they mostly work with Dad in the theatre and express themselves by being what he calls 'queeny', which means a lot of camp humour and a fair amount of bitchiness, which is often very funny.

When I was at Pimlico, the gay thing wasn't something I ever really thought about. It was never discussed, and if anyone was gay they kept it well hidden. Conrad and I were occasionally accused of being 'pooftas', but it turned out the boys who said it thought it meant posh and poncey. At Bedales the situation was altogether different. There were a couple of boys who were completely open about being gay and took a lot of pleasure in camping it up, and no one was bothered either way. One of them frequently turned up to games in a pink Fiorucci jumpsuit and would scream and wave his arms around like a girl every time the football came near him. Another boy persuaded our housemaster, Harry, to rent a film called *La Cage aux Folles* for the sixth-formers' Saturday night film club about a gay couple who run a nightclub in Saint-Tropez. The film has all the charm of the south of France mixed with the farcical adventures of the gay couple. It was so popular with everyone that we insisted on watching it again on the Sunday morning. The boy who organised the screening spent the rest of the term copying all the little screams and rolls of the eyes of Albin, the main character in the film. I couldn't ever have imagined watching this film at Pimlico, where we'd have been lynched by the bullies if we'd been found out.

In my first term at Bedales I actually went on what some people might have called a date. At the time it didn't cross my mind to call it that, as it was with another boy. It came about after a phone call when I was at home for half-term. 'I thought he was dead …' Mum said before handing me the phone and raising an eyebrow, '… it's very strange but I could swear Noël Coward is on the phone for you.' The voice at the other end did sound very grand, almost from another era, as the caller introduced himself as Matthew.

I'd seen him around school, though I hadn't met him properly and was curious to know who he was. Matthew Rice is two years older than me and had left Bedales the previous term but often came back to see friends from his year who'd stayed on to do the Oxford and Cambridge entrance exams. Several of them had suggested to both of us that we might get on as our fathers worked in the theatre, so it wasn't entirely unexpected that I'd get a call from him. We chatted briefly on the phone and decided to meet up at Gloucester Crescent the next day and go to London Zoo.

Tom went to the door when Matthew arrived, and then left him waiting on the front porch while he ran down to the kitchen to get me. 'It's Bertie Wooster for William,' he announced, trying hard not to laugh. 'I always knew when William went to that school he'd end up being a ponce.' Ignoring his tiresome attempt to wind me up, I went to the front door to find Matthew, who was dressed like a country squire from the 1920s in a tweed suit with a polka-dot silk tie. Even though it wasn't raining, he was carrying an old-fashioned black umbrella, which he used like a cane to point out various things as we strolled through the park and on to the zoo.

As we walked, Matthew told me about his parents, who

he lived with next to the river in Chiswick, and how he kept chickens in the back garden which he'd bred at school. He talked a lot about his time at Bedales, which he'd loved, and about the teachers who had inspired him. He was passionate about art, art history and architecture, and he had a real skill in bringing everything to life with stories about the terraces designed by Nash on the edge of Regent's Park, and how in the early 19th century the Prince Regent had bought the park to build a palace for himself, though it had never been built. He seemed so knowledgeable about so many things, and I was surprised when he told me that his A-levels had been a disaster, but it hadn't held him back in any way. He'd always wanted to do something creative and had ended up following in his father's footsteps by studying theatre design at art school, which he was hoping to make a career of. He couldn't believe I didn't want to follow my father into the theatre, but I explained that Dad was constantly warning me off it. However, hearing about Matthew's love of the theatre did make me wonder if I was making a mistake.

I found him very easy to talk to as he didn't lecture me or talk down to me, and I was impressed by how much he knew about many of the things that interested me. But as we explored the zoo and talked, there was this nagging voice at the back of my head questioning what this encounter might really be. Matthew was also wise and perceptive and gave me his thoughts on the girls I liked at school, but I couldn't tell if he was gay, straight or just very theatrical and eccentric.

We returned to Gloucester Crescent, and I was relieved to find that Tom and Kate had gone out. Mum and Dad were settling down for tea, and as we sat with them Matthew took out of his bag a box of eggs from his chickens and gave them to Mum. I noticed he'd painted flowers and chickens over the

Matthew Rice

whole box, which Mum complimented him on. Dad asked loads of questions about Matthew's art school and what he was interested in doing. I didn't feel the usual tension when my friends met Dad; he wasn't lecturing him, perhaps because Matthew was managing to hold his own and keeping Dad amused in the process.

I'd really enjoyed my time with Matthew, but when he left I felt confused by the uncertainty of my feelings – had this been more than just two boys hanging out together? If he was gay, was this how relationships of this kind started? And if it was, could it be what I'd been looking for all this time? Maybe this was why I didn't have a girlfriend, or why I'd bailed out of the brief relationship with the girl from school.

I pushed these thoughts aside, but they came back on my next visit home, when Mum asked straight out if I thought

I might be gay. My immediate response was a perplexed 'What?', but she obviously wasn't going to let it go. 'Dad and I really liked your friend Matthew,' she went on, 'but we did wonder about him. And we wanted you to know that it really would be OK if you liked boys and not girls.' We looked into each other's eyes for a moment, as if to see who'd blink first, then she shrugged and said, 'I've always thought it would be rather nice to have a gay son.' What struck me most about her saying this was that she'd clearly given it a lot of thought since Matthew's visit and almost certainly discussed it with Dad. I wondered whether my being gay might bring us closer together, and that it might even give me an edge on Tom and Kate. Maybe it would make me more than just a son to her: I could become her confidant in the way that some of her gay friends were. I wasn't sure what difference it would have made to my relationship with Dad, other than he might have found a certain pride in telling everyone he had a gay son. The truth of the matter was that the idea of my being gay was something I hadn't come to any firm conclusion about, but I was enormously grateful that Mum didn't seem bothered which way I was leaning and that she wanted me to know it was OK. I explained to her that I didn't think I was gay, but if things changed she would be the first to know. I knew I still fancied quite a few girls at school and that I definitely didn't fancy any of the boys.

For the rest of that term Matthew carried on coming to Bedales to see his friends, and would occasionally take me for lunch with his parents at the cottage they rented near Chichester. In the holidays he came to Gloucester Crescent for dinner and would bring more eggs or bunches of wild flowers for Mum. As we got to know each other, the nagging voice of doubt disappeared and I became more comfortable with the idea that my friendship with Matthew was no more than that and that I still very much wanted to find a girlfriend.

I more or less forgot about the feelings I'd had until a year later, when *Brideshead Revisited* came on TV. My friends and I were glued to it every week. I hadn't read the book, but as the story of Charles Ryder and Sebastian Flyte's friendship unfolded I found there was something about it that I could relate to, and which I hadn't thought about before. When I think back to my first meeting with Matthew, it reminded me of how Charles described going to meet Sebastian in his rooms at Oxford. He said that there was a voice in his head telling him he should hold back, but instead he'd gone out of curiosity, and described searching for a low door in the wall that opened onto an enchanted garden. My first meeting with Matthew and the trip to the zoo had been a little like that, and our friendship had become similar in many ways to the one Charles and Sebastian had.

Some of the boys at school joked about how it was obvious that *Brideshead* was a gay love story, but I didn't see it that way – whether it was or it wasn't didn't matter because to me it said something else. When I thought about Charles and what he was in search of, I found I was able to make comparisons with the things that had happened to me. Like Charles when he first arrived at Oxford, I was incredibly happy to be at boarding school and Bedales felt like a safe haven after Pimlico, but I wasn't feeling inspired. I was also looking for something that would open my mind and enthuse me in ways that hadn't happened to me before.

When Matthew turned up, it was rather similar to the way Sebastian had with Charles. We went on trips to the countryside and visited grand houses and churches. We'd pull over in his car and Matthew would get his sketch pad out and draw while we chatted about art or music or history or architecture. None of these things was new to me as I'd grown up surrounded by extraordinary people who knew everything about these subjects, like Dad, Freddie, the Tomalins and my uncle Karl, but most of the time they only wanted to lecture and there was never a discussion. Matthew turned out to have an incredible knowledge of these things too, but we discussed and debated them as equals, and for the first time I was feeling inspired and wanted to know more. He opened a door to a world that was gentler and more colourful, which I wanted to explore and be part of. This helped me finally to close the door on those brutal years at Pimlico and escape to a place that felt safe and part of another time. I realised I'd been there before with Stella at Stanage, where I'd found a long-lost and romantic version of an England that was so different from Gloucester Crescent or Pimlico and where I was happy and felt secure.

29

THE END OF THE ROAD FOR DR WILLIAM MILLER

I can't remember the moment I decided that I wanted to be a doctor, but it probably came straight after wanting to be an astronaut, which I was perfectly serious about and would probably have been a better reason for doing sciences at school. None of Mum and Dad's friends were astronauts, so it would have been my very own thing, and once I'd actually become one everyone would have been incredibly impressed, including Dad. The problem was that whenever I told someone I wanted to be an astronaut they just laughed like they would if I'd said I wanted to be a cowboy or the next James Bond. Being an astronaut was not very Gloucester Crescent. In the end, I knew becoming a doctor would make Dad happy, but I was also attracted to it because it was a job that got a lot of respect, and in Mum and Dad's eyes it meant you were both clever and giving something back. I would also be carrying on a family tradition, which had started with my great grandfather, followed by my grandfather and then both Mum and Dad. However, there were a few whopping great facts I'd temporarily chosen to ignore: I've always been hopeless with other people's illnesses; I panic at the first sight of blood; and the thought of having to touch an oozing abscess or an open wound made me retch.

The irony is that it's Tom who should have been the doctor. I've always been in awe of his ability to remain calm in life-threatening situations where I would have been a blubbering wreck. He once came home covered in blood, having come across a terrible car crash and a man bleeding to death. Tom climbed into the car, put his hand on the man's neck to stop the bleeding and stayed with him until the ambulance arrived. The sad thing is that in spite of his cast-iron stomach for gore he never gave a moment's thought to being a doctor, and Dad never pushed him to consider it in the way he had with me. I think Tom has always been smarter about this than I have: he knew that if he wanted to be a doctor or anything else that Dad took an interest in it was best to keep quiet about it. He also doesn't have the same unhealthy longing to please Dad all the time, knowing it's better to keep your ideas to yourself if you don't want him interfering. As a result, Tom is more or less left to do his own thing without the same pressures I've always had from Dad.

Tom's big passion is photography. Dad can see he's really good at it, and that makes him an artist, which is something Dad can get his head around. When he told Mum and Dad that he wanted to be a professional photographer, he also said there was little point in his staying on at school to do his A-levels, which, somewhat surprisingly, they supported. They also agreed with him that a summer in New York would be an inspiration for his work and bought him a plane ticket. So he left school, went off to stay with friends in Manhattan, and Keith gave him a job as a waiter in his new restaurant so he could earn a bit of money.

When I first arrived at Bedales, I had so much enthusiasm for being a doctor, but by the second term it was apparent to everyone that I was struggling. Rather than offer extra tuition to help me get up to speed, my teachers decided it might be easier to encourage me to downgrade my career ambitions to meet what they saw as my limited academic abilities. This came as quite a surprise, as I'd thought the main reason for going to a public school was that it would help you fulfil all your wildest dreams – this clearly wasn't the case. When the first summer term arrived, everyone in my year was asked to start thinking about university applications and it was subtly suggested that I think about applying to do psychology instead of medicine. Then, towards the end of that term I sat mock exams for A-levels and did so badly that at the next parents' evening my housemaster, Harry, told Mum and Dad that I might want to think about becoming an agricultural scientist. A look of horror came over Dad's face as he nervously asked Harry, 'Do you mean a farmer?' As far as Dad was concerned, farmers lived in the countryside, which we all knew how much he hated, and that in turn meant they probably voted Tory, which in his mind made it all wrong. When he got back in the car, I could see he was trying his best to smile as he looked at me through the open window. Through gritted teeth he told me everything would be fine. I could tell he didn't really think so and was clearly still worrying about the farmer thing as he drove away.

Just before sitting the A-levels, the following year, my suggested career changed again to something in childcare, which was further downgraded, by Harry, in my school report to 'nanny'. He later confessed that he'd only made this suggestion because I was the only boy in the school he trusted to babysit his unruly children. I didn't particularly like his children or feel an affinity with looking after them; I just had a knack of settling them down quickly so I could watch his television in peace and quiet.

Dad never took this suggestion too seriously, but I knew that if he had he would have probably thought that people in childcare were generally decent people who voted Labour, so, unlike being a farmer, it would have been all right. I was starting to get annoyed with Harry's career suggestions, and the worse they got, the more I felt the urge to follow in Tom's footsteps and head to New York. I probably would have done that had I not being enjoying myself so much at school in other ways. It had also started to cross my mind that being at Bedales was now less to do with getting a good education and more about growing up and convalescing from Pimlico.

The summer holiday came as a welcome break from the disappointment of my mock exams, although I felt sad knowing that my first year had gone so fast and that when I returned in September I'd only have three terms left at Bedales. The holidays kicked off with the wedding of Prince Charles and Lady Diana Spencer, and Conrad and I sat in front of the TV watching Sarah Armstrong-Jones perform her royal duties as a bridesmaid. After our awkward meeting on the dance floor, Sarah and I had become good friends, and I'd promised to watch her on telly walking up the aisle.

A few days later Kate and I boarded a plane to New York with Mum for a trip she'd been planning for some time as the highlight of our summer. The plan was to see Tom, who was finishing off working at Keith's restaurant, and then drive together to Connecticut to stay with the Aldriches on their farm. There was, however, a more pressing reason for me to be in New York, and that was to see Dee and Hylan. They were temporarily staying in an apartment at the Chelsea Hotel, an enormous 19th-century red-brick building on West 23rd Street. According to Dee, it was perfect. 'Hylan and I are living the dream on the set of an old horror movie, and we love it,' she told me over the phone. She rattled off a long list of famous writers, artists and musicians who'd passed through, passed out or passed away in the Chelsea Hotel. This included Andy Warhol, Jane Fonda, Arthur C. Clarke (who'd written *2001: A Space Odyssey* while living there), Janis Joplin, Tom Wolfe, Patti Smith and Arthur Miller, who'd lived there for six years after separating from Marilyn Monroe. Freddie's old friends Jean-Paul Sartre and Simone de Beauvoir had stayed there, and Dylan Thomas had drunk himself to death in the hotel. There was Quentin Crisp and Gore Vidal, and more recently Sid Vicious, who woke up to find he'd murdered his girlfriend Nancy Spungen right there in his room. Dee joked that more people had been carried out in coffins than had walked out of the Chelsea Hotel.

Along with an endless supply of cockroaches and faulty plumbing, the other thing that excited Dee about the Chelsea Hotel was the shabby restaurant on the ground floor, called El Quijote. As soon as I arrived in New York she instructed me 'to get my arse downtown' so she and Hylan could take me to El Quijote for one of their famous $6 lobster meals. As we sat in a cosy booth at the back of the restaurant cracking open the shells of our lobsters, she told me how she'd had enough of 'silly old Freddie', and that England had stopped feeling like her kind of place. I told her how sad and lonely her house looked without them and that I missed having her around, even if I was away at school most of the time. As I climbed into a cab to head back uptown, her parting words were, 'If it gets too much at that snobby private school, come and live in New York.' An appealing thought, but one of those mad ideas I decided not to think about – for the time being.

The Norwegian tall ship *Sørlandet*

After learning to sail in Connecticut when I was fifteen, Nelson Aldrich had tried to encourage my parents to let me continue with it, but there were few opportunities for sailing in London. Then at Bedales I discovered it was offered as a general study in the summer term. The course involved navigation and theory, which we did in the classroom, followed by a weekend sailing on the English Channel. Having got the bug, I'd written to Nelson to ask if he knew anyone who might need a crew at their local yacht club in Connecticut. Before we left for New York, he called to say he'd found a sail training company offering places on an old Norwegian tall ship called the *Sørlandet*. It was a 210-foot, three-mast square rigger sailing from Nova Scotia to England, an Atlantic crossing that would take a gruelling two and a half weeks. Apart from a cross-Channel ferry, the only boat Mum and Dad had ever set foot on was a rowing boat on the lake in Regent's Park, so they had no concept of what sailing across an ocean would involve, or just how dangerous it would be. Dad had romantic ideas of ancient mariners, *Mutiny on the Bounty* and Captain Bligh, and with that booked me a place.

In the middle of August, just as I was getting used to long lazy brunches and the gentle pace of life on the farm in Connecticut, Mum and Nelson drove me up to Boston and put me on a plane to Halifax, Nova Scotia, where I joined the *Sørlandet* for its Atlantic crossing.

The next day we slipped gracefully out to sea and crossed the Grand Banks into the North Atlantic, where for the next few weeks I fought off overwhelming seasickness and incredible storms. I climbed the ship's three 115-foot masts and shimmied along the many yardarms to furl sails in the middle of the night and was nearly washed overboard (twice). I also learned about celestial navigation and tying knots. At one point I was coerced into joining a small group of trainees who'd come on the trip dressed as 19th-century sailors and stood around in a tight circle singing sea shanties.

When we finally sailed into Southampton, there was no ceremony on our arrival; no flags, bunting or brass bands playing on the quayside as I'd hoped. There'd been no way of letting Mum and Dad know the date or time of my arrival, so there was no one there from my family to meet me either. I disembarked from the ship and made my way back to London on a slow train that rattled its way through Hampshire and Surrey. The lush, dense greenness of the English countryside, still basking in a late summer, was like a kind of snow-blindness after thousands of miles of open-ocean nothingness. Back in London I hauled my enormous kit bag up from the Underground station to Gloucester Crescent and walked through the front door to find everyone out. I closed the door behind me and stood, for a moment, completely alone in the front hall. Our hall always felt like the wings of a theatre, where people waited to go on stage for the performance of 'Miller family life', only on this occasion the theatre was completely empty and I felt overwhelmed by its silence. It was the first I'd experienced in weeks. The ground was still swaying beneath my feet, but as I tried to orientate myself I felt strangely lost and subdued. I knew that in a few days' time I'd be back at school, and I suddenly longed for my family to come home from wherever they were so I could tell them my stories from the high seas.

30

THE FINE WINES OF BORDEAUX

I've always found it interesting to look at the contrasts in one's life and see how things can change so completely and unexpectedly over time. In September 1979 Conrad and I were still at Pimlico and started the school year travelling on the 24 bus, where we felt demoralised and intimidated, knowing that when we got off we'd have to slip into school and try our best to avoid running into the waiting bullies. The following September that all changed: we were on our way to Bedales and so excited and full of optimism. Then, another twelve months on, and for our last ever year at school, we were driven by Conrad's mum to the courtyard of Kensington Palace, where we met up with Sarah Armstrong-Jones. From there, along with our trunks, we were driven on to school by Princess Margaret's chauffeur, Mr Griffin, in a shiny black Range Rover.

I started my last year at Bedales with the best of intentions, having taken a long hard look at what my teachers and the headmaster had written in my report the term before. They all said if I just stuck to the facts and focused on answering the questions in a way that related to the syllabus I might actually have a chance of getting the grades I needed to study psychology at university; otherwise it was back to farming. After the disaster of my mock exams I decided to take their advice and commit myself to hours of revision. As I settled down to work, some of the optimism and the dreams I'd had in my first term at Bedales returned. I'd also put Dad's books back on his shelves and knuckled down to reading the ones I'd been given by my teachers.

Knowing that I only had three terms left, I also decided to throw myself into everything else the school had to offer. I joined a committee (to encourage the younger boys to clean their rooms), sang in the chamber choir, performed in another production of *Noah's Flood*, although this time I was a goat and the orchestra were all over the place. I played a mute peasant in a loincloth in a production of *A Passage to India*, and to everyone's surprise, including my own, I took part in team sports. Taking part in sports was non-existent at home. In fact, the words 'team sports' didn't feature in the Gloucester Crescent lexicon: the only people who took any interest in sport (as spectators only) and supported a team were Mary-Kay's two boys, Sam and Will, who were both under ten and mad about football, and – astonishingly – Freddie Ayer, who was a lifelong Spurs supporter. No one in the Crescent took their children to play football in the park, although Hylan once tried to get all the parents together to take the children on in a game of baseball, but that ended when Dad got hit on the head with the ball and he went home in a huff.

When I arrived at Bedales, I was told by various people that the school didn't really do sports. Still, in winter white lines were carefully painted on the games pitches for football and hockey. Then in the summer term the grass was cut and they were converted for tennis and cricket, with nets and sight screens erected on the boundaries. Our despondent games master, Phil, had played for Portsmouth FC and lived for a small group who took sport seriously. He was so desperate to make up a team that if you happened to put your hand up for a game of cricket or football you'd find yourself enrolled in the school's First XI. Having discovered early on that I was rubbish at football, I opted for hockey in the winter and cricket in the summer and became a combination of team mascot and figure of fun. Cricket was the game of gentlemen, and I found I could at least catch a ball. There was the added advantage of teas in the pavilion and, best of all, the chance to stand around dressed in cricket whites, looking like an extra from *Brideshead*. Come the following summer term, I raised my hand and was duly invited by Phil to join the First XI. This turned out to be a smarter tactic on his part than anyone originally thought.

Realising just how dreadful I was, he came up with a cunning strategy which involved sending me out to bat first. This would inevitably lead to me being bowled out first ball, for a 'golden duck'. These two words were often used by the rest of the team to put me down, but they were part of the cricketing vocabulary which I found so appealing. 'Leather on willow' was another, and without my ever getting one to make contact with the other, the opposing team would assume the rest of us were as rubbish at cricket as me. This gave Phil the chance to play his secret weapon – Billy and his gang of Angry Young Men. They turned out not only to be successful with the girls but also reasonably good at sports. Having caught the other team off guard, Billy and his mates would breeze onto the pitch and basically rough the other team up before tea.

Back in the classroom my enthusiasm for my subjects soon started to fade as I fell further behind. When, at the beginning of the autumn term, Harry suggested I think about applying to study psychology, I went to visit universities at York,

Nottingham and Bristol. None of them excited me, and in each case I left feeling that studying psychology for three years was unlikely to set me up for life, and I always felt relieved to get back to Bedales. In an attempt to get me to focus, I was given a new study on the other side of the science block. I shared it with only one other person: a girl called Suzy, whose family lived on a farm in Cornwall and kept horses. She'd brought one of these horses with her to school, a chestnut Arab stallion which she kept in a field between the art block and the headmaster's house. Despite my lack of sporting skills I had at least learned to ride reasonably well in Scotland, and Suzy let me borrow her horse whenever I wanted, so I'd saddle it up and ride for hours in the hills around the school.

One Sunday afternoon I rode across Stoner Hill to visit a girl called Caroline. She was a very beautiful day-girl I had a crush on, who didn't board and lived with her parents in Oakshott. She had rather flirtatiously challenged me to ride over the hill to see her, on the promise that her parents would be out at church. Like a character from a Jane Austen novel, I rode all the way to Oakshott and tied the horse to the fence outside their house. Letting myself in through a side door I crept upstairs to her bedroom. I wasn't entirely sure what I thought I was going to do with Caroline, or expected her to do with me, but before she'd finished showing me her large collection of gymkhana rosettes I heard her over-protective parents' car coming up the drive. Within seconds I was down the stairs, out the door and on my horse, galloping back over the hill before her father could find his shotgun.

One of the other signs of the influence of *Brideshead Revisited* was the desire by some of my schoolfriends to relive parts of it by dressing up like Charles and Sebastian. During the

Left to right: Remy Blumenfeld, Conrad, Stephen Battle, Tom Salter, Joshua White and me

holidays we scoured vintage clothing shops and returned to school dressed in tweed suits or blazers with braiding or white cricket flannels. As we got into character, Conrad and a friend called Julia decided that we should go to one of the famous public school balls. Having studied *The Official Sloane Ranger Handbook*, they fell upon the biggest (and worst) of them all – the Feathers Charity Ball, which took place the week before Christmas at the Hammersmith Palais to raise money for good causes. The Feathers was traditionally attended by boys from Eton, Harrow and Westminster, along with girls from St Mary's in Ascot, Wycombe Abbey and Cheltenham Ladies' College. Up to this point in the Feathers' history I'm not sure a Bedalian had ever attended it, but Conrad and Julia thought it would be the perfect ball to try out and an opportunity to dress up and show other public schools that Bedalians weren't the bohemian rabble most of them thought we were.

Twelve of us bought tickets – six boys and six girls – and the pre-ball dinner was held at Conrad's house in Gloucester

Crescent, where his mother cooked an enormous meal with poached salmon and pavlova, which turned out to be the most enjoyable part of the evening. Everyone made an effort to dress the part, with the boys either renting black tie dinner suits or borrowing them from their fathers. The girls came in ball gowns, which either belonged to their mothers, and had last been worn in the 1960s, or they'd gone to frock shops in Chelsea and spent a fortune.

After dinner, some of the parents agreed to drive us all to Hammersmith and collect us afterwards. As we stood outside Conrad's house waiting to get into the cars, a group of the Crescent's residents, including Tom and Conrad's brothers, came out to watch us leave. We were filled with pride, and to begin with thought they'd gathered to admire our outfits and wish us luck, but we soon realised their intention was to make fun of us and comment on the absurdity of what we were doing. 'Bloody hypocrites,' one of my Bedalian friends said as we got into the car. 'Every one of your neighbours went to public school, and I bet half of them practically slept in their tuxedos when they went to university.'

The first thing that hits you when you walk into the Hammersmith Palais is the sticky heat and a stifling smell of sweat mixed with cheap aftershave and sickly perfume. By ten o'clock it was even worse and the ballroom had become a seething mass of gyrating teenagers, many so drunk they had to be escorted to the bathrooms to throw up. In the darker corners of the hall were girls snogging boys they'd only just met that night.

It doesn't take long to realise that at the Feathers you either dance or stand around looking like a nesting emperor penguin in your tuxedo. With this in mind I decided to pluck up the courage to approach a girl who'd been smiling at me for some time from across the room. To my surprise she said yes and we energetically threw ourselves around the floor, arms shooting into the air then down to the floor as we danced to the Bee Gees' 'Night Fever'. This was followed by a slow dance, which allowed me to put my arms around her waist and pull her close. As we shifted awkwardly around the dance floor, she shouted into my ear over the noise of the music, 'Are you an heir?' To begin with I thought I misheard, but she said it again.

'Heir to what?' I replied, to which she stopped dancing, rolled her eyes and stalked off.

At the stroke of midnight the huge overhead lights of the ballroom came on as if a fairy godmother had waved her wand and put an end to the revelry. The dishevelled and disorderly mass of tuxedos and ball gowns moved slowly and unsteadily out onto the Shepherd's Bush Road in search of the parents who'd been waiting patiently in their cars lined up along the pavement as far as Brook Green.

I was relieved to find it was Conrad's mother rather than my dad waiting for us outside the Palais. There was nothing I liked about the Feathers Ball, but Dad would have found the sight of hordes of overprivileged drunk public-school kids enough to make him get out the car and sing 'The Red Flag' at the top of his voice. He might have had a point, but I was proud of my Bedalian friends, who may not have been heirs to anything but behaved with dignity all evening and knew how to hold their drink.

There was another activity I threw myself into at school that term, and that was learning to drive. I set myself the challenge of passing the test before my eighteenth birthday. I found a driving instructor in Petersfield who gave me lessons every week. He was a man of few words, apart from 'left', 'right', 'ahead' and 'stop' – the rest he left to a series of exaggerated hand movements. We drove for miles around country lanes and main roads and then the back streets of Petersfield, where we practised parking and three-point turns. One day, on about the fourth lesson, we pulled into the school car park and out of nowhere he asked, 'Isn't there a member of the royal family at this school?' And that was it, until a couple of lessons later, when he came out with, 'Aren't there are a lot of theatre types at this school?' This time there was a pause before he asked, 'Your father, I don't suppose it's Arthur Miller by any chance?' I didn't answer but smiled knowingly, hoping he might think I was the secret child of Marilyn Monroe.

On the day of my driving test he let me drive to the test centre in Chichester as he sat silently staring out of the side-window. Other learner drivers at school had warned me about a notorious examiner known as 'the Roundabout Executioner', who liked to fail everyone on their first test. As luck would have it, he was my examiner that day – and I failed. On my second attempt I had a kind lady examiner who passed me, wished me luck and gave me a short speech on how speed kills and how I wasn't to go showing off to the girls.

In the spring term one of the choices on offer for general studies was wine tasting. Its purpose was to teach us to drink responsibly by way of an appreciation for fine wines. Although I'd never been one of them, this course was the tip of the iceberg in a campaign to stop Bedalians sneaking off into the woods with bottles of vodka and getting completely off their heads. The course took place one afternoon a week in the sitting room of a housemistress's flat in the girls' house. Her husband, Keith, taught physics and was an easy-going and much-liked Australian with a passion for wine. Each week the group would show up at their flat to find a large illustrated map stuck on the wall showing the wine region he planned to introduce us to that day. The various wines were set out on the coffee table, along with a wedge of cheese and some water biscuits. This was just enough to give the class a taste of the wines without any of us getting drunk.

His system worked well until the very last class, when Keith invited a salesman from the wine merchants Harveys of Bristol, who turned up with a whole case of wine and a selection of sherries and ports. We started the first bottle, which we sipped, swirled around in our mouths and then dutifully spat into a bucket. By the third bottle Keith was so excited by the variety of wines he'd failed to notice that the rest of us were knocking them back, and by the time we got to the sherry and port we were literally gulping them down. By the end some of us were so drunk we had to be carried back to our dorms to sleep it off and face the inevitable hangovers the following day. I am not sure the course delivered on its purpose, as all we'd learned was that it was a lot more enjoyable to get drunk on wine than on vodka and that it was better to do it indoors than out in the woods.

As with sailing, the wine-tasting general study was a rewarding addition to the curriculum and felt worthwhile to my education – until, that is, my school report, along with that term's bill, turned up in the post. Dad was still coming to terms with the idea that he was having to pay for one of his children to go to a private school, and getting the bill each term threw him into a depression although he sometimes tried to ease the pain with a little humour. On this occasion he read the bill and my school report out loud to everyone around the kitchen table at Gloucester Crescent. Acting out an air of shocked disapproval, he started by reading out each item on the bill: 'A term's fees – £1,500, laundry charges – £20, a set of cricket whites from the school sports shop – £15, and wine – £100.' After this last item his eyes fixed on me with withering displeasure as everyone around the kitchen table fell about laughing and I tried to make excuses for the importance and value of each item on the bill. He then read out my school report. 'Biology: I am afraid William continues to be rather weak and despondent and has difficulty with the fundamentals.' Then he moved on to chemistry. 'William's lack of mathematical ability is a distinct hindrance to his grasp of the subject.' I had now shrivelled with embarrassment and tried to come up with reasons as to why I was failing to grasp the fundamentals of any of my subjects, but it was no use. The next one was my sports report, where Phil wrote: 'This *Body in Question* has more enthusiasm than physical expertise although nothing quite deters his hunger for the philosophy of sport.' Then there was the icing on the cake – general studies. 'William has acquired a taste for the fine wines of Bordeaux.' The evidence was damning, but hearing Dad reading out my report in the manner of a high court judge about to pass sentence, I suppose it was quite funny. The grim reality was that things were not going well with my A-levels and it was likely to go downhill from there.

31

THE BEDALES FINALE: SUMMER 1982

At the end of the spring term our teachers announced that they'd taught us everything we needed to know from the syllabus, and in the final lessons of that term they closed the textbooks, handed us pages of revision plans and sent us home for the Easter holidays. By now Conrad and I had become pretty good at cadging rides to and from London with our trunks, and Sarah Armstrong-Jones was someone we could usually rely on for a lift. So, once again, Princes Margaret's chauffeur, Mr Griffin, turned up in the black Range Rover and the three of us were driven back to north London, via Kensington Palace.

In an attempt to knuckle down and revise, I decided it would be a good idea to go somewhere less chaotic and distracting than Gloucester Crescent and went to stay at Stanage for the first week. As ever, Stella was thrilled to see me, and set me up with a desk in the library, lit a roaring fire, and while I buried myself in textbooks she brought me lunch each day on a tray. I took the occasional break to go for a walk with her and the dogs, and I went fishing on my own on the lake and came back with a couple of trout for our supper. With the best intentions I steadily worked my way through the revision plans, and it seemed like I was making progress of a sort, although I wasn't entirely sure how much of the information was actually sticking in my head.

A few days after returning to London, Sarah Armstrong-Jones called and asked if Conrad and I would like to go to the theatre with her to see *Cats*. I've never been a big fan of musicals, but a night out with her and Conrad would be a welcome break from memorising the formula for photosynthesis and the elements of the periodic table. I also thought if I could borrow a car it would be an opportunity to experience the freedom of driving my friends around town. With a little persuasion my parents agreed to lend me theirs, and Conrad and I set off to collect Sarah from Kensington Palace. We parked in the palace courtyard and walked up the front steps to be greeted by a tall, smartly dressed butler who showed us to the drawing room and then dashed off through a side-door. A few minutes later he reappeared with a tray of glasses and a bottle of champagne.

Although Dad and Alan are the last people to take royal etiquette seriously, just before I left for the palace they thought it might be amusing to give me a lesson in the basics. I think their motive had more to do with the absurdity of it rather than the importance of not embarrassing myself in royal company. Either way, they stood in the middle of the kitchen facing each other and acted it out for me. Dad kicked off with how to address the Queen or Princess Margaret, with Dad playing the commoner and Alan the royal personage. 'Remember,' Dad said, 'it's "ma'am", which should rhyme with "spam", and not "marm" as in "palm".' As he said this, Alan responded with mock-regal squeals of pleasure. Alan went on to explain that girls curtsy and boys bow, which Dad demonstrated with a quick nod of the head. Funny as it all was, I said it was highly unlikely that I'd be meeting Princess Margaret, who would probably be out cutting ribbons or hosting a dinner somewhere for the Girl Guides.

It was perhaps the serving of the champagne that was the first clue that the evening wasn't about to go in the direction Conrad and I had originally been led to believe. Sarah came into the drawing room looking slightly uncomfortable, closely followed by her mother, who was dressed in a pale pink taffeta ball gown. In a moment of surprise and confusion on seeing her mother my mind went blank, and I found I couldn't remember the key points of Dad and Alan's etiquette lesson. As she approached, I found myself curtsying and nodding at the same time, and whatever it was I said it definitely didn't rhyme with 'spam'. Conrad nodded and said 'ma'am', which left me wondering which one of us had got it wrong. Princess Margaret, graciously ignoring my awkward greeting, asked after my father and what he was working on. As I was trying to remember the name of Dad's latest production, the butler returned with more champagne and a tray of canapés, which he proceeded to hold out for each of us. I reached out and took a canapé of beef on melba toast with an unidentifiable garnish. As I bit into it I knew it was a mistake as the beef stuck to my teeth, the toast snapped in two and everything else fell down the front of my shirt, leaving a snail trail of what looked like mayonnaise. The conversation stopped briefly as everyone stared at the remains of the canapé on the carpet. Princess Margaret looked up, smiled kindly at me and said, 'So sad we don't have corgis like my sister – they'd have gobbled it up in an instant.' Then she clapped her hands and shouted, 'Chop-chop, let's go!' I had another one of those moments where my head went blank with confusion and I looked across to Sarah for some kind of explanation.

'Chop-chop who … where?' I jokingly replied, but it soon

became obvious what she was saying – our party of three had become four and she was coming with us to the theatre. By now Sarah was blushing and looking at her feet, knowing she'd left this minor detail of the evening out in case we turned her down.

Our party now walked out of the front door, where Mr Griffin was standing in the courtyard, holding open the back door to Princess Margaret's official car – a brown Rolls-Royce Silver Wraith. Surprisingly, her Rolls-Royce wasn't quite as big inside as I'd imagined, and Conrad, Sarah and her mother squeezed into the back seat, leaving me to go in front with Mr Griffin. 'Well, this is cosy,' Princess Margaret announced as I looked back at them. She was grinning from ear to ear, and somewhere under a mass of taffeta were Conrad and Sarah. As we pulled out of the palace courtyard we were joined by two police cars and two motorcycle outriders. At Kensington High Street the motorcyclists raced ahead to clear the traffic and we drove along the edge of Hyde Park, down Piccadilly and on to Drury Lane.

There is no royal box at the New London Theatre, so we sat right in the middle of the stalls, with Princess Margaret in her pink ball gown, Sarah, still looking embarrassed, and me and Conrad in our casual jackets and jeans. Princess Margaret seemed to be captivated by *Cats* and didn't take her eyes off the stage for a second, whereas there was very little I liked about it other than a couple of catchy songs I'd heard on the radio. As my mind wandered, I looked around the auditorium and noticed that most of the audience were staring at us rather than the stage, and I started to wish the show would hurry up and end.

When the curtain finally came down, an official-looking

man from the theatre made his way down the aisle and politely instructed our entire row to stay in their seats while the four of us awkwardly climbed over their legs. Then he escorted us to a hospitality room backstage, where it had been arranged for us to have drinks with the cast. One by one the performers filed into the room, curtsied or bowed to Princess Margaret and Sarah, and then to Conrad and me. After gushing with praise and congratulating each of them, Princess Margaret announced to everyone in the room that I was the son of Jonathan Miller. I really wished she hadn't – the cat was out of the bag, so to speak, and I was now the centre of attention, with little to say other than lying about how much I liked the show and how sad my father was to have missed it.

I was eventually saved by the familiar cry of 'chop-chop', and we were suddenly back in the Rolls-Royce. Only this time our departure didn't go quite as smoothly as the one from the palace. As I climbed in the front seat I pressed my hand against my chest to check my wallet was still inside my jacket, only it wasn't – it had probably fallen out in the hospitality room, where I'd thrown the jacket over a chair. As our police escorts started to rev their engines, I apologised profusely, leaped out of the car and ran back into the theatre. Sure enough, there under a chair in the hospitality room was my wallet. Back at the car the police were now battling with a crowd of autograph hunters and a couple of drunks who were trying to get to the car for a better look at its occupants. Inside were Conrad and Sarah, looking terrified, and Princess Margaret, who was clearly not amused. Mr Griffin sat calmly at the wheel, and as soon as I was safely inside we sped off up Drury Lane.

There was an uncomfortable silence in the car, then, as we passed McDonald's at Marble Arch, my mind started to wander onto food and the fact that the only thing I'd eaten in hours was the corner of a single canapé. I figured that as soon as we got back to Kensington Palace we could say our goodbyes, then Conrad and I might just make it back to McDonald's before it closed.

The butler was waiting for us on the front steps and we followed him into the drawing room, where he whispered something in Princess Margaret's ear and then scuttled off. By now I had a Big Mac with fries on my mind and was seconds away from saying, 'Thank you for a lovely evening, Ma'am, but we really must be off.' But as the words collected in my head and I tried to remember if it was 'ma'am' or 'marm', the butler reappeared between two double doors which he pushed open with a flourish to reveal another room with a large table laid for dinner.

As we sat down, the butler unfurled our napkins and placed them carefully on our laps, then he poured Princess Margaret a very large whisky and placed a silver cigarette box beside her. Once everyone was settled, he disappeared to fetch the first course, returning a minute later with four prawn cocktails in glass bowls. Princess Margaret lit a cigarette and took a long sip of her whisky pushing her prawn cocktail to the side. Then she said, 'I don't think your father would have liked *Cats*, would he?' She was right; he would have hated it. 'Shame,' she said, 'I went to see *Guys and Dolls* at the National last week and it was wonderful.' She then informed us that she had the soundtrack and wanted to play it to us after dinner.

She didn't seem to have much of an appetite, and as I was trying to extract a second prawn from under its pink sauce her fist came thumping down on a rubber clam shell positioned six inches from her place mat. The shell clearly contained a hidden bell which must have connected to the kitchen, as seconds later the butler came flying back into the room and removed our nearly full bowls. He topped up her whisky then ran off to get the next course, which was petit poulet with roast vegetables, a bread sauce (which I love) and gravy. I'd just started to dissect mine by removing a succulent slice of breast and was lifting it up to my mouth when down came the royal fist, back came the butler and my plate was gone. At first I thought the speed at which we were getting through dinner might have had something to do with Princess Margaret wanting to get to bed, but it soon transpired it had more to do with her wanting to play us her record of *Guys and Dolls*. When the butler returned, he was carrying a tray with four enormous glass bowls, each containing a delicious-looking trifle. As he approached the table, he was met with a steely glare from the Princess, who waved him off announcing 'I really don't think anyone has space for pudding.' As if to keep his balance and the momentum going, he carried on moving all the way around the table holding the tray of trifles and disappeared back through the door. Judging by the look on Conrad's face he was about as heartbroken as I was about the sudden disappearance of the trifle, which would have easily made up for the earlier loss of the prawn cocktail and the petit poulet. Crestfallen, Conrad and I were led back in the drawing room by Sarah and her mother, who was now waltzing her way across the room to the record player, where she carefully placed the needle onto the rotating record. For the next two hours she proceeded to choreograph Sarah, Conrad and me through a series of dance routines from *Guys and Dolls* – a nightmare combination of my two least favourite things: dancing and musical theatre.

It was the eventual return of the butler that saved us when, at around two in the morning, he came in and offered us nightcaps. This was our cue to leave, and within ten minutes Conrad and I were driving up Kensington Palace Gardens towards the Bayswater Road. There was something surreal about having escaped the bubble of royal life at Kensington Palace and finding ourselves back in the real world. It felt liberating to be driving my parents' battered old car without the police escort or the discomfort of Princess Margaret sitting in the back seat judging us. We were now properly starving, and having found McDonald's at Marble Arch to be closed, we carried on driving through the empty London streets in the hope of our finding something to eat at home. As we drove we talked and laughed out loud going back over the unexpected events of our evening.

Before long we were sitting at the kitchen table in Gloucester Crescent picking our way through the remains of a roast chicken we'd found at the back of the fridge. As we polished off the carcass, Conrad told me that he'd been discreetly reminded, before we left Kensington Place, that on writing to thank Princess Margaret we must remember to sign off with 'I remain your humble and obedient servant'. We sat in silence for a while as we picked at the remains of the chicken and reflected on our evening and the somewhat archaic requirements for our thank-you letters. I also thought back to Mum and me listening, last year, to Princess Margaret's *Desert Island Discs* on the radio and how odd it had been. Everyone else tended to chose calming music, whereas she'd chosen mostly music for royal pageantry: 'Rule Britannia' was one of her choices, which left me asking why anyone would want to hear that on a desert island, and another 'Scotland the Brave'. This was played by the Pipes and Drums of the Royal Highland Fusiliers, followed by 'King Cotton', performed by the Band of the Royal Marines, who she said always came with them on the Royal Yacht *Britannia*. At the time I thought it was going to be a very busy desert island and that she wouldn't get much time to sit with her feet in the sand contemplating life. Then again, when Dad did *Desert Island Discs,* one of his choices was a hymn, of all things, called 'Immortal, Invisible, God Only Wise', and his luxury item was a razor blade. When Roy Plomley asked Dad politely if it was to shave with, he said, 'No, to slit my wrists.' Princess Margaret made no such suggestion – in fact, her luxury item was a piano.

A week later we were back at school, and for the next two months, as I waited for exams to start, the summer term began to feel like a car accelerating towards a brick wall. I could see the wall getting closer, but there was nothing I could do other than close my eyes, steer in a straight line and wait for the sound of crunching metal and breaking glass.

Before I knew it I was sitting in the sports hall staring at my first A-level exam paper, which was chemistry, and something called a 'free response' paper. The last thing I needed was the opportunity for any free response, since that always got me in trouble as I drifted off topic. I looked long and hard at the first question but found I couldn't make head or tail of it. I felt physically sick but I had to write something, so I set off like a madman as a stream of consciousness flowed from my head and through my pen to the paper. I wasn't sure if any of what I'd written made sense or went anywhere towards answering the actual questions I was being asked. Whereas everyone else came out of the exam saying 'Well that was easy' or 'That was tough', I found I simply didn't have the first idea what I thought.

The exams went on for two weeks, with essays, multiple-choice papers and something called 'structured questions', along with several more 'free response' exams. At the end of June I sat the very last one. I walked out of the sports hall into brilliant sunshine and lay in the long grass of the orchard. As the sun warmed my face, I tried to take in the significance of this moment – as I lay there, it dawned on me that my entire school life had been one long meandering journey that had taken me to this one single point, where everything to do with school suddenly stopped: Primrose Hill Primary, Pimlico School and then Bedales, with year after year of lessons, evenings and holidays destroyed with endless homework and months of revision – the curtain had come down and it was all over. There would be no more exams and no more school. For the next few weeks I had nothing to do other than enjoy what was left of my time at Bedales and try to forget about the exams. Then it would be the summer holiday and the long wait for the results.

32

THE BEGINNING OF THE REST OF MY LIFE

The children's bath at the Old Manse is massive and made of cast iron; it stands on four big lion's feet and is at least seven foot long. When Tom, Kate and I were smaller, we would sit naked on the back edge of the bath and wait for the water to run out. Then we'd shoot down its slope and along the full length, crashing hard into the taps at the other end. Thanks to years of wear and tear, the enamel on the bottom of the bath has big cracks in it which always left our bums grazed and bleeding. For the brief moment of excitement our injuries were more than worth the pain.

The bathroom, situated on the half-landing to the first floor, is often a sanctuary from the comings and goings at the Manse, and when we were younger it was the centre of our pre-bedtime routine. Easily big enough for the three of us, we would sit up to our necks in soapy hot water listening to Mum reading us stories. Other times, Esther or Jeanie would sit on the loo seat next to the bath and tell us about their life in Jamaica, or Dad would give us one of his talks on the imminent threat of nuclear war. This was usually triggered by our questions about the converted Shackleton bombers we'd seen lumbering over our heads from the airbase next to the beach at Lossiemouth. Dad got pretty excited when he saw them and told us that the sound reminded him of the same planes taking off for bombing raids on Germany during the war. Now the Shackletons have been converted to airborne early-warning planes, and Dad would explain how they were heading out over the North Sea and up to the Arctic Circle to intercept Russian bombers intent on bringing nuclear oblivion on us all. He didn't beat around the bush, and Tom and I would sit silently listening, occasionally asking him about our chances of survival, to which he would respond 'Not good.'

As I got older I found myself on the other side of the bath trying to entertain the children of our house guests, like the two Garland boys, Alexander and Theo, who, encouraged by us, had discovered the thrill of the bath's Cresta Run. Apart from the much-loved cast-iron bath, it's never been that nice a bathroom. There's an airing cupboard with the hot water tank in it and a washing machine between the sink and bath, which tends to tango across the floor when it hits the spin cycle. The only window is a large skylight over the bath, where you can see the occasional seagull circling the house. Mum and Dad have a much nicer bathroom, which they installed off their bedroom, with views all the way down the valley to Knockando and the hills beyond. Here you feel completely cut off from the rest of the house but, like with our old Morris Minor, Mum bought their bath forgetting just how tall Dad is. This means he has to leave one leg dangling out of the bath or sit with his knees tucked under his chin.

It was now the end of August, and I was lying in our old bath trying not to let my head sink under the tepid soapy water. I'd lost track of how long I'd been there, having finally given up any effort to distract myself from the single thought which had been haunting me for the entire summer holiday.

As I stared up at the skylight, I thought about how the school part of my life was over for ever, and the anxiety I'd felt over the summer had been entirely down to the endless guessing of how I'd done in my A-levels and what might come next. I could be going to university, or taking a year off to travel the world, or maybe this was the start of the rest of my life – but what might the rest of my life be? There was, of course, my housemaster's suggestion of a career in childcare, but one thing I knew for certain: a future that involved looking after other people's children was definitely not part of any plan I had.

It had been a long and painful two months since walking out of my last exam, and the endless waiting had given me restless nights filled with confused dreams of both success and failure. There was a recurring dream I kept having – one where I was blissfully happy, having exceeded my wildest expectations and passed all my exams. I was now at Oxford, although I wasn't entirely sure what I was studying. My rooms were identical to Charles Ryder's in *Brideshead* – on the ground floor, they looked out over the quad of my college, and I could see students rushing to lectures or returning from lazy afternoons by the river. When I opened the window, warm air, filled with the scent of flowers from the beds below, drifted into my rooms. Most of my friends from school had come up to Oxford too and were scattered around the town at various colleges. This included Matthew, who was taking his MA in history of art at Christ Church and had rooms that were strangely similar to Sebastian Flyte's, and I'd arrive for lunch dressed in an elegant suit and we'd eat plover's eggs and drink champagne. There was another aspect to this dream which seemed surreal and made me feel calm and happy: my father would drive up to see me, and we'd walk over to the Ashmolean Museum and have tea on Broad Street and discuss medicine and art and I'd be able to tell him what I'd thought and he'd listen.

When I woke and slowly came to my senses, a sinking feeling would take over as I realised it was only a dream and my future had yet to be decided and was very unlikely to be anything like the dream. There were other dreams where failure was the theme which seemed a lot more likely, like the one where I'm waiting in a never-ending queue at the post office in Camden Town. I'm there collecting my dole money with men from Arlington House. I realise that the woman behind the counter is Miss Crosby, the mean and angry teacher from Primrose Hill Primary, and she's tormenting everyone in the queue. I never get any closer to the counter, but outside a crowd of friends from Bedales and Pimlico are laughing and pointing at me.

I'd tried all summer to be patient, knowing that until that little brown envelope with my exam results arrived at Gloucester Crescent and someone called to tell me what was in it, I was going to be at the mercy of these dreams, and the stress of it had left me exhausted and fretful.

Whatever the outcome, I was back at the Old Manse waiting for that all-important phone call, and I knew that, as had been the case with my O-levels, the results would be life-changing either way. As I lifted my hand out of the water and examined the prune-like texture of my fingers, I realised it was exactly two years since I'd gone through this very same torture. Back then the news hadn't been great, but it was at least good enough to change my life and escape the hellhole that was Pimlico.

I'd been in Scotland for over a month, and my family had headed back to London, leaving me to play host to the

Langlands family. Alastair Langlands is the headmaster of Dunhurst, the prep school for Bedales. Mum had been a pupil there during the war, before she went to the Sadler's Wells Ballet School in London. Alastair has always been something of a legend at Bedales; looking and sounding like a character from *The Wind in the Willows*, he could usually be found walking around the school wearing a pale greeny-brown tweed jacket and plus fours, which he sometimes wore with a matching cape.

As with so many Bedalians before me, I'd come to adore Alastair and his wife, Jane, for the simple reason that they treated everyone, whatever age, as equals and adults. In my two years at Bedales I'd got to know his family well as I was often asked to babysit for their three children. Unlike looking after my housemaster's children, babysitting for the Langlandses was a pleasure that meant family life, a home-cooked meal and, as I'd usually stay the night, a break from sleeping in a dormitory. Over breakfast Alastair and Jane would ask how things were going at school and we'd chat. I felt I could talk openly about my hopes and fears for the future, and I always came away feeling inspired – there weren't many teachers at Bedales who did that. Most of them only ever wanted to talk about what was in the coursework and what you were doing wrong, but Alastair talked about what you might go on and do with your A-levels at university and after. He made it all sound exciting, rather than a requirement for whatever came next. They never talked about failure, even though our discussions always centred around getting good A-levels and going to university, which in Alastair's mind meant Oxford. It was fun to play along with the fantasy, even though I knew it would probably only ever be that.

One way or the other, it now felt absolutely right to have

the Langlandses with me in Scotland at the very moment I'd get my results. Whatever they were, I knew Alastair would say the right things and support me, as he always had in the past.

From the bathroom I heard the single loud ping of the phone in the sitting room, followed by the deafening ring that filled the house and Alastair crossing the hall to answer it. Less than a minute later he was calling up the stairs, 'William, it's your mother on the phone.' Shivering from the cold bath, I pulled on my dressing gown and made my way down to the sitting room.

'I think I have your results,' my mother said nervously on the other end of the phone. 'Do you want me to open the envelope?' I could then hear her tearing it open and pulling out the single slip of paper. She mumbled something before screaming, 'Oh my God, William! You've got A's in everything! This is incredible, I can't believe it, clever old you, I'm so happy for you!' Alastair, who had been standing close enough to hear what Mum was saying, was now smiling with his eyes closed and hands pressed hard together – he'd clearly been praying for me.

With all the bad dreams and endless warnings I'd been given by my teachers and housemaster, this was not the result I was expecting. My mind went into overdrive as I tried to process the news and work out the unplanned consequences of these results. It changed everything – it would mean another term at Bedales taking the Oxford and Cambridge entrance exams, which many of my friends would be doing too. I could go back to the original plan and really become a doctor – and I would have those rooms on the quad.

The excitement of all those new opportunities seemed to last for ever, but in reality it was less than a few seconds before

Mum said, 'Hang on, there are two columns here, one says "level" and the other says "grade".' This was followed by a painful pause before I asked her which column all the A's were in. 'Levels,' she replied, 'the A's are in the levels column.' I suddenly felt cold and faint as I dared myself to ask her what was in the other column.

'Oh,' she said in a whisper.

'Oh what? Oh dear, or just O's?'

'Just O's, that's what it says in the grades column – you have straight O's.'

I handed the phone back to Alastair, whose expression had changed to one of abject compassion, as if he'd just heard that I was about to die of some dreadful disease. It had been a fleeting moment of false hope, but the worst part was knowing that Mum was feeling terrible for making a simple mistake. I probably would have done it myself had I been the one opening that envelope, but for a few seconds it was nice to have had the chance to play out one of the positive themes from my dreams.

I needed to be alone so I could digest what had happened, and holding back my tears I left the sitting room. I slowly climbed the stairs to my room, where I sat on my bed with my head in my hands. Pretty soon I came to the conclusion that I would just have to pull myself together and deal with the harsh reality of my situation and come up with a strategy. Straight O's were worse than anything I could have imagined. It basically meant that the last two years of school, studying three subjects I didn't even like, had been a total waste of time. I should never have chosen sciences, and now all I had to show for it were three more O-levels, which I couldn't do anything with. It was like snakes and ladders – I'd got to the top of the board and landed on a long fat snake that took me all the way back to the bottom, where I was sixteen again with nothing more than a collection of useless O-levels.

Realising I couldn't hide in my bedroom for ever, I made my way downstairs to the kitchen, where Alastair and his family were sitting around the table. As I walked into the room, Alastair, his wife and their three children tilted their heads to one side in unison, as if in a show of sympathetic understanding. 'Now, I've spoken to your mother, who's got it all sorted,' Alastair said cheerily as he handed me a cup of tea and plate of toast. 'Get that down you and let's make a plan to get you back to London.' The plan, it turned out, had already been set in motion by Mum and Dad, who had been frantically calling round their friends. Between them they'd come up with a tutorial college in Oxford called Greene's, where I could retake my A-levels. I had an interview there in four days.

While I was sitting on my bed, it had crossed my mind that perhaps the outright disaster of my A-levels was in fact a blessing in disguise. I'd struggled with sciences for so long and had lost all interest in medicine or psychology, and now it suddenly felt like I'd been released from a future I'd had doubts about for a long time. I was feeling so confused; at the kitchen table I'd been carried away by Alastair's enthusiasm for my parents' rescue plan and could just about see myself believing in it too, but that time alone in my bedroom had left me with a nagging thought I was finding hard to shake off. What I needed most was space to think, and the advice of someone I'd always trusted. Later that day I called Mum and told her I would pack up the house and drive back to London, with a minor detour.

I set off from the Old Manse at 6 a.m. the next day, and by

evening I was heading up the long drive at Stanage. As the car crunched over the gravel, Stella came out of the house with the dogs and, after giving me a big hug, led me into the house. 'Well, you've got a lot of thinking to do,' she said as she sat down next to me on the sofa in the drawing room. Stella never lectured or told you what to do – she just planted thoughts in your head and left you to draw your own conclusions. 'Follow your instincts,' she said, 'and this time do what's right for you.' She went on to tell me the story of how she'd done the same: against everyone's advice she'd given up a career in Hollywood to marry Guy, which she'd never regretted for a minute.

I'd driven five hundred miles in twelve hours, passed through the Highlands, across the rolling hills of the Borders and then down the spine of England, past Manchester and Liverpool and on to the Welsh Marches and then Stanage. As I drove, I realised I could pick any route I wanted and could stop wherever I fancied. It was the first time I'd driven so far on my own and I found the freedom of it completely liberating. Now that I was with Stella in the peace and quiet of Stanage I came to a decision. I knew in my heart that the very last thing I wanted to do was retake my A-levels. I'd made a fundamental error in pursuing my father's dreams instead of my own. I loved Dad more than anything, but I couldn't live the rest of my life trying to please him. Surely if I could drive across an entire country on my own, choose the route to take and get to my destination safely, then I could go anywhere in the world and do anything I wanted to do. It was clear what I needed to do, but I had the feeling no one was going to like it, least of all Dad.

Keith had done it, so had Peter and Gully and Dee and Hylan and then Tom, although briefly. They'd all left London and headed to New York – and now it was my turn. Over several years, thanks to a number of Saturday jobs and generous birthday presents, I'd managed to save exactly £500. I worked out this was just enough to buy a one-way ticket to New York and still have a little left over to cover my expenses until I found a job. Stella let me call Keith in New York from the phone in the drawing room. He was initially supportive of my plan but concerned that it might depend on him for its success. When he asked me how long I was planning to stay, he seemed a bit surprised when I said it might be for ever. Keith had been incredibly kind giving Tom a job, but he'd known it would only be for a couple of months. I didn't want him to feel burdened in any way by my decision or to feel I would be his responsibility – I just needed his help and advice. Keith had arrived in New York seven years before, and he'd done it completely on his own without anyone's help and gone on to be very successful as a restaurateur. His tenacity was one of the reasons I'd always looked up to him, and the idea of embarking on a similar adventure with many of the same challenges made me feel all the more excited and motivated.

In the end Keith and I made a deal, which seemed more than fair. His brother, who also lived in New York, was going away for two weeks and I could stay in his apartment until he came back. Keith said he wasn't going to give me a job, so within two weeks I had to find work, and if I hadn't found somewhere to live I'd be on the street and if I didn't get a job I'd be asking Mum and Dad to wire me the money for a plane ticket back to London.

I was right about Mum and Dad; as soon as I got home and told them I was going to America, Dad didn't like it at all. In fact, he went into a depression and blamed himself for everything, although, when pressed by Mum, he couldn't explain what it was he was blaming himself for – which I felt was part of the problem. At the same time Mum failed to grasp the magnitude of what I was doing and kept telling her friends I was going on holiday to New York. They seemed to have forgotten that I was an American citizen and could stay in New York for as long as I wanted and work. This twist in my birthright was something they'd frequently pushed to one side, having let my US passport expire when I was five, probably believing it was of no value to me. Then, when I was nine, I mentioned it to Dee, whose immediate response was, 'Jesus fucking Christ, your goddamn parents are morons.' Before I knew it she was frogmarching me down to the US Embassy in Grosvenor Square, where I was made to stand in front of an official and swear allegiance to the American flag. They handed me a new US passport on the spot, and on the way home Dee told me that one day it would come in useful and that I should never let it expire again.

I knew once I got to New York no one would care about my A-levels: I'd be living on my wits, and on some phone numbers I'd found in Dad's address book, which included his lecture agent, literary agent and the American publicist for the BBC Shakespeare series. I then went to the travel agent on Parkway and bought a plane ticket to New York. As I sat at the desk and wrote out the cheque my hand was shaking, but I couldn't tell if it was out of fear or anticipation. As I finalised everything for my departure I had a few moments of complete panic, which I couldn't reveal to anyone, not even Conrad, who I'd discussed everything with at length. Conrad had triumphed in his A-levels with two A's and a B, and was returning to Bedales to sit his Oxbridge entrance exams. He was surprised by the hastiness of my decision not to retake my A-levels, but also admitted that he wished he was coming with me.

As the day of my departure approached and my mind raced back and forth between thoughts of 'I'm going' and then 'How can I get out of this?', I came across a film called *Midnight Cowboy*, which was on TV the night before I was due to leave. The TV listings described the film as 'Young man heads to New York in the hope of making his fortune'. This is my story, I thought, and surely it was the perfect film to get me into the right state of mind. That evening I settled down to watch it on my own. It started well with the hero, a Texan dishwasher called Joe Buck, packing his bags and getting on a bus to New York City.

As he makes his way to the Big Apple there's this fantastic song playing called 'Everybody's Talkin'', which made me think, 'Wow! That could be my song, and I'm going there too and it's going to be amazing!' However, things start to go wrong for Joe very quickly, and before long I was watching the worst film I could have chosen at this particular moment. Almost as soon as he arrives in New York he becomes a male prostitute, who is robbed and ends up living with a con man called Ratso in a slum apartment. New York soon looked cold, lonely and frightening, and Joe becomes so desperate he's being paid to give blow jobs to strange men in cinemas. I never got to the end of the film as I was so freaked out and confused by what I saw that I had to switch it off. I crept upstairs to bed with my mind spinning. I felt like the ground was being pulled from under me, that I'd naively backed myself into a corner and now had no choice but to go along with Mum and Dad's rescue plan at Greene's in Oxford. As I headed upstairs, I stopped outside Mum and Dad's bedroom door and thought about waking them up to announce my sudden change of heart. I knew they'd be delighted, but I decided to sleep on it and tell them in the morning.

Lying in bed, I couldn't get out of my mind the images of rundown apartment buildings and the dirty streets filled with dangerous men hanging out on every corner waiting to attack you. My chest started to feel tight and my breathing shortened. My bedroom at the top of our house in Gloucester Crescent felt as safe as ever, and I never wanted to leave it again. I felt drained from all this fretting, but I got up and sat in the dark staring out of the window and thought how different it all looked from the world of Joe Buck. There was something comforting about my neighbours in their houses across the gardens in Regent's Park Terrace as they settled down for the night. I could see V. S. Pritchett pottering in his study, the Harrisons chatting as they washed up in their kitchen, and the Harrisons getting ready for bed. As life carried on across the gardens I could feel my breathing start to ease and my body relaxing. Would I really be in New York in just over twenty-four hours? Did I really have to go? As my eyelids got heavier, I climbed back into bed and fell into a deep sleep.

I woke with a start at 6 a.m. and rolled over to see my suitcases lying on the floor waiting to be taken downstairs. I'd spent hours methodically packing my life into those two suitcases. The unpacking of those bags and putting everything away would symbolise a colossal failure that I would find hard to explain to friends like Conrad, Stella and Keith. Everyone would think I was a coward with no stomach for adventure. I'd also had that dream again – the one about standing in line at the post office collecting my dole money – and somehow that seemed a lot worse than Joe Buck's misfortunes in *Midnight Cowboy*.

As I waited for my taxi to the airport I was trying to

remember how many times I'd stood on the front porch of our house about to embark on another phase of my life. There was my first day at Primrose Hill Primary, when Jeanie and our nanny waved me off as I got in the car with Mum. Then my first day at Pimlico and, five years later, hauling my trunk out the door to go to Bedales. The street had been the backdrop for so many transitions in my childhood and happy memories. The races with the Roebers along the pavement and around the block, helping the dads push Miss Shepherd's van up the road, skateboarding with the Haycrafts and getting the car ready before catching the overnight train to Scotland.

Now I was about to start on another journey that would take me far away from all this. Alan and Conrad had joined my parents, and they were all standing on the front steps to say their goodbyes. I could tell my mother was trying not to cry, while my father, who'd never been good at dealing with tears, was doing his best to make everyone laugh with an amusing story about being in New York with Alan and Mum in the 1960s.

As the taxi slowly made its way up the long curve of Gloucester Crescent, I turned back to take one last look at our house and the small leaving party. Mum was smiling at Conrad while Dad and Alan had turned around and were walking back into the house. I had no doubt that life in the Crescent would carry on without me, but as they disappeared from sight I wondered if I'd ever come back again.

EPILOGUE

2018
(Age 54)

In the 1990s the Crescent went through a sad and steady decline. It was as if a long-drawn-out play with many acts had finally come to an end. Most of the original residents had moved on, either finding their houses too big once their children had flown the nest (the Roebers, Claire Tomalin, Mary-Kay Wilmers) or, after a divorce or death (the Haycrafts, V. S. Pritchett), had decided to sell up. There were a few stragglers left to dismantle the sets and switch off the lights. My parents are one of those families who have stoically remained in their house to this day, along with two or three other couples who settled down to a more comfortable and slower pace of life. What was most surprising throughout the 1990s was the complete absence of children in the street. The gardens fell silent, like an out-of-season seaside resort. Gone were the swashbuckling sword fights, the water bombings, tree-climbing and the calling for friends to come and play from across the garden walls.

Out on the street things had changed too, with the regular presence now of young men who would sit in groups on Alan's garden wall, idly threatening all those who passed. They were members of organised gangs and arrived with the clean-up and redevelopment of King's Cross, when the drug dealers and their customers where pushed up to Camden Town. The gangs worked for the drug dealers, who employed them to run errands and pick up and drop off drugs around Camden Lock. The Crescent turned out to be the ideal place to hang out as they waited for the next drop, and the ivy-covered walls of the front gardens provided the perfect place to stash their supplies. They stayed for the best part of a decade before leaving, having either been sent to prison or moved on to ply their trade elsewhere.

Then a strange thing happened as the century turned into the new millennium: with the gangs gone, a new generation of families started to take an interest in the Crescent. Over the following years the houses and gardens in the Crescent came back to life. As the newcomers took up residence, did up the houses and settled in, the volume was gently turned up and the sounds of family life and children playing in the gardens returned.

In 1983 I came back from New York for what I thought would be a short visit to London, followed by a month in India with my mother. I'd been in New York for a year, initially living alone and then sharing an apartment with Remy (from Bedales) and then Conrad. I had two jobs: working for a PR firm by day and an assistant *maître d'* for Keith by night. My intention was to return to New York at the end of the summer, settle down and do more of the same. But at some point, over one of my parents' Sunday brunches, I overheard Dad talking about Patrick Uden, the man who'd so brilliantly turned *The Body in Question* around. Patrick had just set up his own television production company off the back of the newly launched Channel 4. Something about this new venture made me curious, and I went back to Dad's address book and looked up Patrick's phone number. A few days later I went to see him, and he offered me a job as a production trainee. And so, instead of returning to New York, I embarked on what would be a long career in television, of which the next eighteen years would be spent building a large and successful production company with Patrick.

At the end of 1999, on a business trip to New York, I was re-introduced to Nigella Lawson at a dinner held by Keith at his restaurant, Balthazar. She remembered me as an awkward teenager, and this time we hit it off and talked all evening about the old days, the Ayers and our holidays in the south of France. While in New York together we met on several occasions and came up with a plan to work together. On my return to London I quit my job and went into business with Nigella, producing her television programmes as well as creating, launching and running her retail brand.

Over the coming years, as I got on with my life, my father came to terms with the idea that I'd turned my back on ever going to university or getting any qualifications. What he found equally hard to understand was that I'd chosen a career path that neither he nor his friends fully approved of. Although I'd gone into an industry they were familiar with, I'd joined what they felt was the opposing team: the one on the top floor, who wore suits and ran the business – the Establishment. In their eyes this was somewhat grubby and should be treated with an element of suspicion. We were the ones who stopped people like them from getting on and doing the important and worthwhile things. Over family lunches and gatherings I'd argue back that I was, in fact, the person who made their work possible: I kept their shows on the road, closed the deals, fought for them to have bigger budgets and ultimately made it possible to do the work they wanted to do. I don't think my father ever stopped believing that what I was doing was wrong, but as time passed the discussions became fewer, and I found I felt less of a need to justify myself or please him.

In the meantime I got married, divorced and then married again, and with my second wife who I pursued relentlessly for seven years had two wonderful children. Unlike my father, who'd spent his life circling the fringes of Regent's Park, I decided to take an altogether different route. Determined to remain as independent of my parents as I could, I moved to places they tended not to visit, like Fulham and Chelsea and then across the river to Stockwell and Camberwell, before settling down in west London.

In an attempt to lure me back, my mother would occasionally mention that one or other house in the Crescent had come up for sale, and casually suggest that I should take a look at it. I'd brush it off each time, fearing a return to the Crescent would undermine the independence that had become important to me. I'd created my own life on my own terms where I could dip in and out of the old one whenever it suited me, and I was in no hurry to return.

Then, in the spring of 2008, another house came onto the market following the death of Ursula, the widow of Ralph Vaughan Williams. She had moved into the street in the 1970s after the death of her husband in the late 1950s, and quickly become one of the Crescent's much-loved characters. Ursula was a wonderfully elegant woman who, when not entertaining friends, could be seen pruning her roses wearing a straw hat with a colourful Sobranie cigarette hanging from the corner of her mouth.

For several months after Ursula's death a lodger lived in the house and was given the task of sorting out her papers. It was this lodger who came to the door one spring afternoon, when, without me knowing, my wife rang on the bell to enquire about the house. She fell in love with it the minute she entered the hall, and persuaded me to come over and see it for myself later that day. I did this with a certain amount of trepidation, alarmed by the idea of returning and putting myself in such close proximity to my parents and the life I'd worked so hard to get away from. Over the last two decades I'd watched the Crescent's slow decline and the era of my childhood become a distant memory. I couldn't imagine there being another era like it. But I was also curious, and ready to play the game of 'What if?'

The last time I'd walked up the front path of this house was to visit its previous owner, old Mr Pavlovich, with my father when I was six or seven years old. Back then the front garden was completely overgrown but now, after thirty-five years of Ursula's love and care, it was filled with white tulips, hellebores and fragrant flowering bushes that lined the path to the front steps. The house was one of the few in the street with a hall that runs all the way from the front door to the back. When the lodger opened the door, the first thing I noticed was the intensity of the light reflecting off the lush green jungle of the back gardens at the other end of the hall. This drew me straight through the house and into the back garden. There I wandered around taking in the alternative perspective of the gardens and the backs of the houses that I knew so well.

I was used to standing under my parents' magnolia, but from where I stood now, three gardens away, I could see the full scale of the tree my parents had planted forty-five years before and was now as tall as the house. It was in full bloom and dominated the surrounding gardens with its long branches heavy with pink flowers. Through it I could still make out my father's study and his books on the shelves. Above that was my old bedroom, which had brought me so much comfort later in my teens. There were familiar noises like a distinctive door slamming which I knew instantly to be from the Roebers' old house, and for a moment I could have sworn I heard their mother calling them in for supper. The sound of manual typewriters had disappeared, replaced by the barely audible tapping of computer keyboards. I craned my neck to look over the walls to locate the sound of children playing a few gardens away. Then, when I looked back at my parents' house, I noticed my father had entered his study and was reaching up to take a book from the shelves. He then sat down at his desk and started to read. As I scanned the back of the houses and reminded myself of who'd lived in each one and wondered where they were now, I felt an overwhelming desire to be part of it again. This was where I wanted to be and where I wanted my two daughters to grow up. I would always be independent of my parents, wherever I lived. I realised there was a new generation in Gloucester Crescent and a community that I wanted to be part of.

We made an offer on the house, with the belief that it would probably never happen. In the months that followed, as the lawyers got to work, I would frequently ask myself if I had lost my mind. Then one day the call came to say the deal was done and the house was ours. I put the phone down and sat there trying to comprehend the magnitude of what I'd done – after all these years I was really moving back and returning to Gloucester Crescent.

For the first few months I walked around in a daze, bewildered by my decision. Curious to see what had changed, I would take a walk each evening with my wife heading up the Crescent then along Regent's Park Terrace and back down the other side. As we did this, I would peer through people's windows and stop and chat to other residents in the street. I noticed how many of the houses had been smartened up and enlarged, with many having been scrubbed of a century's worth of soot. Even the old piano factory had been cleaned up. Colin Haycraft's publishing company, Duckworth, was gone and the five-storey rotunda was now occupied by architects, film production companies and various designers.

With our evening walks we soon got to know the new

neighbours and before long established a circle of friends in the Crescent and the surrounding streets. It's still a close-knit community, but the new generation is subtly different from the old. Like my parents and their friends, we get together around our kitchen tables and make each other laugh and cry. We talk endlessly about what we want for our children and encourage them to roam free over the walls, climb trees, share meals and cross the same invisible boundaries of the community. The big difference is the approach we take towards our children's education; unlike the *laissez-faire* attitude our parents had, we go in and talk to the teachers and get involved with the schools; we go to every meeting on offer and would like to think we have a plan. We sometimes wish we could be as carefree as our parents had been, but we find it hard to let go: we're concerned about our children's safety, their use of the internet and social media and worry endlessly about their loss of innocence.

On returning to Gloucester Crescent I realised how very young my parents and their friends were when they first arrived in the '60s. It's easy to forget that the current generation is almost twenty years older, and perhaps this is the reason why we are more circumspect. Perhaps the magic and charm of the Crescent has evolved into something more grown up and responsible.

But then, of course, there are times when I realise I've said or done the exact same thing my father would have said or done to me as a child, and then I wonder how like him I've become. My study, like his, is the equivalent of my garden shed, and there are undoubtedly times when I find myself retreating to it to avoid the arguments, discussions about social media and the general noise and chaos of family life.

Living so close to my parents has meant I see more of them than I did before, but we've set our boundaries and the

conflicts and oppressive expectations I feared never material-
ised. When we get together for afternoon tea or a meal, I go
with the knowledge that my father's opinions no longer affect
me in the way they used to. I've never stopped loving him or
my mother and have come to the conclusion that living cheek
by jowl with my parents at this time in their lives is a privilege
which has brought us closer together at a time when it probably matters the most.

Philip Larkin famously wrote 'They fuck you up, your mum
and dad', and I've met many who have been fucked up by
their parents, but I don't honestly think I ever was. The
journey I have taken, with all its highs and lows, has given
me the resolve I needed to get on and make something of my
life, and I am eternally grateful to my parents for the part they
played in that. There may be times when we don't see eye to
eye, but I've never stopped admiring them for standing their
ground in the hope of creating a better, kinder and more just
society. To them their ideology was their religion, and there
was no room for ambiguity. But I like to think I am not that
different and have the same goals. Maybe I've become a mod-
erate who believes you have to be open-minded to both sides
of the argument and be prepared take an alternative path or
even compromise to get there.

Today, happily settled back in the Crescent, I find comfort
in hearing the sound of my father calling to my mother three
gardens away. I can hear my sister arriving for tea with her two
girls, followed soon after by my brother and then Alan. From
my study I can watch my own daughters making their way
along the garden wall, from our house to theirs, to join them,
and I realise that many of the good things I cherished most
from my childhood are alive and well.

Pulling my own two children up Gloucester Crescent, 2009

Outside, I can hear my children playing, and my parents chatting and laughing with my wife. I now know, without a shadow of a doubt, that my decision to return to Gloucester Crescent was the right one.

WHERE ARE THEY NOW?

My parents, Gloucester Crescent, 1961 ... and 2017

My parents have remained in their house in Gloucester Crescent to this day, and very little has changed other than they've slowly taken over the rooms that were once the children's. My old bedroom at the back of the house is now Mum's study, with the same tranquil view over the gardens that helped me to feel safe all those years before. People still come and go, dropping in for coffee or meals, and for as long as I can remember my parents have hosted a Sunday brunch for the family where an assortment of old friends and regulars, like Alan, drop in.

In the early '80s Mum fell in love with India and spent the next decade walking each year in the Western Himalayas as a trek doctor. I accompanied her on her first visit in 1983 to the

Me and Mum, Lahaul Valley, Western Himalayas, 1983

remote Lahaul Valley, near Zanskar. In the late '80s she took a sabbatical to work as a doctor in the hill town of Manali on the edge of the Himalayas, leaving Dad, for the first time, on his own to fend for himself in London. After three months he found her absence so difficult he flew out to beg her to come home, only to be struck down by a crippling case of dysentery, and he swore he'd never visit India again. In 1992 Mum retired as a GP so she could spend more time travelling with Dad when he worked abroad. She also worked part-time with her close friend Anne McPherson helping her to develop a ground-breaking medical web site.

Dad continued to direct both theatre and opera for almost every major opera house in the world until he was 79. In spite of having an enormous list of credits to his name, he's never stopped telling everyone how much he's hated working in the theatre. Over the last three decades he's continued to write and present television programmes, which have included a number of landmark projects for both the BBC and Channel 4. In his thirst to educate, entertain and inform he's tackled subjects ranging from the human brain, in *States of Mind*, to his pet subject, atheism, in *A Brief History of Disbelief*. We've worked together on several occasions, when he fronted a series of masterclasses for the BBC called *Opera Works*, then again for a *Horizon* about Parkinson's Disease called *Ivan*, and another about a man with amnesia called *Prisoner of Consciousness*. These were produced by the company I ran with Patrick Uden, allowing me to work discreetly in the wings cutting the deals and putting the production together while Patrick worked his magic on Dad. In the last five years he has finally started to wind down, occasionally overseeing the revival of an opera, but now spends most of his time in his studio at the top of the house, where he paints, sculpts and creates collages from paper, wood and metal.

In 2002, having been honoured with degrees and fellowships of every kind, he was knighted for his services to music and the arts. When the letter arrived, he spent days locked in his study agonising as to whether he should accept an honour from the establishment he'd spent a lifetime railing against. In the end we coerced him into accepting it, believing it was the recognition *he* claimed never to have had for his contribution to not just the arts but a whole way of thinking. To this day neither he nor my mother have used their titles for anything.

Tom pursued his passion as a portrait and architectural photographer working over the years for magazines, art galleries and architects. His photograph of Gordon Brown now hangs, along with portraits of every other Prime Minister, on the staircase at Number 10.

Kate has worked in the management of a number of large

Mum in the garden at Gloucester Crescent, 2018

television production companies, including five years working with me at Uden Associates. She is married, with two daughters, the elder of whom has finally fulfilled Dad's ambitions for at least one of his children to become a doctor.

Jeanie lived on and off at Gloucester Crescent throughout her twenties, leaving, at one point, to live with a boyfriend and then again to work in a children's home. When she was in her late twenties Mum and Dad helped to buy her a flat in Finsbury Park, and for the next thirty years she worked as an adviser in a number of Citizens Advice bureaux, where she helped mostly black kids who'd got into trouble with the police. She often told me her job had brought her face to face with the ugliness of institutional racism and made her question her own background and experiences. At times it was clear that she felt both guilt and anger for becoming what she described as 'white and middle-class'. Maybe this was the source of the problem, as from about 2005 she started to

Dad and Alan, Gloucester Crescent, 2015

distance herself from our family, in the end cutting herself off altogether. She died in 2012.

Alan closed a chapter in the Gloucester Crescent story by putting the house he had owned for fifty years on the market in 2017. This was the house where Miss Shepherd had lived in his driveway and was made famous by the film of Alan's play *The Lady in the Van* (2015). Alan now lives on the other side of Primrose Hill with his partner, Rupert Thomas, who's the editor of the magazine *The World of Interiors*. Rupert was a friend of my sister's, and it was she who introduced the two of them; they've been together ever since. Alan and Rupert divide their time between Primrose Hill and their house in Yorkshire, but Alan is still a regular feature of our family's life.

Conrad remained at Bedales for one more term in order to sit the Oxford entrance exams but in the end accepted a place at Edinburgh University. He then took the rest of the year

Me and Conrad, 2016

off and joined me in New York. Along with Remy, our friend from Bedales, we lived together in a loft apartment overlooking the Hudson River on the west side of Manhattan. I visited Conrad on a regular basis in Edinburgh, which, in a strange way, afforded me a form of university social life that I might otherwise never have had. It was then, through a close friend of Conrad's from university, that I'd first meet the woman who would become my second wife, Trine Bell.

After university Conrad spent several years working as a television researcher before going to the United States to study for his MBA at Wharton. He then became a successful management consultant and remains one of my closest friends to this day. He's done the brilliant job of being my best man, not only for my first marriage but my second as well. He is also godfather to my eldest daughter. Conrad now lives in London with his partner.

After the Roebers' stepfather, Will Camp, died, their mother, Juliet, sold their house in Gloucester Crescent and moved to their house in Wiltshire, where she lives today with her third husband. The triplets, Bruno, Nicky and James, all live in London.

Dee and Hylan finally moved out of the Chelsea Hotel and into an apartment on New York's West 22nd Street. Back in London, following a fairly acrimonious divorce from Dee, Freddie finally married Vanessa Lawson. Their wedding was a somewhat odd affair, with their Indian maid acting as a witness and the maid's boyfriend stepping in as Freddie's best man. They bought a house on York Street in Marylebone, where they lived with Vanessa's youngest daughter, Horatia. In spite of the blood-letting that went on over their divorce, Dee and Freddie managed to find a piece of common ground where they could be civil to each other: Nick. A little late in the day, this came from a shared concern for his welfare, although it never went as far as an offer of a home. After years of fending for himself he finally moved to New York, where he did various jobs before going on to university.

After only two years of marriage Vanessa tragically died of cancer, leaving Freddie a broken man. Over in New York things weren't going well either, as Dee and Hylan's hopes of a better life, away from the snobbishness of the English, started to look like a pipe dream. As they became more disillusioned, so their relationship began to falter. Then one summer, while Dee was away in France, Hylan packed up his things and went to live in California. Over the next few years, decades of heavy smoking started to take their toll on Dee's health. To everyone's amazement, she suggested to Nick that she might come and stay at La Migoua at the same time as his father. Freddie was surprised to find that her declining health had seemingly taken the sting out of her tail.

Freddie's smoking hadn't done him any good either, and his health was starting to suffer too. In 1988 he was struck down with pneumonia and admitted to hospital. To everyone's surprise he made a remarkable recovery, only to then choke, in hospital, on a piece of smoked salmon and pass out. According to the doctors, technically he had died, and a day later he admitted that in his state of death he'd seen a bright white light which he'd forced himself to turn away from before coming round. He also talked about having seen a river, which he claimed to have crossed. This led some to ask if he'd seen the River Styx as well. Had Freddie finally found God and the afterlife, everyone asked? This was certainly a turning point for a man whose entire philosophical belief had been based on there being no God. He later insisted that through this experience he'd become a 'born-again atheist'. After this life-changing experience Dee wrote to me to announce that 'Freddie had become a nicer person since he died'.

Later the same year, with Hylan gone and Dee spending summers playing happy families with Nick and Freddie in France, Nick persuaded his parents that maybe they should try living together in London. To everyone else's surprise Dee sold her apartment in New York, moved back to London and took up residence in York Street with Freddie. As if that wasn't enough, by the spring of 1989 they had remarried. This time the only people attending their wedding were Iris Murdoch and her husband, John Bayley, along with a woman called Wendy Fairey, a lifelong friend who'd only recently discovered she was in fact Freddie's daughter. Within months Freddie's health had started to deteriorate further, and he was again admitted to hospital. On 27 June, Freddie Ayer passed away, with Dee, Nick and Horatia Lawson by his bedside.

Over the coming years Dee divided her time between London and the south of France, but her smoking had affected her circulation, leading to gangrene in one leg. Eventually she had to have it amputated, but she still managed to find humour in the situation. On one of my visits to see her in York Street I found her standing in the hall brandishing a prosthetic leg with painted toenails. This, she proudly announced, was her 'beach leg', which she'd ordered specially for the south of France. Nick finally moved into the basement of York Street and, in spite of his continuing anger towards his mother, he looked after her while her health deteriorated further. Around this time Dee struck up a close relationship with the infamous Claus von Bülow, who became her constant companion as she went in and out of hospital. In 2003 she was admitted for another operation, but this time she never came round from the anaesthetic. Dee passed away on 24 June. Her memorial service was held at St Bride's on Fleet Street and was attended by all her old friends from Gloucester Crescent and Regent's Park Terrace, along with Hylan and many others. George Melly gave his best rendition of Bessie Smith, and we all sang the American Civil War song 'The Battle Hymn of the Republic'. Nick returned to New York, where he stayed for more than a decade, but now lives back in London with his American girlfriend.

True to her word, Stella remained at Stanage until Jonathan found a wife and then moved into a small but pretty cottage on the estate, where she lived until her death in 1997. I went

Me and Stella Coltman-Rogers, 1984

to visit her as often as I could and continued, into my adulthood, to seek her worldly advice. Although she never lived to meet my own children, my second daughter was named after her.

After leaving my father, Sue ended up working for a literary agency, where she met Michael Bond, the creator and author of *Paddington Bear*, whom she later married. She now lives in Little Venice in London.

Keith became one of New York's most celebrated restaurateurs and at one point had nine restaurants in Manhattan. He now divides his time between London, New York and Martha's Vineyard, and we still speak on the phone most weeks.

Over the years the Haycraft children came and went along with numerous other people. Oli, who now lives with his wife

The Old Manse, by Nicholas Garland

and various children in California, still has the old German army uniform he bought with Nick Ayer from Laurence Corner. It's now worn by a shop mannequin called Herman the German. After Colin died of a heart attack in 1994, Anna sold their house in Gloucester Crescent and moved to Wales, where she died eleven years later.

Matthew Rice and I have remained close friends ever since Bedales. In the mid-1980s Matthew married the potter and entrepreneur Emma Bridgewater and together have built her pottery company, of the same name, into a multi-million-pound business and brand. They have four children and live on a farm in Oxfordshire. Matthew is chairman of the Bedales board of governors and is godfather to my youngest daughter.

At the beginning of the 1980s our gardener Willie Moggach passed away and Mrs Thain decided it was time to retire. Without a gardener or a housekeeper the Old Manse suffered badly from neglect. Our beautiful and much-loved garden quickly turned into an unmanageable jungle, and the house, which constantly needed airing and warmth when empty, started to fall down. My parents made a brief visit in 1983 to find collapsed ceilings, damp floors and the furniture going mouldy. My mother felt Mrs Thain was irreplaceable and that it was her that made having the Old Manse possible. Realising also that it was getting harder to get all of us together for family holidays, my parents decided to put the house on the market. It was sold in 1983 and since then has changed hands several times, but my mother and I, who loved it the most, continue to have dreams that we've returned and have been tempted on several occasions to buy it back.

In 1994 Alan's partner, Rupert Thomas, re-introduced me to Trine Bell, who I'd lost touch with and who was now working with him at *The World of Interiors*. In 2001, after a seven-year courtship, we were married in a small church on the shores of Loch Fyne on the west coast of Scotland. When I came clean and told the Church of Scotland minister, who'd agreed to marry us, that I was both Jewish and divorced, he quietly informed me that 'We don't need to tell anyone about that!' Seven years later we moved to Gloucester Crescent, where we live to this day with our daughters Daisy and Stella, along with a cat and a dog.

My children, Daisy and Stella, Gloucester Crescent, 2015

ACKNOWLEDGEMENTS

In writing my first book I went through all the soul-searching, the pain and the pleasure that so many first-time authors go through: the naive enthusiasm that comes with a strange desire to write a book, then the endless self-doubt which finally leads to the knuckling down to write it, followed by even more doubt and then the euphoria of actually finishing. Without the support of so many who saw me through this process I would neither have embarked on this endeavour nor followed it through to its conclusion. So, to begin with, I would like to thank those who initially coerced and encouraged me to write a book about my childhood: Anita Land, Reggie Nadelson, Jeremy Lloyd, Kaia Bell, Lizzy Moberly and Philip Norman. Without them I would have never had the courage to do it. In the end the final decision to actually lock myself away for a year and write was down to my wonderful agent, Claire Paterson Conrad, of Janklow & Nesbit. Without her this book would never have happened. She had incredible faith in the idea for this book and then guided me and taught me so much in the process of doing it. I would also like to thank Anna Swan for all her help and hard work with the early drafts as well as my editors at Profile Books, Louisa Dunnigan and Rebecca Gray, along with Penny Daniel and Matthew Taylor. I would especially like to thank Andrew Franklin for being the first to believe this book was one worthy of a publishing company like Profile.

In the end, though, the biggest thank-you has to go to my

mother, for giving me her blessing and support and letting me write this book as well as giving me access to all her letters and photographs. I know it wasn't an easy decision, nor was it easy for her to read certain parts of the book, which we discussed and debated at length. In the end she realised it was a story I wanted to tell and that it needed to be written as I experienced it and not as others had. My thanks must also go to Conrad Roeber and Matthew Rice, who have always been there for me, allowed me to include them in this story and then made sure I didn't make a total fool of myself in the process.

Others without whom I couldn't have written this book and who gave their support and input are: Sue Bond and, in spirit, her mother, Stella Coltman-Rogers, Nicholas Ayer, Gully Wells, the Roeber family, Alexandra Aldridge, Alan Bennett and Keith McNally.

I would also like to thank my wife, Trine, and my two daughters, Daisy and Stella, for being there for me every step of the way. Last but not least, I owe an enormous debt of gratitude to my father for being an incredible and unique person, my inspiration in so much and for making things possible without his ever knowing he was doing it.

PICTURE CREDITS

Looking through my family's extensive collection of photograph albums in search of suitable images was to me like dipping madeleines in tea. Without them I couldn't have written this book. The majority have come from these albums or have been donated by family and friends. A million thanks to you all. Those from other sources are listed below:

Frontispiece: Dad, Tom and me © Ian Berry 1967/Magnum

p. 14 Dad's one-man show, *Poppy Day*, Cambridge, 1953 © Hulton Archive/Walter Bellamy/Getty Images

p. 20 Dad at Sue's desk, with the window cleaner, 1968 © Godfrey Argent/National Portrait Gallery

p. 22 'The Stringalongs' by Mark Boxer, *The Listener*, 1968 © Mark Boxer estate

p. 23 Alan Bennett © Ian Berry 1967/Magnum

p. 26 Beryl Bainbridge and Anna Haycraft © Edward Hamilton West/*Guardian* © E. Hamilton West/Guardian News & Media

p. 48 The view from Mum and Dad's bedroom at the Old Manse © Nicholas Garland

p. 101 Sir A. J. Ayer at work © 2006 John Hedgecoe/Topfoto

p. 133 Dad and me in the Cotswolds, 1978 © Judith Aronson

p. 136 Pimlico School, London. Wikimedia

p. 167 Garland car being repaired in Scotland after a crash © Nick Garland

p. 168 The Garland family returning from Scotland without their car © Nick Garland

p. 168 The Garlands and the Millers © Nick Garland

p. 172 The original 1961 *Beyond the Fringe* sketch 'So That's The Way You Like It': Jonathan Miller, Peter Cook, Dudley Moore and Alan Bennett © Lewis Morley Archives

p. 175 Dad in the production office at the BBC for *The Body in Question* © *Judith Aronson*

p. 250 The kitchen, Gloucester Crescent – Alan Bennett, Mum, my cousin Daniel Miller, Kate and Dad © Judith Aronson

p. 332 *The Old Manse* by Nicholas Garland © Nicholas Garland

While every effort has been made to contact copyright-holders of illustrations, the author and publishers would be grateful for information about any illustrations where they have been unable to trace them and would be glad to make amendments in further editions.